The Great Lakes

Sudbury

St. Marys River

O N T A R I O

Bruce Peninsula

Parry Sound

LAKE HURON

Oscoda

Owen Sound

Toronto

LAKE ONTARIO

Oswego

Bay City

Saginaw

Hamilton

Niagara Falls

Rochester

Lake St. Clair

Buffalo

Detroit

Detroit River

LAKE ERIE

NEW YORK

Erie

Bass Islands

PENNSYLVANIA

Toledo

Cleveland

0	50	100	150 Miles
0	50	100	150	200 Kilometers

OHIO

The Late, Great Lakes

The Late, Great Lakes

AN ENVIRONMENTAL HISTORY

William Ashworth

ALFRED A. KNOPF

New York   1988

THIS IS A BORZOI BOOK

PUBLISHED BY ALFRED A. KNOPF, INC.

Library of Congress Cataloging-in-Publication Data

Ashworth, William

The late, Great Lakes.

Bibliography: p.

Includes index.

1. Water—Pollution—Environmental aspects—Great Lakes—History.

2. Lake ecology—Great Lakes—History.

3. Great Lakes—History.   I. Title.

QH545.W3A68   1986   363.7′3942′0977   85-45915

ISBN 0-394-55151-6

Manufactured in the United States of America
Published May 15, 1986
Reprinted Once
Third Printing, April 1988

For Virginia, Karen, and especially Melody,
without whom this book would have been impossible.

They contain round archipelagoes of romantic isles, even as the Polynesian waters do; in large part, are shored by two great contrasting nations, as the Atlantic is. . . . they are swept by Borean and dismasting blasts as direful as any that lash the salted wave; they know what shipwrecks are, for out of sight of land, however inland, they have drowned full many a midnight ship with all her shrieking crew.

Herman Melville, *Moby Dick*

There are two ironies about the Great Lakes: first, that the people who have become most dependent upon them have misused them the most; and second, that despite our abuse of them the lakes remain as wondrous as they must have seemed to Melville and indeed to Etienne Brulé, the first European to see them, when he stood on the shores of Georgian Bay in 1610.

John Rousmaniere, *The Enduring Great Lakes*

Contents

The Late, Great Lakes

I The Fifth Coast

There is a fifth coast of North America, one that lies not at the edge like the other four, not along the Atlantic or the Pacific or the Caribbean or the ice-swept, lonely Arctic, but at the center, along the midcontinental line. It is a spectacular coast, where surf rolls in from beyond the horizon to break upon broad sand beaches at the base of great dunes or crash against tall cliffs and bold, rocky headlands. It is a valuable coast, cradling a fistful of great port cities and dozens of smaller ones along its more than 10,000-mile length. But it is also a freshwater coast, the coast of those five enormous, closely connected bodies of water we call the Great Lakes, and because of this it has been belittled, abused, misunderstood—and now may be about to die.

The misunderstanding runs very deep, as deep as the name itself: Great Lakes. In no conventional sense are these lakes. Back in the early days of Fifth Coast exploration, in the seventeenth century, there was a French explorer named Jean Nicolet who set out by canoe one fine summer morning to find out what lay west of the Strait of Mackinac. Arriving several days later off the far side of Lake Michigan, he paused long enough to put on a damask robe before going ashore so that he would be properly garbed to greet what he presumed would be the Chinese. The robe was bright red, and heavily embroidered in yellow with twining poppies and birds of paradise. The explorer was dirty, unshaven, in buckskins, and untroubled by any sense of incongruity. He had just crossed an ocean, after all, and he knew what he ought to do.

That is closer to the mark; but Nicolet misunderstood, too. These are no more oceans than they are lakes. They are something else, something separate and unique and wonderful. The first European to make note of them, the French explorer Samuel de Champlain, called them *mers douces*—sweet seas. That is the closest of all, and is probably the closest we are going to come without a new word altogether.

Despite the fact that they have long been called "lakes," they have also long been treated as though they were infinite. That is the second misunderstanding. Their waters, their fishes, their furs, their woods —all at various times have been thought to be in such large supply as to be undamageable, and all have ultimately proved very damageable indeed. The furs went first, skinned out and shipped off to Europe, the animals that bore them pushed farther and farther off beyond the horizon until the "infinite" furs of the Great Lakes were being taken on the Missouri River and Lake Athabaska and Hudson Bay, and only a whim of fashion that cast aside the beaver hat in the 1830's in favor of silk and woolen kept them from being pushed off the continent altogether. The trees were next: big trees, four feet and more through at the base, trees that went on "forever." Beginning in about 1835 they were mowed down in a massive orgy of sawmilling known as the Big Cut, and by 1900 they were, nearly everywhere, only a memory. Then it was the fishes' turn. Great Lakes fisheries, we were told, were "exhaustless." Sturgeon were so thick in the Lakes as to be a genuine nuisance: Their carcasses were taken from the nets set for more desirable species, piled on the beaches in great maharajan pyres, and torched. Steamboat firemen fueled their boilers with them. Now they are next to nonexistent. The Atlantic salmon is extinct in Lake Ontario, where it once darkened the water with its schools, and the Lake whitefish and Lake trout of the upper Lakes —overfished, shut out of their spawning streams by pollution, and preyed upon by salt-water lampreys, which have sneaked into the Lakes through the navigation canals dug by humans—have nearly followed the salmon into extinction. Fishing used to be one of the Lakes' major industries. Now it is almost gone. Traveling the length of the Fifth Coast one recent summer, I looked every day for commercial fishing boats. In all that time, I saw only one. It was at anchor.

Related to this belief in the Lakes' unbounded resources is the belief in their agelessness, their changelessness through time. This is perhaps the largest and most pernicious misunderstanding of all. Because of it, we fail to see the changes that have happened and will continue to happen. We take refuge in "always." The Lakes have "always" been the way they are, since the dawn of creation; they will "always" be that way. Geography is immutable. As it was and ever shall be, world without end, Amen. This is false. The Great Lakes are young: They were formed a geologic eyeblink ago, and they can be destroyed just as quickly. They are constantly changing. The ecology of the Lakes is totally dissimilar to what it was when the first explorers came upon them, and that was different from what it had been a few centuries before they arrived. Four thousand years ago there were whales in the Great Lakes, and walruses sported on now-vanished shorelines along the northern part of Michigan's Lower Peninsula. The shorelines continue to alter today, adding beaches here and subtracting them there. The species-mix within the Lakes changes; the chemistry of the water changes. Even the elevation above sea level changes. For centuries the northern part of the Lakes region has been slowly rising in a process known to geologists as "isostatic uplift"—a rebound from the compression of the land caused by the great weight of the continental glacier that carved the Lakes' beds. This rising is still going on. Accurate elevation measurements here require the specification of a year as well as a measurement in feet and inches. Sault Ste. Marie, Michigan, is creeping upward more than eight inches each century. Thunder Bay, Ontario, is nearly two feet higher above the Atlantic today than it was in 1900.

For a little while back in the 1960's, it appeared that this belief in the Great Lakes' immutability would be challenged and demolished. That was the time when Lake Erie turned green and opaque, and word went around that it had died. This was itself a misunderstanding, a failure to grasp the meaning of the scientists' explanation of the process known as "eutrophication," which had run wild here; but the misunderstanding was compounded a few years later when the Lake turned blue again. Word is now going round that we were right the first time—that the death of Lake Erie was temporary and reversible, and that nothing ever really changes. Thus are dangerous misconceptions reinforced. The fact is that the Great Lakes as a whole—not just Erie, but including it—are in far worse condition now than they were in the 1960's. The damage to them has reached crisis proportions; it is compounding annually; it may be irreversible; yet still the politicians congratulate themselves for building their little sewage-treatment plants and "saving" the Lakes, and still the signboards by Ohio's Sandusky Bay shout LAKE ERIE IS ALIVE AND WELL. It is such stuff that dreams are made on. How can Lake Erie be alive and well with the oil-black Rouge River flowing into it? Or the brown Maumee, or the turgid Thames, or the flammable Cuyahoga? Near Sandusky Bay, there is a town called Bellevue, which for years got rid of its sewage by simply dumping it into limestone caverns beneath the community. Now there is a huge fan of cavern-borne pollution reaching from Bellevue toward the bay and creeping closer each year. Eventually it will get there. What will they do then with all those rosy billboards?

I spoke not long ago with the man who programs the computers on board the LANDSAT satellites—the ones that control the cameras that broadcast those remarkable photomontages of the earth's surface back to those of us who crawl about upon it. He said, "We can't program the computer to recognize the Rouge River as water. The Rouge is so filthy that if the computer recognizes it as water, it won't recognize anything else in the world."

The other Lakes are, if anything, worse off than Erie. At the southern end of Lake Michigan, near Chicago, there is a harbor with a floor that is half PCBs, and another in which the bottom sludge is 40 percent mud and 60 percent a sort of twentieth-century witch's brew involving PCBs, chromium, zinc, lead, oil and grease, iron, and various compounds lumped together into the general category of "volatile solids." The floor of the western arm of Lake Superior is carpeted with asbestos fibers from the processing and transshipping of iron ore. Love Canal, that monument to modern disposal technology gone awry, drains into Lake Ontario, along with similar dumps at Oswego, Port Hope, Welcome, and other places too numerous to mention: Over 60 million gallons of wastewater polluted with dioxins and PCBs and upwards of 40 other toxic chemicals pour into the Tittibiwasi River—a tributary of Lake Huron—from just one industrial facility, the Dow Chemical plant at Midland, Michigan, every day. Over all the Lakes hangs the specter of the most frightening form of pollution of all: toxic rain. This is not just acid rain, though the acidity readings of rainfall in the Indiana Dunes area of Lake Michigan are among the highest found anywhere in North America and the entire region around Sudbury, Ontario, in the Lake Huron basin, has been denuded of vegetation for decades by acid rain from the nickel smelters there. Acid rain is bad enough, but rain over the Great Lakes carries toxic organic chemicals as well. Fish from remote wilderness lakes on Isle Royale, in northern Lake Superior, show PCB levels in their flesh twice those considered acceptable for human consumption, and Toxaphene—a pesticide not commonly used near the Great Lakes at all—has been found in dangerously elevated levels in the flesh of fish from Lakes Superior, Michigan, and Huron.

That is one way to kill a coast: by polluting the waters off it to the point where they are no longer much good for anything, while you labor under the misconception that conditions are improving. There are other ways. You can fill coastal wetlands, for example: This is done under the misguided assumption that wetlands are waste-lands. In fact they are an important part of the coastal zone, acting as water filters and fish producers and nesting sites for insectivorous birds. Because the Great Lakes are geologically young, however, wetlands are poorly developed here. Estimates are that only 7 percent of the coast has ever been natural wetlands, and that percentage is rapidly decreasing as dredge-and-fill projects take their toll. Much of Chicago is built on filled Lake Michigan wetland; half of Ontario's extensive Pelee Marsh, on the north shore of Lake Erie—one of the most important stopping places along the great migratory bird flyways of central North America—has been drained and converted to cropland. Seventy-five percent of the wetlands that once existed within the state of Michigan have been destroyed. The pace of wet-land destruction has slowed somewhat of late, and many of the more important areas have been protected (the remainder of Pelee Marsh has been a Canadian national park for over half a century), but dredge-and-fill operations have by no means stopped entirely. Per-mits are required, but are largely a formality. "It seems as though they can always come up with some reason to make a landfill," laments an environmental engineering consultant from Cleveland, "and of course there's always something available to put in it." Often what they put in it comes from elsewhere along the coast. Much of the dune belt at the southern end of Lake Michigan has disappeared that way—dug up, dredged out, and hauled off by the trainload to dump in marshes to build something on.

And we are always building something: That is still another part of the problem. Eighty-six percent of the shoreline of Lake Michigan's southern end is covered by housing, commercial, or industrial development; the figure is 70 percent for Lake Erie, more than 40 percent for Lake Ontario, almost that much for Lake Huron, and a good 30 percent for "undeveloped" Lake Superior. Much of this building has actually taken place *in* the Lakes rather than beside them, on fill; much has also taken place on areas that, in the natural course of things, are soon to become lake through erosion and mass wastage—landslides and other large-scale earth movements—of the shore. This leads to the strange human activity of trying to deny change on some parts of the coast even as we create change on others. *We* can remove beaches, or sand dunes, or marshes, but Nature had better not try it. So we build $100,000 homes on bluffs that may fall into the Lake when the next wave hits, and then we spend another $500,000 (largely of tax moneys) trying to keep that wave from hitting. Erosion is the biggest nonproblem in the Great Lakes Basin. When people have the sense not to build within the erosive zone, erosion is merely geology.

Navigation works have altered rivers, changing them to shipping channels and eliminating the bars at their mouths and the entire ecological communities that once dwelt in their bottom muck. Canals built for shipping have allowed access to the Lakes by exotic species such as lampreys and alewives, which have thrived, multiplied, and permanently changed the ecology of the entire Fifth Coast region. Navigation continues to be extended into the winter months, despite the pleas of scientists—and even some shipowners—that not enough is understood about the winter ecology of the Lakes to predict the effects of winter-long icebreaking and shipping activities. "We know nothing—it's just a virtual black hole," complained one Wisconsin government biologist a few years ago. This was at a time when the Reagan Administration, claiming that "we know all we need to" about the Lakes, was attempting—unsuccessfully, as it turned out—to remove all Great Lakes study moneys from the federal budget.

(Sadly, the administration officials who pushed that attempt probably believed exactly what they said.)

All these problems, however, are pallid indeed beside the threat looming on the western horizon, where mining and agricultural interests are readying large-scale plans to lay pipelines to the Great Lakes, supplying by pump and pipe the water God doesn't supply by rain to the arid reaches of Montana and Kansas and Nebraska and Arizona. The concept is simple. The need is *here;* the water is *there;* and the shortest distance between two points is a straight line, preferably a round, hollow one, made of concrete and filled with water. This is what is known in the trade as "out-of-basin-diversions," a rather innocuous name that manages to overlook or hide the fact that if water is diverted *out* of the basin it will no longer be *in* the basin; it will be, in fact, drained off. The plans to pump water west amount to nothing short of a plan to drain the Great Lakes.

Drain the Great Lakes? It sounds preposterous, and it is, but not because it cannot be done. It can. The technology exists; the need exists. The greatest output of agricultural products in the United States comes from the irrigated lands of Nebraska and Kansas and Colorado and the Texas Panhandle. Virtually all of this irrigation comes from a single aquifer known as the Ogallala—and the Ogallala is running dry. If irrigation is to continue in this huge multistate area, another source of water must be found. The Great Lakes are the most visible source, and the one being ogled most lecherously. The preposterousness of the idea does not come from its technological infeasibility, or from its unlikelihood. It comes from the assumption, basic to the idea of diversion, that the water can somehow be put to better use on the Plains than it can be in the Lakes.

And make no mistake: Diversion means drainage. We are not talking here about small amounts of water. When the Ogallala Aquifer was full, some forty years ago, it held roughly the same amount of water that Lake Huron holds today; and if we refill the Ogallala from the Great Lakes, it will take all of Lake Huron to do it. Will we be better off then? Or is Lake Huron more important to us where it is?

Without the Great Lakes, the iron ore of Minnesota could not get cheaply to Cleveland and Gary to be made into steel.

Without the Great Lakes, the climate would change over eastern

North America: It would be dryer, with greater swings of temperature. The tornado belt would shift north, and the rain-washed forests of New England and the Laurentians would gradually be replaced by mesic, dryland vegetation.

Without the Great Lakes, Niagara Falls would run dry. This would be more than a disaster to the honeymoon industry. Niagara is the largest generator of hydroelectric power in the Western world. It may help to recognize the importance of this if you remember that the great East Coast Blackout of 1965 was caused by the failure of a single small relay in the Sir Adam Beck Power Station at Niagara Falls.

All these things can happen. All of them *will* happen, if the massive transfusion of Great Lakes water into the economy of the High Plains—now being so carefully planned—should take place. To assume that it cannot happen—because it is too expensive, because political pressure from the Great Lakes states will prevent it, because Canada will not stand for it—is to fall prey to the greatest misconception of all: the misconception that reason, despite the clearly unreasonable human mind, will somehow automatically prevail.

Will the Fifth Coast of North America become a coast without water? The answer to that question, ultimately, is up to all of us. And like everything else about the Great Lakes, it is very much up in the air.

Back in the still-innocent year of 1820, in the month of May when the ice had gone and the wilderness was all in bloom, a young glassmaker and geologic dilettante from Watervliet, New York, named Henry Rowe Schoolcraft set out from Detroit with a federal survey expedition under the command of General Lewis Cass to spend all of one long golden summer rambling through the Great Lakes. Paddling northward up the Detroit River in three large canoes, the Cass expedition crossed Lake St. Clair, ascended the St. Clair River into Lake Huron, and turned west, along the United States shore. Up the east

coast of Michigan, through the Neebish Channel, around the great
Sault de Sainte Marie, and along the wild south shore of Superior to
Fond du Lac they went, traveling fifty to one hundred miles per day,
laying over when the rains came or the winds were against them,
exploring the marshes of Saginaw Bay, the gardens of Mackinac, the
great dunelike banks of Le Grand Sable, the islands òf Chequamegon
Point, the copper country around the Ontonagon River. Schoolcraft
was expedition mineralogist. He went about happily with his rock
hammer and collecting bag, picking up pebbles from the beaches,
sampling the outcrops along the shores and on the islands, rambling
through the uplands. The Indians called him Paw-gwa-be-ca-we-ga,
which translates freely as "destroyer of rocks." He recorded this with
ill-hidden pride. Gliding along in his canoe with a team of voyageurs
paddling, he watched the shores sweep by and read Johnson's *Lives
of the Poets*; by the firelight in the evening camps, swatting mosquitoes and black flies, he worked on his journal. He was keeping an
extensive journal, and by and by, when he came home again, he
published it. In it one can read today of the Great Lakes as they once
were, when all possibilities were still golden and none had yet turned
upon us to demonstrate that even golden tigers have teeth and must
eat and excrete like all other creatures.

Two fragments will have to suffice here. The first describes Saginaw Bay, which Schoolcraft found to have

a broad beach of sand intervening between the woods and the water,
which affords innumerable harbors for encamping. . . . The navigation is safe for vessels of any burden, and its numerous coves and
islands present some of the best harbours in the lake. At its southern
extremity it receives Saganaw river, a large and deep stream with
bold shores, and made up of a great number of tributaries, which
irrigate an extensive country, reputed to be one of the most fertile
and delightful in the Territory of Michigan. . . . From the terms of
high admiration of which all continue to speak of the riches of the
soil, and the natural beauty of the country, and its central and advantageous position for business, we are led to suppose that it presents
uncommon incitements to enterprising and industrious farmers and
mechanics.

The second excerpt is a note Schoolcraft jotted down on the banks of the Ontonagon River, which flows into Lake Superior just west of the Keweenaw Peninsula in western Michigan:

> One cannot help fancying that he has gone to the ends of the earth, and beyond the boundaries appointed for the residence of man.

One summer not long ago, Schoolcraft's journal in hand, I followed the Cass expedition's route westward through the Lakes. The Ontonagon had a town on its banks and a mouth full of dredge spoil —the abandoned dredge was still sitting there—and on that "broad beach of sand" bordering Saginaw Bay, at precisely the spot where the Cass expedition had shoved off to make the dangerous crossing of the bay's broad, unprotected mouth, someone had yielded to the "uncommon incitements" of the place and established one of the most dreary and depressing trailer parks I have ever seen.

II The Deep Past

The town of Grand Marais, Michigan, sits at the eastern foot of the Grand Sable Banks on the south shore of Lake Superior: If you think of Michigan's Upper Peninsula as a running rabbit, as Michigan schoolchildren are taught to do, then Grand Marais comes right at the point where the rabbit is arching his back to draw his legs up. It is a quiet little backside-of-nowhere sort of place, huddled among sand hills at the end of a twenty-five-mile spur road out of Seney, its weatherbeaten buildings carrying the air of proud but desperate poverty that is called "picturesque" by those who have never had to endure it. A hundred years ago, during the heyday of the Big Cut, this was a major lumbering port, its harbor crowded with schooners, its streets busy with trade. But the trees were all cut down and shipped out, and the logging moved west. Then it was a fishing port, but the lampreys came in and finished that. Now it is not much of anything. Two paved streets, crossing at right angles just above the harbor: a handful of stores, a double handful of houses, a low line of dunes, and beyond the dunes and the wind that sings among them, the restless, boundless world of the infinite sea. Learned men with no learning call it a lake. They have never been to Grand Marais.

Early one Saturday morning in late July, 1983, chemist Rod Badger and I stopped for coffee and sweet rolls at a tiny little hole-in-the-wall Grand Marais restaurant called Shirley's Sweet Shop. We were the only customers. The high school girl behind the counter polished her nails and watched us out of the corners of her eyes: A smell and sizzle of hot grease wafted past her over the kitchen wall. The coffee was excellent. Afterwards, I sought out a telephone to make a call to Marquette, eighty miles west along the rugged Michigan coast, and Rod wandered across the street to the general store. When he came back a few minutes later, he was carrying a pair of small waxed-paper parcels. He unwrapped them and showed them to me. One had smoked Lake trout in it. The other contained smoked whitefish.

"Whitefish" is a name commonly given to two unrelated fish of the Great Lakes. One, the round whitefish or menominee *(Prosopium cylindraceum)*, is a small animal shaped rather like a baby torpedo; it rarely exceeds thirteen inches in length. It makes an adequate smoked fish but is otherwise largely useless as human fare. The other, the Lake whitefish *(Coregonus clupeaformis)*, is a gift of the gods. It is not a beautiful fish, but it is among the most delicious on earth. The flesh is soft and delicate, with a subtle, almost pastrylike flavor—like a trout with the troutiness removed. If you think of a fine French Sauterne and contrast it with a California Mountain White Wine purchased in jugs off the bargain shelf at the discount store, you will get some idea of the comparison between whitefish and other fish. Smoked, salted, boiled, baked, fried—there is nothing, simply nothing, quite like it.

In times past—and not so long past, at that—there were millions of these big, salmon-like relatives of the common fresh-water chub scattered throughout the Great Lakes system. The English trader Alexander Henry, traveling through the Lakes in 1762, found them "crowded together in the water in great numbers" below the rapids of the St. Marys River, between Lake Superior and Lake Huron: "a skilful fisherman," he reported, "will take 500 in two hours." Nearly eight million pounds were taken from Lake Superior alone in 1903, and the total Great Lakes whitefish fishery remained above five million pounds as late as 1950. Then the collapse came. By 1960 the catch had declined to below 500,000 pounds, and most of the commercial fishermen around the Lakes had scrapped their boats and gone out of business. Smoked whitefish has always been a delicacy; today it is also a rarity.

Wordlessly, reverently, Rod rewrapped his treasure and placed it in the little portable icebox in the back of my station wagon. We drove down to the beach, parked at the edge of the sand, got out the fish again, and shared a tiny amount of it, sitting in the car, gazing out across the white and restless breakers toward the blue, transparent, impossibly far-away horizon.

To understand the present, it is first necessary to understand the past; and in the Great Lakes, the past goes very deep.

The Great Lakes are geologically recent, but they have a history that stretches far back into the early Precambrian, three billion years and more ago. In that dawn-time, what is now the Lakes region was on the active edge of a young and growing continent. Shallow seas spread over the continental shelf; their shores lapped an east-west coastline that lay in a great arc through the area that would one day become southern Ontario. An archipelago of volcanic islands lay offshore. Life had not yet been born.

Details of that distant era are, not surprisingly, confusing and uncertain, but geologists have been able to piece together enough to give us the major outlines. There were magmatic intrusions and lava flows; there was rapid erosion from the highlands, where no plants yet existed to hold back the flow of surface water, and rapid deposition of sediments on the sea floor. Continents collided and rebounded. Mountains rose and eroded back to plains. There are at least three separate episodes of mountain-building, known as *orogenies*, detectable in the Pre-Cambrian rocks of the Great Lakes region; only remnants of these mountains are visible today.

The earliest range, the result of an uplift called the Laurentian Orogeny, has been eroded down to its roots—a vast undulating expanse of granitic rock centered in mid-Ontario and known today as the Canadian Shield. It forms the Canadian shores of Lakes Superior and Huron and crops up in scattered places on the American side, notably at Sugar Loaf Mountain near Marquette, Michigan, and in the Thousand Islands at the entrance to the St. Lawrence River.

The mountains of the second uplift, the Algoman Orogeny, are poorly represented on the current land surface; they are known mostly through the sediments that eroded from them and were later uplifted in the third and final mountain-building episode, the Penokean Orogeny.

The Penokean Mountains were spectacular. They were Alplike in scale and probably in appearance, and they lay in a broad band from Minnesota eastward through Wisconsin and Michigan and southern Ontario into northern New York. The core of this mountain system still exists in Wisconsin and Upper Michigan, though it is now greatly diminished: It is known today as the Gogebic Range, and is rich in iron—iron laid down among the ancient sediments from the eroding Algoman Mountains. There were the beginnings of life on the earth by this time. It is thought that the iron of the Gogebic is the result of the actions of iron-fixing algae or other primitive life forms in the shallow waters of the ancient, long-vanished Great Michigan Sea.

None of the events to this time—roughly 600 million years ago—contributed anything other than raw material to the actual shaping of the huge basins that were to become the Great Lakes. But now, as the Pre-Cambrian drew to a close and the Cambrian began, that shaping started. For reasons that remain obscure, the landmass of North America was seized by the forces of continental drift and nearly pulled in two. The great North American Rift developed deep beneath the surface, extending in a huge ragged line from the Atlantic at least as far west as Kansas. The stretched-out crust of the continent sagged downward over the rift, forming great structural basins, or "synclines"; arms of the sea spread inward, reinvading the continent, filling the structural basins with water. At that time, the water was salt. It received the sediments from the eroding Penokean Mountains, and the weight of these sediments caused further downwarping along the rift.

In the bottom of what is now Lake Superior, the weakened crust tore. The fissures released lava flows; the lava flows spread outward, covering hundreds of thousands of square miles beneath many layers of basalt. Still the downwarping continued. The layers of basalt bent, their centers depressed, their edges tipped up, like sheets of paper resting in a hole. Today those tilted layers of basalt make up some of the most spectacular landforms of the Great Lakes region. On Brockway Mountain Drive on Michigan's Keweenaw Peninsula you drive your car along the edge of one of these ancient, tilted lava flows. To the north the land slopes off at a forty-degree angle, steep but smooth, sweeping down past green forests to the endless blue expanse of Lake Superior; to the south it ends abruptly in a cliff hundreds of feet high. The cliff has a broken appearance about it, as if someone had taken an Oreo cookie and snapped it in two and you were an ant crawling along the crazy edge of the break. That is approximately what happened. The entire Keweenaw is made of ridges formed of the broken edges of a layered structure not unlike an Oreo; so is the nearby Porcupine Range, where the spectacular Lake of the Clouds escarpment is now the centerpiece of Michigan's largest and most scenic state park.

The various north shore mountain ranges, and the offshore mountains of Isle Royale, look much like the Keweenaw Peninsula, but in reverse: The slope of the layers lies to the south, the cliffs face north. They lie in the opposite limb of the Lake Superior Syncline, and are in fact the other end of the downwarped Keweenaw flows. Between the two limbs, in Cambrian times, stretched an alluvial plain, its lower-level sediments slowly turning to shale. A great river flowed eastward across it in a broad valley not unlike today's Mississippi.

In eastern Lake Superior the North American Rift, for reasons of its own, developed a substantial offset, and a subsidiary rift came into being, heading south at right angles beneath what is now Lower Michigan to connect to the main rift's continuation along the axes of Erie and Ontario and the St. Lawrence Valley. Over this offset a second huge syncline, the Michigan Structural Basin, developed, but this time the crust did not break. The land simply kept warping downward, forming a huge bowl. A shallow arm of the sea came in and filled the downwarping bowl with salt water; sediments filled the sea, forming layers that bent like the basalts of the Keweenaw as the land continued to sink beneath them. At least once, the channels connecting this Michigan Sea to the Atlantic were cut off. The sea dried up, leaving behind huge deposits of pure salt. That salt is mined today in—among other places—downtown Detroit, Michigan, and Cleveland, Ohio.

By the end of the Pennsylvania period, 280 million years ago, the slow downwarping of the Michigan Structural Basin had created what is one of the most striking bedrock formations in the world. Centered near the tiny town of Barryton, Michigan (population: 420), lies a gigantic bull's-eye of sedimentary rocks hundreds of miles across. The rings march outward like ripples from a stone dropped into a pond, leafing back through older and older geologic ages as they do so. The rocks near Barryton—the target circle—are the Grand River formation, of upper Pennsylvanian age. Ten miles out, the rock type changes abruptly to the Saginaw formation, a lower Pennsylvanian rock group. There are six rings of Mississippian sediments: Beyond them, mostly submerged beneath the waters of Lakes Michigan and Huron, are seven rings of Devonian. Beyond the Devonian rings the Silurian rings begin; there are eight of these, mostly formed of a particularly erosion-resistant type of limestone known as dolomite. The hardness of these Silurian dolomites has largely determined the shape of Lakes Michigan and Huron, and it has contributed to the shapes of the other three Great Lakes. On a map they show up plainly, forming the Door and Garden peninsulas that separate Green Bay from Lake Michigan, arcing around the north shore of the Lake and through the Strait of Mackinac into Lake Huron, forming Manitoulin Island and the Bruce Peninsula, separating Georgian Bay from the main Lake. Like Isle Royale and the Keweenaw Peninsula on Lake Superior, the Door Peninsula and the Bruce Peninsula are strikingly similar but reversed. The Door slopes to the east, slanting up from Lake Michigan and dropping off into Green Bay in a cliff 300 feet high; the Bruce slopes west, slanting up from Lake Huron and dropping off into Georgian Bay. That is because the layers of the Michigan Structural Basin slant toward their sinking centers and break off abruptly at their edges, like the rims of a series of gigantic nested bowls.

The Silurian dolomites continue southward from Owen Sound, forming an escarpment across Ontario known variously as "The Ridge" or "The Mountain," and then turn east. Lake Erie is dammed up behind them; and where Lake Erie empties over them into Lake Ontario lies the single most famous tourist attraction in North America. It is called Niagara Falls, and it has given its name to the entire ring of Silurian dolomites. Geologists call it the Niagaran Cuesta.

But the Niagaran Cuesta is not the outer edge of the Michigan Structural Basin. Beyond it, the concentric rings continue: two more Silurian rings, five Ordovician rings. The three outermost rings are Cambrian: The middle ring of the three, the Jacopville Sandstone, forms the south shore of Lake Superior from Marquette around past

Grand Marais to Whitefish Point. That is why, on a map, the south shore of Lake Superior and the north shore of Lake Michigan have such strikingly similar arcs.

It is believed that the Michigan Structural Basin stopped sinking at the end of the Pennsylvanian, but this is not known for sure: because with the Pennsylvanian the bedrock record stops. There is, incredibly, no rock in the entire Great Lakes region less than 280 million years old. Gaps such as this in the geologic record, called "unconformities," are common enough, but they are almost never more than a few million years long—a geologic period or two at the most. This Great Lakes unconformity, known among geologists as the Lost Interval, covers not only periods but entire geologic eras: the end of the Paleozoic, the entire Mesozoic, and nearly all of the Cenozoic. Only in the Pleistocene, near the end of the Cenozoic, does the record begin again. Elsewhere life climbed out of the sea; elsewhere dinosaurs rose, flourished and fell, or took to the air and became birds; elsewhere mammals evolved. There is no trace of any of that here. The fossil record leaps directly from the trilobite to Man.

The agent that caused the Lost Interval was the same agent that formed the Lakes as we know them today: Pleistocene ice.

About 500,000 years ago, a change or series of changes occurred in the climate of the Northern Hemisphere that caused a slight cooling and an increase in precipitation in the upper latitudes. Snow fell, did not melt, and turned to ice. Year upon year, century upon century, the ice accumulated; eventually its own enormous weight caused it to flow outward, as a lump of soft clay left on a table slowly flattens itself into a disc. The edge of it crept south, leveling the landscape as it went. That is why there is a Lost Interval. All the evidence of the intervening millennia was scraped off by the glacier and deposited as unsorted piles of rubble in New York and Ohio and Illinois and Indiana.

No one can ever be certain, but it is believed that there were no Great Lakes before the glaciers came. Instead, there was a broad, branching network of river valleys, following the courses laid out for them by the Superior Syncline and the Michigan Structural Basin. The main stem of this river system seems to have begun near the head of Lake Superior; the St. Louis River, which empties into the Lake at Duluth, may be a truncated remnant of its headwaters. It flowed eastward down what is now the axis of Superior on a bed made largely of shale and soft sandstone. Entering upper Lake Huron over the same course taken now by the St. Marys River, this pre–Ice Age stream joined with a major tributary flowing in from the Michigan basin and another, forked tributary rising in twin headwaters at the south end of Lake Huron and in the upper Saginaw Valley—but the Saginaw River is not a remnant of this stream—before flowing through the gap in the Niagara Escarpment now occupied by what is known as the Main Channel and turning south once more into Georgian Bay. It crossed the neck of the Ontario Arrowhead, entered the Ontario basin at about the site of present-day Toronto, curved gently eastward along the base of the Niagaran Cuesta—where it took on a third major tributary, this one draining what would eventually be the Lake Erie basin—and headed for the Atlantic down what is now the St. Lawrence Valley.

The land surrounding the river and its tributaries was probably generally low and rolling. It may have been grassland, or forest, or even desert. No one knows.

The ice changed all that. It was more than two miles thick at the center and at least a quarter of a mile thick at the leading edge, and it came down on that gentle landscape like a combination bulldozer and battering ram. The shales and sandstones in the Lake Superior Syncline and the soft Devonian sediments along the limbs of the Michigan Structural Basin were scooped out like so much ice cream; the edges of the nesting bowls forming the Basin were sheared off flat. The hard basalts of the Keweenaw and Isle Royale and the dolomites of the Niagaran Cuesta resisted the ice, but they were scoured and gouged and polished, their surfaces ground down as a craftsman grinds down a piece of wood with a file or a sheet of sandpaper. At least four times the ice advanced, and at least four times it retreated, leading to ice-free periods known as "interstadials" when soils formed and forests grew on the clean-scraped rock (preserved remnants of one of those forests can be seen today near Two Creeks, Wisconsin). Finally, about 12,000 years ago, the ice withdrew for what we presume to be the last time. Left behind were five gigantic holes, hundreds of miles across and up to a quarter of a mile deep. The holes filled up with water. The Great Lakes were born.

It is fascinating to compare the landforms of the Great Lakes region with the landforms of the alpine-glacier regions of our western mountains. The same features are found in both places, but the scale is enormously different. Glaciers—all glaciers—build up ridges along their margins known as "moraines," formed of unsorted chunks of the material the glacier has been excavating from its bed. In the western mountains these moraines may be as much as three or four miles long and perhaps 70 feet thick. In the Great Lakes there are moraines a hundred miles long and 500 feet thick. The southern end of the Lake Michigan basin is ringed by these massive moraines, which have largely determined the Lake's shape in this area: Dammed up behind the moraines, it is the same shape as the lobe of the glacier that left them. Moraines also form most of the south shore of Lake Erie and lie in a jumbled mass over much of central Michigan, where they stand against the sky like young mountains. I once drove through central Michigan with a geologist from the West who has spent much time in alpine glacial terrain. He knew about the continental glacier moraines in this region and was looking for them, but so vast is their scale that we had traveled most of the day among them before he dared to recognize that these tall tree-covered ridges that had been getting in his way all day were in fact the very things he had come two thousand miles to see.

A glacier flowing over resistant bedrock leaves scratches in its surface known as "striations," produced by the grinding of stones caught in its undersurface and dragged like the teeth of a file over the unmoving rock of the bed. In the western mountains, these striations seldom exceed an inch in depth. In the Great Lakes they may be considerably larger. Striations two and three feet deep are found commonly in the hard Silurian limestones of the Bass Islands in western Lake Erie, and on nearby Kelleys Island, at Glacial Grooves State Monument, their depth exceeds six feet.

Other glacial features here are on a scale similar to the moraines and the striations. There are whole fields of drumlins—streamlined hills of glacial debris, formed in the lee of bedrock obstructions beneath the glacier—more than a hundred feet high. There are kettle lakes five miles and more across, filling holes made by melted blocks of ice fallen from the 3,000-foot-high face of the great glacial wall. There are outwash plains that cover whole counties: There are kames like small mountains, and eskers, the sinuous sediment-filled tunnels of streams that once flowed under the glacier, that may be traced for mile after winding mile across the landscape. This is not just esoteric knowledge. The kames and eskers make excellent sources of sand and gravel: The Blue Ridge Esker, near Jackson, Michigan, has been quarried for that purpose for years.

West of Grand Marais the vast, lonely bluffs of the Grand Sable Banks rise suddenly from the Lake Superior surf like ruined battlements, blurred and fuzzy and blown about by mists as though posing for a Turner landscape. Henry Schoolcraft, in common with others of his day, thought they were a set of huge sand dunes. They are not; they are the monstrous filling of an ancient crevasse. There was, geologists are now certain, a persistent crack in the body of the great continental ice sheet here where it had to flex as it came up out of the bed of the Lake and headed south across the flat landscape of the eastern Upper Peninsula. The crack collected windblown sand and other small debris from the glacier's surface. When the glacier melted away, that debris was left behind as a giant ridge, 300 feet high and more than six miles long—a sort of reverse mold of what must have been one of the largest holes-in-the-ice the world has ever seen.

The most striking glacial features of this landscape, however, are undoubtedly the Great Lakes themselves. They are like glacial lakes everywhere, but on a stupefyingly enormous scale. They are oceanic: They have tides and surf. You cannot see across them. Lake Ontario, the smallest of the five, is 50 miles wide and nearly 200 miles long; its surface area is 7,550 square miles, larger than the states of Connecticut and Delaware put together. Lake Erie is 240 miles by 60 miles and has an area of nearly 10,000 square miles—Lake Ontario plus two Rhode Islands and the District of Columbia. Those are the small fry; the upper three Lakes are much larger. Lake Michigan is 300 miles long and 120 miles wide, with a surface area of 22,400 square miles, roughly the same as the province of Nova Scotia. Lake Huron is shorter but considerably wider—roughly 200 miles each way—and its area is slightly larger than Michigan's. Of Lake Superior there is no way to speak except in superlatives. It is not only the largest of the Great Lakes, it is the largest body of fresh water on earth: 350 miles long and more than 150 miles wide, it has roughly 32,000 square miles of surface area—larger than New Brunswick, or about the size of New Hampshire, Vermont, Connecticut, and Massachusetts rolled into one. Its nearly 3,000-cubic-mile capacity is well over ten percent of the world's total supply of fresh surface water, and is larger than that of the other four Lakes combined.

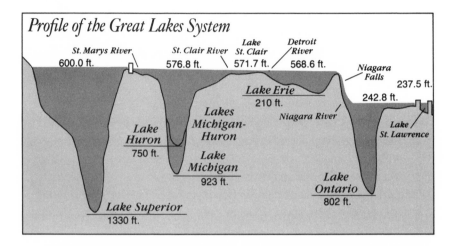

Profile of the Great Lakes System

Today the Great Lakes are unique, or nearly so, but this has not always been the case. Like the forests that surround them and the sturgeon that inhabit their depths, they are remnants of a vanishing class. At the close of the Ice Age there were many Great Lakes; they lay scattered across the continent like ghosts of the departed glaciers. Lake Shoshone covered southern Idaho; Lake Bonneville inundated much of Utah, and a much larger, fresh-water version of today's Mono Lake rolled from the foot of the Sierra far out into what is now Nevada. Lake Ojibwa-Barlow spread in a rough crescent across the valleys of the Moose and Albany rivers south of James Bay, and Lake Wisconsin lapped gently across the center of the future Badger State from the Baraboo Range to the vicinity of Stevens Point. Lake Missoula, four times as big as Lake Erie but confined to a maze of canyons and at no place more than a few miles wide, fingered octopus-like through the Montana Rockies.

Largest of all was Lake Agassiz, named for the Swiss geologist Louis Agassiz, who in 1840 first propounded the theory of continental glaciation. At its height, Lake Agassiz covered most of southern Manitoba and large parts of Ontario, Minnesota, and North Dakota.

For part of its life it drained into Lake Superior via the Pigeon River, making it a sort of super-Superior—a part of today's chain. At other times it emptied down the Minnesota into the Mississippi, or down the Red River du Nord into Hudson Bay. Villages were built along its coasts by ancestors of the Dakota Indians. When the French entered the present-day Great Lakes in the seventeenth century, they found a Dakota-speaking people, the Winnebagos, living on the western shore of Lake Michigan, surrounded by Algonquin-speakers. They had a tradition that told of once living on a "great water" to the west. The French thought the "great water" had to be the Pacific Ocean, and redoubled their search for the Northwest Passage. Eventually they decided it was the Mississippi River instead, and gave up. They were wrong both times.

What happened to these early, numerous Great Lakes? There are various answers to that question, depending upon which of the early, numerous Great Lakes you are referring to. Lake Bonneville simply dried up, leaving a saline remnant behind that we know today as Great Salt Lake. Lake Shoshone eroded its northern lip away and escaped down the Snake River. Lake Agassiz silted in, leaving big puddles here and there about its bed, including one "puddle"—Lake Winnipeg—which has a larger surface area than Lake Ontario, though it contains considerably less water.

Lake Missoula's fate was the most spectacular. It was a so-called *proglacial* lake, backed up behind a lobe of ice in what is today the Clark Fork Valley, and when the ice gave way it gave way all at once. The water thundered westward in a series of gigantic, inundating waves called the Spokane Floods, breaking out of the Rockies onto the plains of eastern Washington and scouring most of them bare right down to bedrock in an area now known as the Channeled Scablands before rushing on down the Columbia River to Oregon and the sea.

The Great Lakes survived this post-glacial period of lake destruction, but they didn't survive unscathed. Their boundaries changed numerous times. At first they were proglacial lakes, backed up against the retreating lobes of the great glacier; there were only two of them then, Glacial Lake Maumee (Erie) and Glacial Lake Chicago (Michigan), and they drained to the south, down the Illinois and Maumee rivers. (On a map, the tributaries of today's Maumee River look very odd: They seem to enter the river backwards. That is because when they were formed the river ran the other way. It was continuous with what is now the Wabash, and it drained into the Mississippi.) Later, Glacial Lakes Saginaw (Huron), Duluth (Superior), and Iroquois (Ontario) formed in the other three basins. Lake Duluth drained westward into the upper Mississippi; Lake Iroquois overflowed the low divide at the head of the Mohawk River and drained that way, down the Mohawk and the Hudson to New York Harbor. Lake Maumee's drainage had changed; its waters now flowed north along the ice margin into the new Lake Saginaw, which drained westward down what is now the course of the Grand River into Lake Chicago and onward to the Illinois.

Geologists have adduced numerous further stages of the ancestral Great Lakes. Beach terraces and wave-cut shore features—sea stacks, cliffs, and caves—lie about the region in bewildering variety, and they have been associated with a bewildering variety of ancient lake levels. Most of these can be passed over here, but two are important. One, the Chippewa-Stanley stage (9,500 years ago), represents the smallest dimensions the Lakes have had in their short lives; the other, the Nipissing stage (4,000 years ago), represents the largest.

The ice had gone during Chippewa-Stanley, but the land was still compressed from its weight, and the area around what is now the town of North Bay, Ontario—on the east shore of modern Lake Nipissing atop the 700-foot-high divide between Lake Huron and the Ottawa River—was close to sea level. An arm of the Atlantic—known variously as Warren Gulf, the St. Lawrence Embayment, or the Champlain Sea—extended far up the St. Lawrence Valley, probably into the current bed of Lake Ontario; the upper Lakes, reduced to relative puddles, drained through the North Bay outlet and into the Champlain Sea. The Strait of Mackinac was a canyon 300 feet deep with a river flowing through it; Lake Erie drained, by way of a much reduced Niagara Falls, over the Niagara escarpment. During the earliest part of this stage, the waters of Niagara may have fallen directly into the sea.

With the ice gone, isostatic uplift began. Little by little, the North Bay outlet rose; little by little, the Lake waters rose behind it. By 4,000 years ago, the North Bay outlet was more than 400 feet above sea level, and the waters had backed up so far that they were overflowing through the old Lake Chicago outlet at the southern end of Lake Michigan, down the Illinois and into the Mississippi. Some water was also escaping down the current route of the St. Clair River into Lake Erie. Lakes Erie and Ontario were roughly the shape and size they are today, but Lakes Huron, Michigan, and Superior were a single gigantic body of water. The Nipissing stage had begun.

Because both the Chicago and St. Clair outlets are south of the so-called "hinge line"—which separates the isostatically rising northern Great Lakes from the isostatically stable southern portion, where uplift is no longer going on—it was inevitable that Lake Nipissing would shrink again, as more and more of the land to the north climbed above the level of the two outlets. It was also inevitable that one of those outlets, eroding faster than the other, would eventually capture all of the outflow. This happened roughly 2,500 years ago, when the St. Clair River shifted sideways a few hundred feet from a bedrock sill to an area of soft, easily eroded glacial till; at roughly the same time, the continuing uplift to the north raised the north edge of the Michigan Structural Basin—with its relatively resistant ring of Jacobean sandstone—above the level of the down-cutting St. Clair. Lake Superior stabilized above the falls at Sault Ste. Marie, and Lakes Michigan and Huron—connected through the Strait of Mackinac and hydrologically a single body of water— sank below the Chicago outlet and took their current form. In far-off Egypt, the Pyramids were already ancient history. Knossos had risen on Crete, Moses had led the Children of Israel to the Promised Land, and on the rocky Acropolis in the center of Athens the Parthenon was going up.

(Interestingly enough, the abandonment of the Chicago outlet was never fully completed. Only six feet of elevation separate the "datum" level of Lake Michigan from the floor of the old outlet, near what is now the intersection of Interstate 55 and Illinois State Highway 43 in the Chicago suburb of Forest View. During early historical times, this outlet, known then as the "Mud Lake Swamp," was still inundated at times of high water; and during our own time it has been reactivated by human design. The Chicago Sanitary and Ship Canal runs through here, reversing the Chicago River so that it flows out of the Lake and into the Illinois—as it did on its own not so very long ago.)

.   .   .

Because the Lakes are so new, and so huge, their hydrology and ecology present some unique features. Their waters contain relatively few species of fish (though these few species have historically appeared in abundant numbers). Some normally anadromous species —those that live most of their lives in salt water, coming up rivers to breed—are adapted here so that they live through their normally salt-water stages in the Lakes' vast oceanlike spaces. Benthic drift organisms—the microscopic life forms upon which the smaller fish feed—are also of relatively few types, and these types seem more like those typically found in rivers than those found in lakes. The food chains are simple, short, and easily disrupted. The Lakes' tides are small—measurable in inches rather than feet—but there are tidelike motions called "seiches," which are caused by differences in barometric pressure at various points on the Lakes' enormous surfaces and which, once started, can oscillate from end to end of a Lake for days, like water sloshing in a bathtub. These are common enough that the benthic drift organisms have adapted to them: Those that contain chlorophyll do most of their photosynthesizing during the first three hours of their exposure to sunlight, as if they were hurrying up and getting it out of the way before a seiche came along and mixed them down out of the zone of sun.

Seiches have been known to raise the water level by as much as thirteen feet in a matter of minutes. In 1954 three people on a Chicago dock failed to scramble to safety as a seiche approached and were drowned.

A particularly noteworthy feature of the Lakes is the so-called thermal bar. Normally in a lake there will be a horizontal interface known as a "thermocline" between the warm, circulating water at its surface (the epilimnion) and the colder, still water in its depths (the hypolimnion); the thermocline forms during the spring as heat from the air penetrates into the water and breaks up again in the autumn as the water cools. The Great Lakes are so vast, however, that the thermocline is often ill defined, its depth fluctuating radically from place to place and even from time to time under the influence of currents, seiches, tides, waves, and the Coriolis effect (the swirling motion caused by the earth's rotation on its axis); and because of this, it is equaled in importance by another temperature-dependent

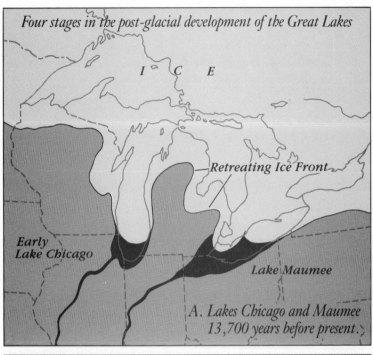

Four stages in the post-glacial development of the Great Lakes

I   C   E

Retreating Ice Front

Early
Lake Chicago

Lake Maumee

A. Lakes Chicago and Maumee
13,700 years before present.

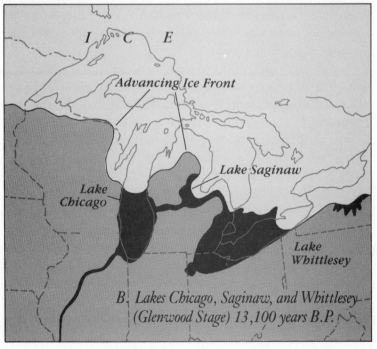

I   C   E

Advancing Ice Front

Lake Saginaw

Lake
Chicago

Lake
Whittlesey

B. Lakes Chicago, Saginaw, and Whittlesey
(Glenwood Stage) 13,100 years B.P.

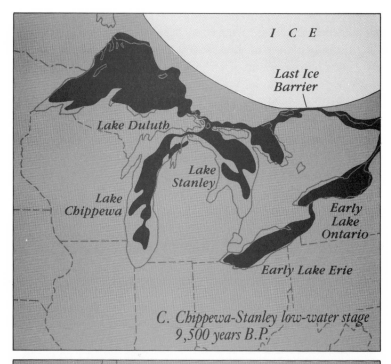

C. Chippewa-Stanley low-water stage
9,500 years B.P.

Lake Duluth

Last Ice
Barrier

I C E

Lake
Stanley

Lake
Chippewa

Early
Lake
Ontario

Early Lake Erie

D. Nipissing high-water stage
4,000 B.P.

Modified from Hough, 1963, "The Prehistoric Great Lakes of North America,"
permission of *American Scientist.*

phenomenon that hardly even exists in smaller bodies of water. Since the great mass of deep offshore waters warms much more slowly than the waters lying over the nearshore shallows, the Great Lakes tend to warm from the shore out, forming a vertical cold water/warm water interface, the thermal bar. The thermal bar starts near the shore and moves slowly offshore as the summer progresses. This change from a horizontal to a vertical interface has profound effects on the life within the waters, the breeding cycles of wetland-dependent animals, and even the climates of nearby coastal cities.

That, in a nutshell, is the natural history of the Great Lakes. That is the storehouse of incomparably varied and delicate treasures that the devout Visigoths of Western civilization have been piously plundering for the last three and a half centuries.

III Contact

The first recorded contact of Old World civilization with the Great Lakes was in 1615. That was the year Samuel de Champlain, the Father of New France, came in through the North Bay gap, where the waters of the ancient Lakes once surged out to join the vanished St. Lawrence Sea, and "discovered"—the word is a condescension, but we will let it stand—Lake Huron.

It is largely a historical accident that the first Europeans to enter the Great Lakes Basin did so through the Basin's abandoned drain instead of its active one. Champlain, like most explorers of his day, was seeking the fabled Northwest Passage to the "Great South Sea" —the Pacific Ocean—and the distant riches of Cathay. He had heard rumors of a "Great Water" lying somewhere to the west of his post at Montreal, and he was determined to find out if it was the Great South Sea. He needed a route westward. And the obvious one—the great westward-tending valley of the St. Lawrence—was closed to him. The French had come into the region through the lower St. Lawrence Valley, and the first Indians they had encountered were the Hurons. The Hurons were at war with the Iroquois, who controlled the upper St. Lawrence. Therefore the French, accompanied by Hurons, could not go that way. They would have to find another.

It was a nuisance, but it could be worked around. Champlain and his men made a wide circle to the north, ascending the Ottawa and then the Mattawa to the short portage at North Bay, over the old

Chippewa-Stanley outlet channel where whales once swam, to modern Lake Nipissing. Lake Nipissing empties into a westward-flowing river, known today as the French. Champlain descended the French. The barren, polished rocks of the Canadian Shield closed in on him. The riverbed was full of rapids. Canoes overturned; supplies were lost. Finally, toward evening of their second day on the river, Champlain and his party floated out onto a broad blue sheet of water where gulls wheeled and surf crashed loudly against bold rocky headlands. The horizon was a thin blue line on the distant water; the far side could not be seen. The Great South Sea? Champlain tasted the water. It was fresh. Not the Great South Sea, but something else, something that had never been seen before. He named it *La Mer Douce*—"the Sweet Sea"—and turned south along its coast, winding in and out among the Thirty Thousand Islands. Eventually he found his way back through the country of the Iroquois enemy to Montreal. The Northwest Passage remained undiscovered; but the first of the Great Lakes was on the books.

On the books. That was the key. The Indians had, of course, known of the Lakes for centuries, and there is some evidence that a party of Vikings may have visited them in the days of Vinland, traveling westward along the north shore of Lake Superior all the way to Duluth and beyond into central Minnesota. There had even been at least one Frenchman there before—a shadowy renegade scout named Étienne Brulé, whom Champlain himself had sent out to look over the country three years earlier and who was now, in 1615, acting as a guide. But of all these, the Father of New France was the first one capable of writing down his experiences. On such small distinctions does fame ride.

Perhaps we should take a look, before going any further, at the thriving human cultures that existed around the Great Lakes at the time of Champlain's arrival, and at some of their long history before a Frenchman with a pen came along to "discover" the place.

Human history in the Great Lakes region goes back at least as far as the Lakes themselves. There is little question that there were already people living here at the close of the last Ice Age. Artifacts have been found beneath glacial deposits associated with the final southward thrust of the ice—known as the Valders Advance—and

a cave on an Ohio River tributary in western Pennsylvania, the
Meadowcroft Rock Shelter near Eldersville, contains cultural remains dating back at least as far as 14,000 B.C. Archeologists call
these early peoples Paleo-Indians; they made a type of chipped-
stone spearhead known as a Clovis point, and they hunted masto-
dons and barren-ground caribou along the ice margins through
what are now the fertile farms and fields of the American Midwest.
It is thought that they were not related to the later Indian cultures
of the area.

The Paleo-Indians were succeeded by the Aqua-Plano culture,
the Boreal Archaic Culture, and eventually, around 5000 B.C., by the
Old Copper Culture, which persisted for at least 3,500 years. Here,
for the first time, the archeological record is extensive: There are Old
Copper sites scattered all over the Great Lakes Basin, usually near
shoreline features associated with the ancient levels of the Lakes,
which were undergoing drastic change during this period as the land
warped upward following the retreat of the ice. Old Copper Indians
undoubtedly hunted deer in the canyon where the Strait of Mackinac
now stands and followed trails through forested hills that now lie far
beneath the surface of southern Lake Michigan. They were, for their
time, a culturally advanced people. They lived in large villages and
buried their dead in cemeteries; they had domesticated the dog, and
were beginning to make a few stabs at agriculture. They were excellent boatbuilders who may have been the inventors of the birchbark
canoe. And they were—as their name implies—extensive users of
metal. They were, in fact, probably the first extensive users of metal
anywhere in the world.

The mountains around Lake Superior once contained vast deposits of what are known to geologists as "native copper amygdules"—
pockets of pure copper enclosed in the holes of vesicular volcanic
rocks. The Old Copper Indians mined these. Their method was
crude but effective: They heated the rock containing the copper
amygdules and then dashed cold water on the hot rock face to crack
them free. This was done most extensively on Isle Royale in the
northern part of the Lake, where hundreds of shallow prehistoric
mine pits pockmark the island. The copper thus obtained was dis-
tributed throughout the Great Lakes Basin and beyond. It was cold-
worked into knives and axes and spearpoints and jewelry. Many of

these items still exist and are still usable, though no archeologist would dream of doing so.

Around 1500 B.C., for reasons that remain uncertain, the Old Copper Culture declined, to be succeeded by the richly varied Woodland Culture. Possibly a main cause for the change was that the mines were giving out, making the metal harder to obtain and therefore more valuable: Woodland Indians used less copper than their predecessors, and most of what they did use went into jewelry rather than implements. But they made excellent pottery, built large structures (including the famous midwestern "effigy mounds"), and brought the extensive practice of agriculture into the Great Lakes region for the first time. It is difficult to say to what cultural peaks these changes might ultimately have led. The Woodland Culture was at its height, and still developing, when Champlain arrived and set in motion the course of events leading to its end.

It is necessary here to dispel a couple of common myths about Indian cultures in America prior to European contact.

The Woodland Culture Indians whom Champlain encountered were not "primitive savages"; they were not backward peoples with a lower level of culture than the Europeans. Their culture was different, but "different" is not necessarily the same as "inferior." The Indians could not read and write, of course, but neither could many of the French. They did not make use of the wheel—so their land transportation was less efficient than that of the Europeans—but they had the canoe, which was so superior in design to Old World small boats that Old World denizens immediately adopted it, and, given the abundance of watercourses in the region, including the Great Lakes themselves, a lack of efficiency in land transport was hardly crippling. Woodland farmers grew as large a variety of crops as did their European counterparts, and they understood the principles of crop rotation and fertilization at least as well. Their various tribal territories had no fixed boundaries—that was a major difference in philosophy that would eventually cost them dearly—but they were similar in size and function to European nations, and when Champlain arrived they were in the process of being united under the Iroquois Confederation, a government that the English, at any rate, clearly thought of as equals: The Iroquois exchanged ambassadors for years with the Court of St. James. They had no gunpowder, but that was hardly a sign of backwardness. All that meant was that in wars with the European powers they were likely to lose.

On the other hand, if the Indians were not the Primitive Savages the explorers and missionaries thought they were finding, they were hardly the Noble Savages of Romantic lore, either. Theirs was not a mythic Golden Age when Nature smiled and humans lived in harmony with the earth: Exploitation of the Great Lakes started well before the arrival of Old World civilization. It is probable that the Old Copper Indians, with their (relatively) high-tech weapons, were at least partially responsible for the extermination of the mastodon and the mammoth in North America. The Indians fished the Lakes to the limits of their technological ability, and they burned the surrounding forests to drive game from them. Their sanitation practices were, to put it delicately, crude. The early French explorers who traveled with them on long canoe voyages noticed that the Indians would carry small waterproof baskets for use as chamber pots so that they wouldn't have to stop paddling to attend to bodily functions; the pots, when full, were merely emptied over the side. That wasn't so bad, of course, by the standards of the day; the French did it too. But then the Indians used the same baskets, unwashed, to eat their dinners from. The French drew the line at that.

So Champlain came, and traveled among the Indians who had known Lake Huron for generations, and "discovered" it all over again; and, a few months later and in like manner, "discovered" Lake Ontario. Slowly over the next fifty years the remaining three Lakes crept out of the wilderness and into the geographies. Champlain was responsible for two more of these, though he didn't actually go to either of them. Back in Montreal after his failure to find the Northwest Passage, he got to wondering about possible relationships between his *Mer douce* and the Great South Sea. Could they possibly after all be one and the same? Had anyone tasted the waters off Cathay? He sent Étienne Brulé off to investigate further. Seven years later, in 1622, Brulé came wandering back with a tale of a new and even greater *mer douce* to the north of the old one. He had discovered Lake Superior, which temporarily became known as the *Mer douce du Nord*. Huron was rechristened the *Mer douce du Sud*.

Brulé also reported the existence of the Strait of Mackinac, and hinted of another Great Water opening beyond it to the west. Champlain's dreams of Cathay were rekindled. In 1634 he sent his young protégé Jean Nicolet westward through the Strait in a canoe with seven Hurons and that incongruous mandarin's robe of red damask. Crossing the Great Water, Nicolet entered a large bay on the far side and expectantly donned his mandarin's robe before stepping ashore. The land was not Cathay, however: It was Wisconsin, and the bay was Green Bay. Nicolet had discovered Lake Michigan.

There were rumors of a fifth Great Water, deep in the Iroquois country. The Hurons had heard of it, Brulé claimed to have glimpsed it, but no one could pin it down, because everyone was afraid of the Iroquois. Finally, in 1669, Nicolet's nephew Louis Joliet, a fur trader and ex-priest who was later to become famous as the "discoverer" of the Mississippi, came upon an Iroquois held prisoner in a Chippewa village at the Falls of the Saint Marys—today's city of Sault Ste. Marie—and obtained his release on the grounds that Joliet himself would take him down to the French settlement at Quebec. The grateful Iroquois, who might have been eaten by his captors—that is what had eventually happened to Brulé—guided Joliet across Lake Huron and down the Detroit River to Lake Erie.

Meanwhile, a couple of teenagers named Radisson and Groseilliers, known to present-day Minnesota schoolchildren as Radishes and Gooseberries, had stolen away from Quebec strictly against orders to go exploring on the North Sweet Sea, known by that time (1658) as Lac Supérieur. They circled around the west side of the Lake and paddled up the north shore for some distance, perhaps as far as today's Minnesota/Ontario boundary, pursuing a last fading chimerical hope for a passage to Cathay. They found no passage, but they did find furs. The two truants returned triumphantly to Quebec at the head of a convoy of 360 fur-laden canoes. The expropriation of the Lakes' resources had begun.

From that day to this, it has never stopped.

IV Furs

The trader feels the effects more keenly, he sees the ruination of his character, health and fortune; but circumstances are such that he cannot remedy the evil, and their brightest prospects are crumbled in the dust; and many promising young men have been driven to dissipation, from which it is impossible to extricate themselves. The blame rests on the heads of the principals, and they will have to answer for it some day or other.

William Johnston, *Letters on the Fur Trade* (1833)

Radisson and Groseilliers's 360 canoe-loads of furs—or rather, the profits from them—were a revelation. Before that, the predominant European view of North America had been that it was in the way. It was a barricade across the western trade routes to the Orient, and everyone was looking for a way through it. The continent's intrinsic value seemed low—a place for colonies of social outcasts, a land full of heathens where God's work of conversion to Christ could be done, but of no great financial worth. Standing offshore in the *Mayflower*, William Bradford observed "a hideous and desolate wilderness, full of wild beasts and wild men" and feared for the future of the Pilgrims he was about to land. There was some small trade with the Indians—the Dutch founded New Amsterdam as a trading post, and a few furs had trickled east across the Atlantic out of New France every year since the beginning of the colony—but it was largely incidental. The main task was to get the hell through the place and reach the Orient, where the money was, as rapidly and efficiently as possible.

The two truant Québécois changed all that. Suddenly the New

World looked much more inviting; suddenly it was apparent that one needn't go to the Orient for profitable trade. Who needed a Northwest Passage? One could get extremely wealthy right here.

The fur trade spread across North America, eventually reaching all the way west to Oregon and California, south to Arizona, and north to the Arctic Ocean, but the center of this immense, far-flung industry—its soul and throbbing heart—was always the Great Lakes Basin. Geography guaranteed that. The Great Lakes not only provided furs themselves; they provided a water route three thousand miles long deep into the heart of the continent, making transportation easy and cheap. How important this is can be judged from the settlement patterns of the two major colonial powers, England and France. While the English, landing on the Atlantic coast, were moving slowly and painfully inward through the tangled forests of Virginia and New England, the French—who controlled access to the St. Lawrence River and the Lakes—were already planting colonies halfway across the continent. There was a mission at Midland, Ontario, before the Pilgrims landed at Plymouth Rock. La Pointe, Wisconsin, was founded before the discovery of Lake Erie; Sault Ste. Marie, Michigan, is older than Philadelphia.

Radisson and Groseilliers, it should be mentioned in passing, received none of the benefits from their history-altering voyage. The two were charged with traveling without a permit, and their furs were confiscated. The Company of New France got the profits. The two young men protested loudly, to no avail, and went off angrily to join the British, with whom they helped found the Hudson's Bay Company. The Hudson's Bay Company eventually drove the Company of New France right off the continent. Revenge is sweet.

The fur trade was an extractive industry. It chose a natural resource—beaver—and took it away from the area in which it was found, to be made use of elsewhere. As in most extractive industries, little care was taken for the preservation of the area the resource came from. That was unimportant. There was no profit in caring about the beaver mine that was the Great Lakes Basin; the profit lay in transporting the mined products away from the mine to the seats of civilization, where they could be properly used. After all, they were just going to waste out there in the wilderness. So, little by little the beaver were trapped out, up the streams and over the ridges, beyond the Great Lakes Basin and far, far away. Their reproductivity could not keep pace with the demands of European dandies. With the beaver gone, the beaver dams deteriorated for lack of maintenance; they washed out and were not replaced. Flow rates on the suddenly unprotected tributaries sped up, and spawning beds were wiped out. Waterfowl, deprived of nesting marshes, declined. Siltation increased; so did floods. Rivers widened as the flooding waters took out the root systems of bankside trees. The fur trade was, in its own minor way, hell on the landscape; it was the beginning of the destruction of the Great Lakes Basin. It was premonitory; its cut-and-run, take-the-resource-elsewhere-and-get-out attitude would set the pattern for future attitudes toward the Lakes, the northern forests, and, in a sense, the whole continent. And it was big business.

Very big business.

At the extreme northeastern tip of the Minnesota coast, beneath a small mountain called Rose, on the shore of a bay called Portage, stands an imposing porticoed building out of another age that is known as the Great Hall. Surrounding the hall, which is made of logs, is a large open space like a parade ground; and around this is a palisade fifteen feet high. The palisade is also made of logs, peeled picket logs of cedar connected by slender horizontal poles known as walers. The walers and the picket logs are held together by wooden pins. In front of the palisade is the water; behind it, so close as to seem almost touching, is the steep, forest-covered wall of the little mountain. Between palisade and mountain a modern two-lane highway slashes like an anachronistic knife.

Early one cool summer morning in 1983, Rod Badger and I walked up Mt. Rose in company with historian Don Carney of the National Park Service. The paved trail wove back and forth across the steep face of the little mountain, climbing over ledges of slate among birches and spruce and squat, bushy thickets of red alder. From the top the view was big. Off to the east, beyond the headlands enclosing the bay—Hat Point on the north, Raspberry Point on the south—the wide waters of Lake Superior swept off, table-flat, to the distant blue horizon. Directly below, the Great Hall and its surrounding stockade spread like a map. And to the west, where the basaltic mass of Mt. Maud capped the smooth, nearly even range of hills that were once called the Cabotian Mountains, but are today nameless, the skyline was cleaved abruptly by a narrow, steep-sided little defile called Portage Gap. That was why the Great Hall was there.

It was also why Rod and I were there. Rod is an organic chemist by vocation, but he is a canoe salesman and wilderness outfitter by avocation, and this journey to Grand Portage—so he had been saying for the last several weeks—had for him overtones very like those of a devout Muslim's pilgrimage to Mecca. He had opened his shirt in response to the heat generated by the exertion of the climb, and I could see his pilgrim's outfit beneath it—a T-shirt, beige in color, across which was emblazoned in black the image of a birchbark canoe.

It was the canoe that made Portage Gap so important. Two hundred years ago, that inconspicuous break in the horizon was a key link—*the* key link—in the greatest transportation network of the Western Hemisphere. Eastward the water routes lay open, voyageurs' highways, the broad roads via the Great Lakes and the French, Ottawa, and St. Lawrence rivers to Montreal and Quebec and the distant, glittering cities of ancient Europe. Westward lay other highways, the complex, intricate web of lakes and channels and streams that began on the Quetico Highlands and spread outward like the veins of a hand through the vast, fur-rich forests of the North. Down from the Quetico to Lake Superior flowed the Pigeon River, but it was no highway. Beginning at the Cascades, thirteen miles above its mouth, the Pigeon cut through the Cabotian Mountains in a series of gorges and rapids and waterfalls that absolutely prevented navigation. There was no way through it.

There was, however, a way around it. Portage Gap was that way. A nine-mile trail through the gap linked the upper, navigable portions of the Pigeon River to Portage Bay. The Chippewa Indians, who built the trail, called it Kitchi Onigum, the "Great Carrying Place"; and when the voyageurs—the "French Indians," the canoe-borne, sometimes canoe-born, rangers of the North Woods waterways—came along, they appropriated both the trail and the name, which was translated into French without change. Kitchi Onigum became Le Grand Portage.

It was neither the voyageurs nor the Chippewa, however, who

built the Great Hall and its surrounding stockade. It was the voyageurs' employer, an English common-stock corporation known as the North West Company. The Company needed a field headquarters from which to direct its far-flung fur-trading operations. Le Grand Portage—or, as the officers of the Company anglicized it, Grand Portage—seemed the logical place for that headquarters. The Great Hall was built.

Gesturing with his broad-brimmed Park Service hat, Don Carney explained how the scene below us would have looked back in the heyday of the North West Company. It was an active and colorful operation, hectic-looking to an outsider but amazingly well-coordinated if you knew what was going on. Canoes arriving and departing at the long hooked dock; baggage coming and going along the Portage Trail; the jostling crowds of colorfully dressed voyageurs with their peaked hats and clay pipes, the crowds of equally colorfully dressed Indians of various Nations mingling with them; while inside the palisade, in the Great Hall, in an island of calm, the Company Partners, in their European finery, tight jackets, and lace shirts, debated policy in a dignified manner around a long table or were served dinner, equally dignified and at a table equally long, dining on steamed poultry and imported wine while the voyageurs beyond the gates messed on pemmican and boiled gooseberries. . . .

There would be several thousand people at Grand Portage during the high point of a summer season, the annual July Rendezvous, and despite the appearance of disorder, events would be proceeding in a remarkably smooth manner to execute the North West Company's carefully conceived plan of operation. That plan depended entirely on the voyageurs, who were the arms and legs and even the eyes of an enterprise for which the Partners were merely a few square inches of the forward lobes of the brain.

There were, for the fur trade, not one but two separate and distinct networks of voyageurs: the *bivernants* (winterers) and the *mangeurs de lard* (lard- or pork-eaters). They had certain things in common, among them small stature (to fit better in the canoes); great strength (to carry more than one ninety-pound bundle at once, thus increasing efficiency); good singing voices (to join in the paddling songs that made the work seem shorter); and—surprisingly, at first glance—an almost universal inability to swim (the Partners wanted to make sure the canoes stayed upright and the furs inside, and so they chose men who would be *exceedingly* careful to keep from tipping over); but there were major differences as well.

The *bivernants*, as their name implies, spent the winter in the north country, living with the Indians and collecting the furs that were the basis of the Company's prosperity. They took Indian wives, often several at a time, and they traveled about in small, maneuverable *canots du nord*, "northern canoes," shallow of draft and easily portaged. These were ideal craft for this country of small interconnected lakes but of no use at all on the big water of the Great Lakes, and the *bivernants* did not go there.

The *mangeurs de lard* handled that part. Their big *canots du maître*, or "Montreals," were 36 feet or more in length and weighed nearly half a ton—almost completely unportageable, but solid and stable in big water. They wintered in Montreal, coming to the north country only in summer and then only as far upcountry as Grand Portage.

Around the beginning of May each year, dozens of brigades of *canots du maître*—twenty or thirty to a brigade—would leave Montreal for the west, bearing trade goods and supplies made up into large bundles weighing roughly ninety pounds each. At approximately the same time, the *canots du nord* would come trickling down by ones and twos from the north country—from as far away as Lake Athabaska, in the Mackenzie River drainage some 3,000 miles beyond Grand Portage—bearing the winter's catch of furs. Like the trade goods, the furs were made up into ninety-pound bundles.

The northern canoes would converge on Fort Charlotte, on the banks of the Pigeon River west of Portage Gap, where they would be unloaded and the bundles of furs would be carried the nine miles down the portage trail to the stockade on the Lakeshore. The Montreals would unload at the stockade, and the bundles of trade goods they had brought would be carried up the nine miles of trail to Fort Charlotte. At Grand Portage the now empty Montreals would be loaded with the furs; at Fort Charlotte, the northern canoes would be loaded with the trade goods. The two groups would part again, the pork-eaters heading back with the furs to the comfort of the city, the winterers fanning out once more into the wilderness by twos and threes for another season of trapping and bartering with the Indians.

The Partners and their clerks—known as *bourgeois*—would ride up with the pork-eaters to oversee the transactions at the portage, and ride back with them again when they were done. They were of a higher social class, and a different nationality, than the voyageurs, and they held themselves aloof, doing none of the paddling or camp work, being generally waited on as if they were royalty, and incurring plenty of displeasure in the process. That is why the stockade was there. The Partners and the *bourgeois* were not afraid of hostile Indians. The stockade existed to keep out hostile voyageurs.

By the time the short active life of Grand Portage was over—the post lasted just twenty years, from 1783 to 1803—the great era of the fur trade was about over as well. The beaver mine had lasted 150 years, but the vein was played out. The beaver was nearly extinct; so was the Indian, at least as a culture. The Indians of the Great Lakes Basin had been drawn early into the game of hunting furs, and the diverse social structures of the various tribes had all melded into a single supertribal system that was dependent on the fur trade. When the trade collapsed, the Indians could not go back to the old ways. They collapsed, too. For a while there was a painful attempt to maintain the culture the fur trade had brought; after that, only silence. The settlers were coming, and there was nothing left to resist with except pride—and that was in short supply. "What is an Indian?" asked Henry Schoolcraft, back on the Lakes as Indian Agent at Sault Ste. Marie and Mackinac in the 1830's, and he answered his own question:

> A man spending his time painfully to catch a beaver, or entrap an enemy, without stores of thought, without leisure, with nothing often to eat and nothing to put on but tatters and rags, and withal, with the whole Anglo-Saxon race treading on his toes. . . .

The powerful Iroquois had been vanquished, the strength of the Five Nations broken. The French and Indian War was over, and the American Revolution, and the War of 1812; the lines of political power in the Great Lakes had evolved into much the state they maintain today. The beaver were gone, and that had had its effect on the rivers, but the Lakes themselves were still clean and open, their waters fair, their prairies and forests intact under clean skies. They could still reasonably be termed pristine. It was a condition that could not last. The axes and the plows were waiting in the wings: The era of development was about to begin.

V Pioneers

The first European settlers along the Fifth Coast were, in a sense, the French missionaries, the priests of the Jesuit and Recollet orders who very early on took up residence among the Indian tribes, choosing habitations in the wilderness and living there year-round as they went about sowing the seeds of Christianity in the fertile fields of the New World. They were there on the heels of the explorers, carrying their Bibles and their chalices, chanting their Latin hymns, and wearing the robes—black for the Jesuits, gray for the Recollets—by which the Indians identified them. At times they were there *before* the explorers. When Champlain arrived at the southern end of Lake Huron on his voyage of discovery in 1615, he found there a Recollet friar, Father Joseph Le Caron, living in one of the Huron villages. The Father had seen Champlain's *Mer douce*, but hadn't thought a great deal about it. He had other things on his mind.

The missionaries usually did; that was their problem. Much has been written—justly—about the bravery of these good, Godly men; about the sufferings of those who were martyred, usually at the hands of the Iroquois, who perceived (rightly, as it turned out) that these Black Robes and Gray Robes were merely the first wavelets of an advancing tide that would steal their country from them; and about the contributions made by various individual priests such as Jacques Marquette and Louis Hennepin to knowledge of the Great Lakes region. The fact is, however, that the missions seldom led directly to much of anything in the way of settlement. That was not their purpose. They may have grown corn, but only for the purpose of saving souls—not for the purpose of growing corn. One cannot exploit a wilderness that way. The siting of the missions, with few exceptions, was not suitable for commerce. Most of the villages that surround the old mission sites—places like La Pointe, Wisconsin; St. Ignace, Michigan; L'Anse, Michigan; and Penetanguishine, Ontario —are not much larger today than they were when the missions were founded.

The cities that grew up to serve the fur trade were another matter. These were specifically and shrewdly sited for commerce, and the sites they occupied are, with few exceptions, major cities today. Detroit; Chicago; Green Bay, Wisconsin; Duluth, Minnesota; and Thunder Bay, Ontario, all have beginnings that are deeply rooted in the fur trade, and the record of regional settlement can properly be said to begin with these.

The pattern of settlement for these early Fifth Coast cities was that common to most frontier regions. An advantageous site would be located, usually with a good harbor and at an already established Indian commercial crossroads. A small post would be built: If the post was successful, a military fort would be established next to it to protect it. The fort's garrison would need food, dry goods, and the services of blacksmiths, coopers, and other civilian craftsmen, and a town would spring up around the fort to provide these. Fields would be chopped from the forest or broken from the sod of the prairies. Roads would be cut; satellite towns would spring up. By this time the furbearing animals would usually have taken to their heels and run, and the fur take would have trickled off to nothing, but this never seemed to matter very much. The towns had become self-sustaining. Civilization had come to the wilderness.

Occasionally there were moderate departures from this norm. Sault Ste. Marie and Green Bay were missions before they were trading posts; the strategic position of Detroit was spotted by the French government before it came to the attention of the fur traders, and the fort established there in 1701 under the direction of Sieur de la Mothe Cadillac was a deliberate move by the military to a desirable trade location before the trade developed. But by and large the pattern held.

Detroit was a departure in another, more important way as well: The development of the village surrounding the fort was aided and abetted by the French government. This was decidedly abnormal. While the French held the Fifth Coast, the settlements that inevitably grew up around the frontier posts were at best only tolerated; more often, they were actively discouraged. There was a decided philosophical gulf here between the French and the English. The English moved to America: They planted colonies on the Atlantic shore, beating back the wilderness with settlements that spread slowly up the coastal rivers toward the Appalachian Divide. The French stayed in France, or in the extensions of France that were Quebec and Montreal. Mostly this was simply a difference in approach: The French wanted to rule an empire of subject peoples, while the English wanted to drive out the subject peoples and live in the empire themselves. Partly, however, French self-restraint can be looked on as an early conservation move. Where settlement came, beaver went. The French preferred the beaver. The exception of Detroit was made because it was thought that a city there would be the key to a "chain of forts" stretching from the mouth of the St. Lawrence to the mouth of the Mississippi, consolidating the French hold on the region and keeping the British colonies on their own side of the mountains.

It didn't work. There was war between France and England, the Seven Years' War of 1756–63, which spilled over into America as the French and Indian War. When it was over, the French were gone. All of New France—now Canada—had been ceded to the victorious British.

If there was rejoicing at this news by potential Fifth Coast settlers, however, it was premature. The British continued the French tradition of discouraging settlement in the Great Lakes Basin. The Iroquois had been major allies in the British victory, and the Lakes belonged to the Iroquois; and the British, while claiming the Lakes in principle, were reluctant to claim them in practice until a decent bargain could be struck with the original owners. A royal proclamation was issued:

. . . no governor or commander-in-chief of our other colonies or plantations in America do presume, for the present, and until our further pleasure be known, to grant warrants of survey or pass patents for any lands beyond the heads or sources of any of the rivers which fall into the Atlantic Ocean from the West or Northwest. . . .

The reasoning behind this policy was laudable, but it failed to sit well with the colonists, to whom word of the rich undeveloped lands around the great fresh-water seas in the midst of the continent had been leaking forth tantalizingly for years. "I can never look upon that proclamation in any other light . . . than a temporary expedient to quiet the minds of the Indians," wrote George Washington privately in 1767. Seven years later that "temporary expedient" suddenly looked alarmingly permanent. The Quebec Act, passed by the British Parliament in 1774, extended the boundaries of the province of Quebec westward and southward to take in all of the Great Lakes and the Ohio Valley, cutting off expansion in that direction by the Atlantic coast colonies. Like the more famous Stamp Act of 1765, it was an action Parliament would live to regret: It was, as it turned out, one of the major precipitating events of the American Revolution.

The fighting of the Revolution swept over the Great Lakes without touching them, although the British did maintain fleets of warships on Ontario and Erie and send out raiding parties from the fort at Detroit to harry the illegal settlements in the Ohio Valley. But if the war bypassed the Lakes, the peace afterward definitely did not. Astute diplomatic work by the American delegate to the Paris peace talks, Benjamin Franklin, assured the colonies not only of their independence but of their right to expand westward. The boundary between British and colonial rule was placed down the center of the continent's inland fresh-water seas: The rights of both Britain and its newly independent colonies to navigate those seas were assured. Their south shores and contiguous lands were declared open for settlement.

This part of the Treaty of Paris, which ended the Revolution, was considered so sensitive that it was placed in a separate, secret codicil, and was not revealed to the French—who would have protested it —until well after the treaty was signed.

. . .

The Treaty of Paris seemed to guarantee fair access by the new American nation to the lands around the Great Lakes. But there were lingering problems—problems that simmered to the surface when the Americans tried, once more, to move into the Lakes region. The Iroquois had largely deserted the area, moving north into the country of their British allies at the close of the Revolution; but others among Britain's Indian allies continued to resist. The Miami, who held most of western Ohio and southern Michigan, were provisioned by the British from Detroit and fought on until their decisive defeat at the Battle of Fallen Timbers, on the Maumee River near present-day Toledo, in 1794; the Seneca, who held western New York, continued to raid American settlements until a separate peace was achieved with them in 1797. Meanwhile, the British themselves, though clearly called to do so by treaty, refused to abandon their Lakes posts, maintaining or increasing their garrisons at Oswego, Niagara, Mackinac, and Detroit. Hotheads among the Americans counseled further war. George Washington thought otherwise: He sent his friend John Jay to London to find a peaceful solution. A further treaty was negotiated, and the troops were grudgingly withdrawn—but only just as far as the new Jay Treaty called for. They remained within striking distance, in new forts built just beyond the Paris boundaries, on St. Joseph Island near Mackinac; Amherstburg, near Detroit; Fort George, across the Niagara River from Buffalo; and Fort Henry, on the Canadian side of the St. Lawrence where it flows out of Lake Ontario through the mazy, myriad channels of the Thousand Islands. The Americans garrisoned the abandoned British forts and glowered across the water at the British; both sides moved forward furiously to build navies to patrol the fresh-water oceans each side claimed the freedom of. The Lakes region had become a bomb, armed and ready to explode.

Sixteen years later, in 1812, the bomb went off.

It is a measure of North America's attitude problem regarding the Great Lakes that we have forgotten, these days, just how much of the War of 1812 revolved around the Lakes and was fought near or upon them. We remember the Battle of New Orleans, fought two weeks after the war was over; but we forget the Battle of Amherstburg, which began it. We remember the British sacking and burning of Washington, but forget that this raid was in retaliation for the American sacking and burning of Toronto, known at that time as York and serving as the capital of Upper Canada. We remember the great naval victory of Oliver Hazard Perry, reported to his superiors in that famous laconic phrase, "We have met the enemy and he is ours," but we forget that this victory—and most of the other crucial naval victories of the war—took place on fresh water.

It would take us too far afield to discuss in detail the tangled course of the War of 1812 and the numerous battles that were fought on or around the Lakes, but a few hints can be given. There was, for starters, General William Hull's idealistic foray into Canada from Detroit: He went expecting the Canadians to rally to him against England, and was amazed when they failed to do so, forcing him to surrender Detroit to the British forces without firing a shot. Mackinac Island was also taken bloodlessly, by British troops who stole onto the island at night, climbed to its peak, and set up a cannon behind a hastily thrown-up earthwork; the cannon was aimed down into the stockade at Fort Mackinac, and would have devastated the place had it been fired. The sensible thing was to surrender, and that is precisely what the garrison's commander did. Mackinac had just fought a war without any victims.

Chicago was not so lucky. The recently built stockade there, Fort Dearborn, was alone in the vast wilderness of the Lake Michigan shore. The garrison, accompanied by the residents of the surrounding village, attempted to move overland to Detroit at the outbreak of the war. They got two miles. Among the lonely dunes where the 18th Street railroad yards now spread, they were set upon by Potawatomi Indians allied to the British. Eighty-four people had set out from the fort. Eight survived.

Numerous battles raged back and forth across the Niagara River, with invasions and repulsions on each side. Sacket's Harbor, the principal American naval yard on Lake Ontario, was attacked unsuccessfully several times. Naval skirmishes were fought on all the Lakes. American ships-of-war harried the coasts of Georgian Bay; a British fleet threatened the young settlements on the south shore of Lake Erie. The British schooner *Perseverance* was captured in Lake Superior and run over the falls at Sault Ste. Marie. The *Perseverance's* sister Lake Superior trader, the *Recovery*, was sailed into a cove on the northeast side of Isle Royale; there, her masts unstepped and her decks camouflaged beneath cut branches, she waited out the war, useless but safe.

It was the Battle of Lake Erie, however—where Commodore Oliver Hazard Perry's squadron of nine American ships defeated the six-ship Royal Navy squadron commanded by Commodore Robert Herriot Barclay—that is generally considered the turning point of the war. It was a battle the Americans probably should not have won, despite their three-ship advantage. Six of Perry's ships were brand-new and untried; they had been built hastily at Presque Isle, Pennsylvania, by a crew of house carpenters from Buffalo. The fittings had been hauled in overland from Pittsburgh; the lumber was standing trees that had to be felled and cut into boards on the spot. The bar at the mouth of Presque Isle harbor was so shallow that the ships could not simply sail into Lake Erie but had to be worked out by lines, leaving them vulnerable to enemy fire for long periods, and it was only the inexplicable disappearance of Barclay's roaming squadron—which had been lingering about as preparations were made to attempt the crossing—that allowed the crossing to be made at all. The wind was against the Americans, who nearly failed to get out of Put-in-Bay, where they would have been sitting ducks, on the morning of the engagement. Perry's flagship, the *Lawrence*, was cut to pieces by Barclay's *Detroit* early in the battle, forcing him to remove his commodore's flag with its boldly emblazoned message DON'T GIVE UP THE SHIP and do precisely that. But after Perry and a few of his officers had made a daring escape to the nearby *Niagara* in a small boat through cannonading and small-arms fire from the enemy fleet, the tide of battle turned: The *Niagara* had been hanging back from the engagement, and she was fresh. Perry drove her right through the British line, cannon blazing from both sides. Barclay's *Lady Charlotte*, maneuvering to cut her off, swung into the *Detroit*; their riggings became entangled. Both ships were raked clean by the *Niagara*'s guns. Barclay hoisted a white flag. British power on the Lakes had been broken—as it turned out, forever.

The Treaty of Ghent, which terminated the war, made a few minor changes in the American/Canadian boundary through the

Great Lakes but generally left things as they had been before the war. Like most wars, it had gained precisely nothing.

Or perhaps not quite nothing. The actual political status of the land west of the Appalachians was no different, but British resistance to the westward movement of American colonists was dead. The north coast of the United States had at last been fully opened for settlement.

And almost as soon as the guns were silent, the settlers were on their way.

VI The Great Wave

I t is difficult for us today to appreciate the impact of that great human seiche that poured forth from the east in the mid-nineteenth century to people the unpeopled reaches of Ohio and Wisconsin and Michigan and Indiana and Illinois. It came from the Atlantic seaboard states, from the South, and from New England; it came from Canada; it came from Scotland and Ireland and Norway and Germany and all the ancient, overcrowded continent of Europe. Developing cities on the Lakes, cities with a plat and a prayer and nothing much beyond that, hired agents to prowl the docks at New York and Charleston and Providence, uttering the magic words "free land," inducing emigrants who had just disembarked to get right back on another vessel for a trip up the brand-new Erie Canal to the Lakes and the waiting lands beyond. Some agents went further, traveling to Europe to take their sales pitches to the emigrants before they had become emigrants. No one was to be left behind. The barges with their human cargoes crawled up the canal; the cargoes unloaded themselves for transfer to Lakes passenger ships at Buffalo; Buffalo was a polyglot warren of kaleidoscopically shifting humanity. The ships, their holds packed stinking-tight with emigrants, traveled over the Lakes like fleas on a gigantic watery wolf, riding low. Some rode too low, going down with all aboard to colonize dark realms from which there was no returning. Some were cast onto reefs in storms; some burned like gigantic Egyptian pyres, sending up fountains of flame and showers of billowing sparks in the dark night to illuminate one last glimpse of water and sky for the screaming, living cordwood packed in their keels. The *Ogdensburg* and the *Atlantic* collided off Erie, Pennsylvania, in 1852, with the loss of perhaps four hundred lives. The *Phoenix* went up in flames like her namesake bird off Sheboygan, Wisconsin, in 1847, but unlike her namesake did not return from the ashes: Nearly all three hundred aboard her were lost. The *Gold Hunter* disappeared off the Bass Islands in 1869 with an unknown number of passengers, leaving only a bottle to float ashore with a desperate message: "Mast gone. Sinking fast. Goodbye all. Gold Hunter." These are merely examples. Almost three hundred ships were recorded lost on the Lakes every year during the latter half of the nineteenth century. Many of them—perhaps most of them— were emigrant craft. The lives lost were literally uncountable.

But for every ship lost, dozens more got through.

The Lake Erie shore of Ohio was the first of the North Coast emigrant regions to be settled. Here the settlement began even before the War of 1812—before the British had relinquished full claim, before the "Indian problem" had been solved by methods reminiscent of Alexander the Great's solution to the Gordian knot. That shore had been ceded to Connecticut during the 1790's as a "Western Reserve," a place for resettlement of citizens whose properties had been destroyed by fire during the Revolutionary War, and though the "Firelands," as they were called (and still sometimes are), were dangerous places in that era, the settlers came. Ashtabula was founded in 1801, Huron and Sandusky in 1805. Cleveland dates itself back to a boatload of settlers brought over the bar into the mouth of the Cuyahoga in 1796 by one General Moses Cleaveland, who stayed four months and left forever; the people he had chosen to bring with him, fortunately, turned out to have more staying power. (The extra "a" in "Cleaveland" was dropped in the middle of the nineteenth century—so the story goes—by a newspaper editor who couldn't fit it onto his masthead.) The place was already thriving by the time Perry took on Barclay off Put-in-Bay, and Clevelanders spent most of that splendidly clear day on the waterfront listening to the sounds of cannon drifting toward them like cloudless thunder from beyond the western horizon.

Toledo's settlement came later. The earliest emigrant waves had passed by this low-lying area at the mouth of the Maumee River with

hardly a second glance; it was a part of the bed of ancient Lake
Maumee, and it often seemed as though the old Lake were coming
back to claim it. It was damp, mosquito-infested, partially inundated
at high water, and filled with a particularly nasty thicket of tangled
vegetation known as the Black Swamp. But there were settlements
upstream, above the swamp, and the sluggish, meandering Maumee
was too shallow for ships to reach them. In 1836 a town was platted
at the edge of the swamp and drainage began. This very nearly led
to war—not Americans against British or settlers against Indians, but
Ohioans against Michiganders. Both states claimed the area. Outright
fighting between their militias was narrowly avoided when Congress
stepped in and, in return for Michigan's relinquishing claim to
Toledo, gave the infant state a slice of Wisconsin—a large, scenic
slice, rich in minerals and timber, caught between the north shore of
Lake Michigan and the south shore of Lake Superior. It is known
today in Michigan as the Upper Peninsula, or simply the U.P.

Congress's gift to Michigan came just in time; a few more years,
and Wisconsin would have been in a position to contest the issue.
Leapfrogging most of Michigan, the next tide of emigrants was
landing there—there, and along the neighboring Illinois and Indiana
shores. One of the greatest resettlement movements in history was
underway.

The pace was dizzying. In 1820, the Cass expedition had camped
the night of August 26 "at the mouth of Milwacky River," finding
—according to Schoolcraft—"two American families, and a village
of Pottowatomies, at its mouth." By the beginning of 1833, a full
thirteen years later, the population had increased by exactly one. But
by the end of that year, four more people had arrived, the first trickles
of the coming flood. Incorporation came in 1835, with the population
at a few hundred; the population of the entire Territory of Wisconsin
at that time was about 11,000. The next summer, sixty buildings went
up in town in seven months. There were 10,000 people in Milwaukee
by 1845, 21,000 people by 1850, and 46,000 by 1851. By then Wisconsin
had a population of over 300,000 and had been a state for three years.
There had been some talk of making it an independent country; more
than two-thirds of the inhabitants were German, and there were large
areas where English was neither spoken nor understood.

Ninety miles to the south, Chicago was growing even faster than

Milwaukee. Like the U.P., this was an area that had been stolen from Wisconsin, cut off and given to Illinois in 1818 to provide the new state an outlet on Lake Michigan. At that time Chicago barely existed; the reinvested relic of Fort Dearborn stood beside a tiny, struggling hamlet with perhaps twelve families in it. There was no harbor. Prospects looked so bleak that when Chicago residents approached the bankers of Shawneetown—the state's leading city—for development loans, they were turned down flat.

The boom began in the 1830's. At the beginning of the decade, the same twelve families were still living by themselves on the banks of "Checago Creek." Three years later the number of residents had risen to 500, and four years after that, to 5,000. Twenty years later the population passed 100,000, bowed once, and never looked back. By 1900 Chicago had reached the two million mark and was the nation's second largest city—a position it held until 1980, when it was passed, barely, by Los Angeles.

Shawneetown today has a population of just over 1,700. So much for the intelligence of bankers.

Development elsewhere around the Lakes went forward considerably more slowly than at Milwaukee and Chicago, but it went forward nonetheless. There was a boom-and-bust feel to much of it, at least on the American side. The northern half of Michigan's Lower Peninsula, the region of jumbled moraines known to geographers as the High Plains, was too rocky and hilly to make good farming country; but it had trees, and the trees could be cut down and sold at an enormous profit in places like Milwaukee and Chicago and Cleveland and Toledo. Boomtowns sprang up, lived their brief, dazzling lives, and faded away again to next to nothing, leaving a few hardy survivors to stay on and be called settlers. On the Upper Peninsula and in northern Wisconsin, trees were cut, too, but real development had to wait for the arrival of the mining boom in the second half of the nineteenth century. There the same boom-and-bust cycle went on as had been seen in the timber country; there, too, the little cities managed to hang on after the boomers left, slowly growing toward something resembling permanence.

Weighted down by the legacy of the Quebec Act and by George III's cautious settlement policies, Canadian development proceeded at a much more deliberate pace than that of the American side. It did, nevertheless, proceed. Hamilton was founded in 1778, Toronto in 1793, Goderich in 1828, Windsor and Sarnia between 1833 and 1836. By the time the British North America Act was passed in 1867, granting independence to Canada, all of these had grown into respectable small cities. That growth would continue, although—perhaps because it had come through an orderly, dignified transition of power rather than through revolution (or perhaps because the American experiment had already shown that headlong development was unwise)—independence did not bring the same waves of settlers to the Canadian south coast as it had to the American north. Growth increased quietly instead of spurting. This quiet increase, however, was quite enough. Today, there are 15 million people—roughly 60 percent of the country's population—crowded along the shores of Canada's side of the Great Lakes. Toronto alone has 2.2 million residents, and has replaced Montreal as the nation's largest city. In Canada as well as the United States, the Quebec Act has long since proved precisely that "temporary expedient" that George Washington said it would be.

All this development was, of course, not without its problems.

There was, to begin with, the problem of pollution—and we are not speaking here of the pollution brought in by industry, substantial as that has been. We are speaking of the plain, everyday pollution produced by human beings in the process of living their lives, including but not limited to sewage, garbage, smoke and soot, and just plain dirt. Pollution has been a problem in Fifth Coast cities from the beginning. Settlement requires the removal of ground cover: the clearing of timber, the breaking of prairie sod, the destruction of water plants within what will be the settlement's harbor. Large areas of the landscape are covered over and made impervious to rainfall, a process that increases runoff. The runoff carries things with it—dust and ashes, dirt from the city streets, and soil from the denuded and vulnerable ground. If there are horses—and there were, everywhere, during the period of intense settlement of the Lakes—the runoff will also carry manure. It will not generally carry human feces, but these—or at least the effects of them—will get into the water anyway. During the first stages of settlement, human feces will be deposited in pits; groundwater will leach through them, carrying bacteria into nearby watercourses. Later, the route will be more direct. "Modern conveniences"—central plumbing—will arrive, to replace the outhouse by piping all wastes to one centralized location for disposal. Usually "disposal" simply means dumping them into a river or lake and letting the currents carry them away. Out of sight, out of mind.

In the Great Lakes region, water pollution problems were compounded early by two unusual geographic features. One is the poor development of the region's drainage system—the small size and uncertain watersheds of its streams. The second is the huge size of the Lakes themselves. This size was deceptive; it gave them an appearance of invulnerability they did not possess.

The poor drainage system is the result of the recent abandonment of the area by the continental glacier. Old drainages were wiped out by the ice, and new ones have not yet had time to develop. Watershed boundaries, in this flat, new landscape, are indistinct; streams tend to wander from one watershed to another. The effect is a chaos of sluggish little rivers, their courses short, their tributaries intermingled. There are more than 100 rivers flowing into Lake Michigan; of these, only eight have an average flow greater than 1,000 cubic feet per second, and the largest—the Fox, which falls into the Lake at Green Bay—averages just 4,300 cubic feet per second. To get some idea what these figures mean, it may be helpful to realize that the Potomac flows past Washington, D.C., at 11,200 cfs; the Ohio River flows past Louisville at 114,000 cfs; and the Mississippi flows past Vicksburg at more than 1,000,000 cfs. The Hudson is already almost twice as large as the Fox before it reaches Albany.

Small, sluggish streams like those of the Great Lakes have neither the capacity nor the power to move the amount of sewage even a little city will produce; and that is where the second problem, the great size of the Lakes, comes in. The streams might be getting rapidly polluted, but with a seemingly infinite supply of water next door, who cared? Cities turned their backs on their rivers. When the rivers produced fans of pollution out into the Lakes from their mouths, the cities turned their backs on these, too. It was easier simply to move the intakes of their water systems—and there were always plenty of places to move the intakes to. You could usually simply move them along the shoreline (there are 10,000 miles of Great Lakes shoreline). But if that didn't work—if the immediate shoreline got too built up, and you didn't want to pipe water in past the suburbs—you could always move the intakes further out into the Lake instead. As time went on, that was the course most often adopted by the larger Great Lakes cities. Chicago's principal water intake today is three miles offshore; so is Toronto's. Cleveland's is five miles out.

Pollution of the region's rivers was noticeable early. In the first accounts of settlement in northern Ohio, prior to 1825, the word most often used to describe streams and rivers was "fair," which meant clear; by 1850, most of them had been downgraded to "turbid." Fish were having trouble spawning in the Saginaw River and nearby areas of Saginaw Bay, on Lake Huron, by 1845. An 1899 book by J. B. Mansfield, *History of the Great Lakes* (J. H. Beers & Co.), gives the following account of the condition of the Chicago River:

> The Chicago River has been improved, docked, dredged, and bridged by the city of Chicago and by the riparian owners, as the city grew to keep pace with their requirements for commerce primarily and for sewage disposed for convenience incidentally . . . until it has grown to be a great artificial waterway, without public landings or docks, defiled and putrescent with sewage and filth. . . .

Along with the problem of pollution came the problem of direct environmental alteration. Fifth Coast cities filled wetlands, dredged bars and harbors, constructed breakwaters, paved soils. They did these things on a massive scale, a scale that was particularly disruptive because of their locations. The prized sites for cities—protected harbors and river mouths—were precisely the areas of richest environmental diversity and value. They were the areas preferred by spawning fish and waterfowl as well as by city builders. Silt-laden waters slowed down in these areas, dropping their silt and keeping it out of the Lakes. The great mats of aquatic vegetation served as gigantic water filters, through which the stream water would slowly percolate on its way to becoming lake water, leaving behind most of its suspended solids and even large numbers of its resident bacteria. Modern studies of wetlands have documented great dollar values for these so-called wasted areas. A 1978 look at Great Lakes wetland values by

the Michigan Department of Natural Resources, for instance, established a figure of $490/acre, or roughly $52 million for all coastal
wetlands remaining in the state at that time. Other estimates have
been considerably higher. Joan Dent of the Michigan Sea Grant
Program has used the figure $86,000/acre—a bit elevated, perhaps,
but certainly not impossible. Salt marshes along the Florida coast are
known to be that valuable.

The value of wetlands is not widely recognized even today; and
so it is not too surprising to find that it was not recognized at all back
in the nineteenth century when settlement was going on around the
Lakes. Perhaps it would have been ignored even if it had been
known. Cities need harbors, after all; they need land adjacent to rivers
to build buildings upon. There is generally only one way to get these
things, and that is to dredge and fill the rivers and the wetlands. And
that is precisely what happened.

The record of changes wrought on Great Lakes rivers by the
beginning of the twentieth century is staggering. Nearly every
watercourse along the U.S. north coast, and most of those along
Canada's south coast, had been dredged; many had been straightened
for long distances. Bars at their mouths had been removed. Especially
at the southern end of Lake Michigan, where the rivers—after centuries of having their mouths moved sideways by shore drift—usually
ran parallel to the Lake for distances of a mile or more, they were
shortened significantly by cutting through the narrow necks of land
where the first close approach between river and Lake was made.
Breakwaters and groins were built off their mouths, preventing normal shore-drift action. By this means the harbors became usable.
They also became ugly, dirty, and largely sterile.

Buffalo was the first city on the Lakes to improve its harbor. In
1820, locked in a struggle with nearby Black Rock to decide the
western terminus of the Erie Canal, Buffalo got together a public
subscription, lobbied the legislature at Albany for assistance, and
hired a "harbor engineer" at a monthly salary of $50 to turn the
Buffalo River into an anchorage. A few months later they dismissed
the engineer for incompetence and did the job themselves, digging
out the bar at the river's mouth by hand and cribbing the channel
with wooden piers to keep it open. Further improvements came
apace. By 1900 the river had been deepened to 14 feet for more than

a mile upstream from its mouth; a 13-foot deep canal ran parallel to the river, halfway between the river and the Lake, and a masonry breakwater with passages cut through it for ships ran along the shore of the Lake for nearly two miles at a distance of 2,500 feet out. Black Rock had given up on its own harbor work, and in fact had been part of the expanding City of Buffalo for nearly half a century.

The Milwaukee River, at the time the city was settled, was a "curved stream, filled with grass, [and] almost impassable"; surrounded by marsh, it ran parallel to the shore behind a narrow sand dune for more than half a mile. Clearance over the bar at its mouth was less than five feet at the deepest point. In 1846 the channel was deepened to 11 feet; in 1852 the dune was cut through 3,000 feet above the river's natural mouth, and dredging began to a uniform depth of 13 feet. Fourteen years later the depth was increased to 19 feet, and half a mile of wooden cribs was built on each side of the deepened channel. By the turn of the century more than 1,000 acres of Milwaukee Bay surrounding the river mouth had been enclosed by a mile-long breakwater of cribwork on a stone foundation, and the "curved stream, filled with grass" was only a dim memory. In the meantime, the wetlands beside the river had been filled. Much of Milwaukee today rests on that fill, creating severe foundation problems for the city's downtown buildings.

At Marquette, on Lake Superior, the situation was somewhat different. The dark, glacier-polished Pre-Cambrian rocks of the Superior shore rise abruptly from the water; the two little rivers that enter Marquette Bay drop over that rise with rapids and small waterfalls. They could not be improved into harbors by any stretch of the engineer's tape measure. Nevertheless—as the principal port of entry for the Marquette Iron Range—Marquette needed a harbor. At the earliest time of settlement, in the late 1840's, ships were anchored well offshore and their cargo transferred to small boats; animal cargoes—horses and mules and cattle—were simply shoved overboard and made to swim ashore through the cold Superior waters. In the early 1850's an attempt was made to build a dock. A handsome stone-filled crib was extended out to deep water in the bay. The night before it was to be dedicated there was one of Superior's better storms: Marquette woke up the next morning and found itself back where it had started. All traces of construction had disappeared. The Lake had won the first round. Nature never wins for long, however; by 1895 there was a long, stormproof concrete breakwater enclosing the part of the bay immediately in front of the city, and the sheltered cove behind Presque Isle had been dredged out and threaded with ore docks. Where there was need for a harbor there would be one, natural inclination or no.

The stories of Buffalo, Milwaukee, and Marquette were repeated, with variations, all up and down the Fifth Coast: at Duluth, Minnesota, where the great bar of Minnesota Point was cut through in defiance of a court order, issued at the request of neighboring Superior, Wisconsin, to leave it alone; at Toronto, which faced the unusual situation of a moving island that had begun life as a peninsula, detached itself from the mainland, and gradually extended itself into the harbor channel; at Parry Sound, where channels had to be incised into Canadian Shield granites so hard they shattered carbon-steel drill bits; at Toledo, where the first "improvement" was a wooden dock extending several hundred yards through the Black Swamp to the relatively open waters of the Maumee, and given the hopeful name of Manhattan; and at hundreds of other places around the Lakes, the work went on. Even tiny towns, towns often no longer on today's map, got into the harbor-improvement act. Fairport, Ohio, was once considerably larger than Cleveland; it had a mile and a half of docks and an eighteen-foot channel dredged into the Grand River through a bar that had once been so shallow that in the dry seasons it was used as a road. Nearly $400,000 had been spent there for improvements by 1900. Today it is a ruin. White Lake, Michigan, once had a dredged harbor and twin piers, each nearly 2,000 feet long, built at a total cost to the taxpayers of $287,000 in 1880's currency. It is a ruin, too. Marine City, Grindstone City, Cedar River, Port Burwell—the story goes on and on.

Chicago is a special case. So much change has gone on in the Chicago area, so much filling and dredging and changing of the landscape, that it might well be called, not the Windy City, but the Engineered City.

The best place to get a feel for what has happened to this "Place of the Wild Garlic"—the meaning of the Indian word *Checaugou*—is from the Skydeck at the top of the Sears Tower, the World's Tallest Office Building, at the corner of Jackson and South Wacker

Drive in the center of town. To the north and east are the John Hancock Tower, the Standard Oil Building, the First National Bank Building, and the other square, brawny, Chicago-style skyscrapers that make the city's bulky skyline even more impressive than Manhattan's. To the west lies the tangle of freeway interchanges where the Kennedy and Eisenhower and Dan Ryan expressways all come together in a gigantic heap, a jumble of bridges and ramps and intertwining concrete arches known to Chicagoans as the Spaghetti Bowl; to the south, beyond the Congress Parkway, spread the flat, bleak Railroad Yards. To the east lies Lake Michigan, fronted by Grant Park. The Adler Planetarium, the Field Museum of Natural History, and Soldiers' Field Stadium line the Lake's rim like mites on a distant plate.

Two hundred years ago, most of what you see wasn't there— not just the buildings, but the land itself. The park, the museum complex, the stadium, the railroad yards—all of that is fill. Most of Chicago is built on fill. What isn't filled lake is filled swamp; the land here at this old Lake Michigan outlet was so low and marshy that when sewer lines were put in for the first time, back around 1900, they couldn't be dug into the ground because the water table was too high. The city laid its lines on the streets and then covered them with fill. Buildings in Chicago dating from before the sewers were put in often have their entrances on what used to be the second floor.

Curving around the base of the Sears Tower, right at your feet —if your feet were 1,300 feet long—flows the Chicago River. It, too, has changed—more significantly, perhaps, than anything else in sight. In 1820 it was a small, sluggish, meandering stream, with "a bar at its mouth, which prevents ships from entering, but . . . deep within," flowing into the Lake a few hundred yards south of Fort Dearborn. Today the bar and most of the meanders are gone; the river connects to the Lake directly east of the site of the old fort, and it no longer flows into the Lake, it flows out. The change was made in 1900. At that time the river was the city's principal sewer, and it wasn't up to the job. It was carrying typhoid germs, and diphtheria germs, and all sorts of other friendly animalculae. Worse than that: It was carrying raw turds, which were washing up on the beaches in front of the upper-crust apartment buildings along the Gold Coast, north of the river's mouth. That was unsightly as well as unsanitary. Something had to be done.

Fortunately for Gold Coast residents, something was available. The river could not be easily cleaned up, but it could easily be reversed. Lake Michigan came incredibly close, even in its natural, pre-engineered state, to overflowing its basin in the south. There are no mountains here, not even hills—only low, flat morainal deposits left by the glacier when it withdrew 12,000 years ago. The drainage patterns are poorly developed and indistinct. At one point, the watershed boundary between the Lake Michigan drainage basin and the Mississippi River drainage basin is within five miles of the lakeshore; at another point it is barely six feet high. Cutting a ditch through those swampy soils to a point on the Illinois River that would be lower than the Chicago's mouth on the Lake was a simple task, indeed: All the engineers had to do was to duplicate the old Lake Chicago outlet. They did. It is called the Chicago Sanitary and Ship Canal, and it flows out of the Lake, up the old South Branch of the Chicago River, across what used to be the Mud Lake Swamp— which, in times of high water, drained both ways—and into the Des Plaines. Lake Michigan water drains through it, flushing the Great Chicago Toilet on the way, and ends up in the Illinois. Let other people worry about the turds.

In point of fact, they have. Chicago has been sued over the Sanitary and Ship Canal, not once but several times. The interesting thing about these suits, though, is that most of them have not been filed by the residents of the Illinois Valley—where the flush goes—but by those of the Great Lakes Basin, where it comes from. Ever since the canal was put in, there have been recurring fears that it would divert too much water from the Lakes, lowering their level and significantly damaging uses of them by others. Diversions reached a high point in 1928, when the amount of water flushed out of the Lake and down the canal was roughly 10,000 cubic feet per second; since then it has been limited, by court order, to roughly one-third that amount.

By the early decades of the twentieth century, settlement patterns in the Lakes region had taken on much the shape they have today. It is a conspicuously two-tiered arrangement. Below a clearly defined straight-line demographic boundary running roughly from Madison,

Wisconsin, to Ottawa, Ontario—referred to by population experts as "The Line"—development has been intense. In this "working tier" lies the greatest industrial concentration on the North American continent. The third, fifth, tenth, and twelfth largest cities of the United States are in this region below The Line; so, in a curiously parallel arrangement, are the first, sixth, tenth, and eleventh largest in Canada. (For the curious, these cities are Chicago, Detroit, Cleveland, and Milwaukee in the United States; and Toronto, Hamilton, London, and Windsor in Canada.) The automotive industry, as everyone knows, is centered in the working tier of the Great Lakes, principally in Detroit and Windsor; so is the steel industry, though it is more spread out, occupying places like Gary and Hammond, Indiana; Detroit; Cleveland; and Hamilton, Ontario, known among its Canadian neighbors as Steeltown. Chemical plants share shore space with the steel plants in most areas, and other manufactured goods—refrigerators, outboard motors, cameras—are produced in profusion, mostly in smaller cities like Kenosha, Waukegan, and Rochester. There is some sense of the region being a national sacrifice area for two nations. Legend has it—for instance—that the profusion of ugliness that is the mill areas of Hammond and Gary and South Chicago came about because the steel executives, who lived in Chicago, preferred to build their plants out there among the dunes where they wouldn't have to look at them, rather than in the city, where they would.

Above The Line, things are vastly different. This is the Midwestern Outback, the area once referred to by Henry Clay in a famous Senate speech as "a place beyond the remotest extent of the United States, if not in the Moon." This is an American region whose citizens still sometimes talk about trips "back to the States"; it is a Canadian region which didn't get its first through highway until 1960. It is not only not urban, it is not even—for the most part—rural. The word "rural" implies agriculture. Most of the agriculture in the Great Lakes Basin is south of The Line. Above it, the principal crops are timber and minerals.

And scenery, of course. And clean air.

There are, nevertheless, cities above The Line—some of them of considerable size and age. Duluth was settled as a fur-trading post named Fond du Lac in the eighteenth century; it now has a respectable 100,000 people in it, and an inland seaport that moves more freight than any other port in the United States except New York City. Thunder Bay, Ontario, formed as late as 1970 by the merger of the twin cities of Fort William and Port Arthur, nevertheless has a history that goes back to 1803. Again, it began life as a fur-trading post; again, it has flourished lately as a port. Marquette, Michigan; Sault Ste. Marie, Michigan/Ontario; and Ashland, Wisconsin, all have some claim to city status. Sudbury, Ontario—off the Lakes but in the Basin—has a more than just claim: At 100,000 people, it is among the ten largest population centers in the Province.

The development of the Lakes was a necessary part of the development of the continent, and in itself cannot reasonably be called an evil. The Lakes are the economic heart of two nations; we all depend on them. Settlement has been part of this pattern, and has generally been a social good. It would be foolish to argue otherwise. At the same time, however, development has brought with it certain serious environmental disruptions, and these have not been good. The Lakes, we must never forget, are young and therefore—despite their great size—fragile. Settlement has in many cases failed to take this into account. The result—looked at strictly from the standpoint of the Lakes—has been a disaster, the full effects of which are still developing.

Up to this point, I have purposely said little about industry's contribution to the Lakes' problems, preferring to concentrate on the direct impacts of settlement—the land alterations to accommodate cities and the pollution produced by great agglutinations of people living in one place. It is now time to remedy that. The people who live in cities, after all, must make a living—and how they do that can be extremely troublesome. In the Great Lakes, it has been so from the beginning, when, as the fur trade drew to a close, incoming entrepreneurs cast their eyes on the region's next most obvious extractive resources—its vast, prolific, and seemingly infinite forests— and settled down to doing to those forests precisely what their forerunners had done to the beaver that had once inhabited them.

VII The Big Cut

The hemlock bark was piled in long rows of stacks, roofed over
with more bark, like houses, and the peeled logs lay huge and
yellow where the trees had been felled. They left the logs in the
woods to rot, they did not even clear away or burn the tops. It
was only the bark they wanted for the tannery at Boyne City
. . . and each year there was less forest and more open, hot,
shadeless, weed-grown slashing.

Ernest Hemingway, *Fathers and Sons*

The ears of the running rabbit that is Upper Michigan are
formed by the Keweenaw Peninsula—a 20-mile-wide sliver
of rock and pine jutting northeastward 60 miles off the
Fifth Coast into the icy heart of the world's largest freshwater ocean.
The Keweenaw is a hard, awesome place, its mountainous backbone
thrusting nearly 800 feet above Lake level, its rocky, lonely shores
pounded by surf and cupping, here and there, exquisite little beaches
of sand or small pebbles. It receives, in the course of an average
winter, nearly twenty feet of snow, and it has been known to get as
much as thirty. There are few places in the contiguous United States
more remote and less hospitable—or, to the lover of wild places, more
starkly and supremely beautiful.

Out at the extreme tip of the Keweenaw the small town of Copper Harbor sprawls among scraggly pines on a tiny shelf at the foot
of hulking Brockway Mountain. Copper Harbor is literally a wilderness outpost: The small rockbound bay here is the primary jumping-off place for Isle Royale National Park, and most of the several
thousand tourists who pass through town each summer are going
there. Rod Badger and I were going there, too, but there was some-

thing else we had to do first. Just outside Copper Harbor there is a small nature sanctuary called the Estivant Pines, which contains—so we had been told—one of the last stands of virgin white pine in Michigan; one of those pines, the Leaning Giant, was reputed to be the second largest of its species in the nation. Like the smoked white-fish Rod had purchased at Grand Marais, it was a remnant of a fast-vanishing past. A view seemed essential.

We found the parking area for the sanctuary easily, parked the car where the signs said to, and started walking, west, down an old logging road framed by hardwoods and dappled underfoot by bright, tremulous patches of moving sun. . . .

So much has been said in the past about the immense raid on the forests of the Great Lakes region by nineteenth-century loggers that it is difficult to write about it today without running head-on into clichés—most of them false. There is an immediate temptation to speak of "unbroken canopies"; of "cathedral-like groves" made up of "huge, ancient trees"; and of "wholesale destruction" by "greedy, rapacious timber barons." In fact all of these existed, but not quite as they are popularly imagined. The "unbroken canopies" usually ex-tended no more than a few square miles before yielding to natural openings caused by fire, windthrow, or unproductive soils; the "cathedral-like groves" were kept open and cathedral-like by human intervention—understory fires set deliberately by the Indians as a game management tool—and were already fading away, along with the Indians, when the first settlers arrived. The trees were "huge" and "ancient" enough when compared to the second-growth forests of today, but they were young and puny indeed compared to the redwoods and Douglas firs of the west coast. And the "timber bar-ons"—wealthy as many of them became—were driven as often by altruism as by greed. The "rapacity" they have been accused of was more often simply ignorance—ignorance, carelessness, and a mis-placed confidence in the exhaustlessness of forests whose beginnings had not been seen and whose end could therefore not possibly be imagined.

Wholesale destruction, however, there was. That cannot ever be denied.

·   ·   ·

There were three separate and geographically distinct forests in the Great Lakes region when the loggers arrived early in the nineteenth century. To the north there was the taiga, the boreal forest, clothing the north shore of Lake Superior and reaching far down the east shore of Lake Huron; it was composed mainly of spruce, fir, and tamarack, with a small admixture of pines, hemlock, and hardy broadleaf trees such as beech, birch, aspen, and northern maple. To the south, around Lake Erie and the southern tip of Lake Michigan, the so-called central hardwood forest was predominant—an association of oak, ash, dogwood, southern maple, and other broadleafed trees, festooned by trailing vines and broken by scattered grassy savannahs and plains, some of fairly great extent. And in the middle, between the sunny expanse of the central hardwood forest and the dark, brooding immensity of the taiga, was a broad band known to plant geographers today as the "transition forest" and to those who live in it simply as the "North Woods." The North Woods surrounded Lake Ontario, skirted the north shore of Lake Erie and the south shore of Lake Superior, and lay across the broad midsections of Lakes Huron and Michigan like a great, graceful Diana's girdle. There was some oak and dogwood in its southern portions and some spruce and birch and hemlock scattered through the north, but its characteristic trees were pines—white pines and red, four feet thick and more than a hundred feet tall, straight-grained, easily worked, and strong. Very strong. It was these pines that were the preferred prey of the self-styled "timber beasts" in the lumber business, and it was therefore the North Woods that bore the brunt of the logging —the wide-open, cut-it-all-down extravaganza of destruction we know today as the Big Cut.

It started out innocently enough. Human settlement always requires lumbering and the clearing of forests; it is necessary to provide building materials and to open the land for the creation of fields and cities. This was going on along the Fifth Coast long before the Europeans arrived. Axes made of Lake Superior copper are among the most common remains of the Old Copper Culture; the Iroquois and the Hurons lived in fortified towns of wooden houses surrounded by log palisades and cleared fields, and the Chippewa, Potawatomi, and other western tribes regularly set fire to portions of the North Woods to improve the hunting by providing increased deer habitat. When the settlers came, they were content at first merely to follow the Indian pattern. The earliest European settlements on the Great Lakes were at places like Detroit and Green Bay, where they could take advantage of large natural savannahs; and even later, as the settlers moved into the forests, they began by creating openings no larger than they could immediately use. That first big wave of settlement had landed in Ohio, in the midst of the central hardwood region. Clearing the hardwoods was hard work, and, even after the trees were removed, they were a nuisance. There was at that time no market for hardwoods. Thousands of them—millions of dollars' worth, by today's standards—were killed by girdling, chopped down, piled in the centers of the clearings they had once occupied, and burned on the spot.

The settlements in northern New York, on the south shore of Lake Ontario, were in a band of modified North Woods that was rich in pine, and here there was some logging early on; the first building at what is now Rochester was a water-powered sawmill at the Falls of the Genesee, and nearby Auburn had three sawmills operating by 1820. But the markets were over the pass at the head of the Mohawk and clear away down the Hudson to New York City, and the wide-open logging in the pines of Maine, where the transition forest of the Great Lakes region jumped over the mountains and came down to meet the Atlantic, was saturating them all anyway. It wasn't until the timber industry was well established in Michigan that the loggers would come back, almost as an afterthought, and take all the pine out of Lake Ontario and the Finger Lakes.

Not that it took a long time. The key year, as it turned out, was 1835. That was the year an out-of-work timber beast named Harvey Williams cruised up the coast of Lake Huron, turned the corner into Saginaw Bay, took one look at the tall, straight pines with their thick boles marching off, row upon row, into the muted and misty forest distance, and decided that he had found paradise.

Harvey Williams's timing was perfect. The Erie Canal had been opened, providing the missing transportation link to the big eastern seaboard markets; the great pineries of Maine were almost gone, and the timber barons were looking around for new opportunities. The techniques of mechanized, mass-production logging—the log boom and the peavey hook, the steam-powered mill, the circular saw—had been developed and tested in Maine and were ready for full-scale deployment. And the Great Migration was getting underway, that massive mid-century wave of settlement we have already spoken of that poured through the Lakes region and beyond, onto the prairies of the Midwest, of Iowa and Illinois and Kansas and Nebraska—prairies that were open and free of trees, prairies where virtually every stick of building timber would have to be imported. Prairies that came right up to the Lakes at Chicago held out their treeless arms, and cried for succor from the rich green woods of Michigan.

Michigan, as it turned out, was all too ready and eager to provide it.

That first Saginaw Bay mill was a small one, powered by an old steamboat engine and able to turn out only about 2,000 board feet a day. A single big pine would occupy the mill for nearly three days. At that rate the forests might truly have lasted forever; but it didn't take long before that rate was reached, passed, superseded, and generally left in the dust. By 1850, sawmills lined both sides of the Saginaw River for several miles upstream from its mouth; by 1880 the number of mills had passed sixty, and in the mid-1890's it reached 100. By that time the cut had peaked out at over a billion board feet a year and Saginaw Bay was the busiest harbor, in terms of tonnage, on the Lakes. It was not, however, alone. The same year that Harvey Williams founded his mill on Saginaw Bay, a group of timber beasts from the woods around Augusta, Maine, established the town of Augusta, Michigan, on the upper Kalamazoo River. Four years later the first mill was built at nearby Muskegon. Growth in this area was nearly as rapid and intense as that around Saginaw Bay: By 1900 there were fifty-two mills ringed around Muskegon Lake, a landlocked embayment of Lake Michigan, and the city had become the self-proclaimed "lumber queen of the world." It was not a title that remained uncontested. Alpena, on the Lake Huron side above Saginaw Bay, cut 200 million board feet of pine in 1889; Menominee, on the Michigan/Wisconsin border in Green Bay, cut three times that the following year. Five years later, a single Upper Peninsula mill—the Cleveland Sawmill at Marquette, on Lake Superior—was cutting fifty million feet a year. The loggers had reached deep into Wisconsin and Minnesota by this time, and were beginning to abandon the denuded lands of lower Michigan. The cut was moving west and north. Soon—though this was not yet clear—it would move out of the area altogether.

The Big Cut was an era of extravagance. There was a road from Saginaw to Flint literally paved with clear pine, and a mountain of sawdust at Cheboygan 40 feet high and nearly a mile around. There were clearcuts that covered entire townships, the moraines and kames and drumlins (elongated or oval hills) left by the continental glacier sticking up obscenely through the naked soil like the ribs of a shaved dog. Cedars were shriven for matchsticks; hemlocks were felled, stripped of their bark for its tannin, and left to rot where they lay like so many buffalo. Land was cheap—good pineland in the Lower Peninsula was going for as little as $1.50 per acre in the 1830's, and it was not much more expensive in 1900—but it was not cheap enough for some of the less honest lumber operators, who not only cut over their own land but pirated that of their neighbors: Men were hired to file homestead claims on prime pinelands and then sign them over to the timber companies, and the "round forty"—buying forty acres and cutting the trees off all around it as well as on it—became a standing national joke.

There was show. The timber barons, newly rich and getting richer, vied with each other to build the biggest mansions, give the most extravagant dinners, and fund the most spectacular exhibits of mostly tasteless art and statuary. In the woods, the loggers vied, too, chasing records for the biggest tree, the greatest cut made in a single day, the largest boom driven to the mill in the fastest time. For the Michigan exhibit at the Chicago World's Fair in 1893, a mountainous pile of logs 16 feet wide, 18 feet long, and 33 feet 3 inches high was loaded on a lumber sleigh by the Nestor Logging Company of Ewen, Michigan, and pulled out of the woods around the Ontonagon River by a single pair of draft horses. The sleigh and its load, which later scaled out at more than 36,000 board feet, required nine railroad flatcars for transportation to the fair.

It was also, however—along with the show and the extravagance and the chest-thumping, macho exhibitionism—a period of great innovation in logging practices. The loggers of the Big Cut started out wielding double-bladed axes like the ones their predecessors had used in Maine. About 1880, though, they moved to two-man crosscut saws (the well-named "misery whips"), and then, toward the closing years of the devastation, to an early version of the chain saw. The circular saw had been developed in Maine, but the mechanized head saw—a band saw that is the first cutting device a log meets in the mill —had to wait for the inventiveness of Lakes States loggers. At the Muskegon mills they came up with automatic headrigs and bull chains—log-handling devices—and "hot ponds," steam-heated log ponds that allowed the mills to remain active year-round.

Logging itself also became active year-round. In the beginning, the loggers had moved into the woods only in the winter, when snow on the ground covered the undergrowth and previously cut stumps and allowed easy "yarding," or hauling of the logs, to the rivers where they could be made up into the great log booms that would be driven down to the mills when the ice broke up. But around 1870 someone in Michigan came up with a rig known as the "Big Wheel" —a wheel-and-axle combination five feet high at the hub, which could suspend logs high enough to clear the stumps—and after that, logging could be done without snow. "Horace Butters' Patent Skidding and Loading Machine," the first skyline lead, was invented in Ludington, Michigan, in 1886; it extended the range of summer logging even further. Dependence on the rivers for transport to the mills ceased with the coming of railroad logging, first practiced out of Averill, Michigan, by a firm called Wright & Ketchum in the 1870's.

The effect of all these mechanical innovations was to make the cut more efficient: to speed it up, to allow it to reach more of the timber, and—ultimately—to kill the industry. By the 1920's nearly every last toothpick had been cut in lower Michigan, and the cut in Wisconsin had fallen to 300 million board feet—the lowest since 1850. The Big Cut waved goodbye, leaped the Plains, and landed among the Douglas firs of Oregon, Washington, and British Columbia. The "inexhaustible" North Woods of the Great Lakes were exhausted; in their place was one vast wasteland, a land so thoroughly cut over, so wide-open-bare, that the great geologist Frank Leverett managed to do nearly all the field work for his landmark 1915 study of Pleistocene glaciation in Michigan by simply driving a horse and buggy around the Lower Peninsula and keeping his eyes open. Everything was right out there in plain sight; all it took was a little observation.

. . .

It is important to note that this thoroughgoing devastation was, at the time, not thought of as devastation at all. The timber barons were not trying to destroy the Great Lakes; they weren't even destroying them carelessly, as a by-product of trying to get the logs out as quickly and cheaply as possible. Their intentions were to create, not to destroy. The goal was permanent settlement, and permanent settlement required clearing the land for fields and cities. Even the great fires that swept the region in the late nineteenth century, killing thousands of people and hanging curtains of smoke so thickly over the Lakes that navigation was curtailed for weeks at a time, were looked on as ultimately beneficial: The slash, after all, had to be cleared some way, and wasn't ash good fertilizer? The *Detroit Post* certainly thought so. "These lands are now in such a condition that they are all ready for seeding to wheat," they editorialized after much of Michigan was burned over in the summer of 1881:

> . . . The rich salts of the former vegetation are preserved in their ashes, which are an excellent top-dressing of manure, soon to be washed into the earth by rains. . . . The trees, the underbrush and all the impediments to agriculture, it usually costs so much toil for the pioneer to remove, have been swept away, and the rich land lies open and ready cleared for the settler. . . .

In fact, the settlers never came or, if they came, lasted only a few seasons before going bankrupt and leaving the area forever. The boomers had missed an important point: Michigan was not Ohio. In the rich oak bottoms of Ohio, clearing the forest for agriculture yielded bumper crops; in the sandy soils of Michigan, it yielded only disappointment. Michigan had the leftovers, the sandy drift that remained behind after all the good soil had been carried to Ohio and Indiana by the glaciers, and it would grow nothing well but pines. Perhaps things might have been different here and there, in the low-lying areas where some thin organic soils had developed; but the loggers and the fires that followed them had pretty well taken care of that, too. Rain on the cleared lands had washed most of what little soil there was into the rivers, and the fires had taken the rest. They had been so hot that the organic soils had literally burned off, right down to the sand and clay beneath. There was nothing left to grow crops in—nothing at all.

The loggers might have foreseen some of this, had they been alert. There had to be a reason that Ohio grew oaks while Michigan grew pines, after all, and it might have been a valuable reason to know. In fact, the southern border of the pinelands—the area known among biologists today as the "pinelands/oak ecotone"—corresponds almost precisely to the furthest southern margin of the Valders Advance of the continental glacier. South of that, the land is good for agriculture; north of it, it is not, and nothing can make it so. That is the way the region divides today. "The Line" spoken of by modern demographers, separating the urban and agricultural southern Great Lakes from the Outback of the north, is almost exactly the same as the pinelands/oak ecotone along the old glacial margin. Those who feel that humans have indeed conquered nature and can now operate independent of its influence should spend some time pondering that striking alignment.

Insofar as logging was a land-management tool, opening the Lakes States for settlers, it was a failure. But if that failure were its only flaw, it could be forgiven. Worse things have happened than the mere opening of land to settlers who will not or cannot make use of it. What made the Big Cut truly a disaster was not just its effect on the land, but its effect on the Lakes themselves.

The Lakes and their tributary streams were absolutely essential to the early logging operations. They were transportation corridors; they were storage areas and power sources and waste-disposal units. Mills would be located near the mouths of major rivers; the logs would be floated down the rivers from the woods in great loose rafts known as "booms," and the planed lumber from the mills would be loaded on ships in the river mouths for transport to market. When a mill had used up the trees in its own watershed, it would purchase timber from others, and this timber would come to the mill across the Lakes in huge booms pulled by steam tugs. Bark would fall off the logs during transport, littering large areas of Lake bottom with coarse woody debris, covering the spawning gravels and feeding grounds of bottom-dwelling fish and using up the scarce dissolved oxygen of the depths as it decayed. Bark would also fall off in the streams, but a worse effect, there, was the scouring of stream channels and banks. The logs would remove bankside soils and streambed spawning gravels. They would rub like giant cats against the exposed roots of streamside vegetation, killing it, broadening the streams and exposing them to more sunlight. These broader, shallower streams with their increased loads of sediment and their lack of overhanging trees would warm significantly, altering the types of life forms inhabiting them; since most stream-spawning fish require clear water within a certain narrow temperature range for successful reproduction, the ability of the streams in these logged-over areas to produce fish declined drastically and in some cases was eliminated altogether.

If the loss of spawning gravels and the change in temperature and chemistry of the water wasn't enough to stop stream spawning, the dams were. Before the advent of steam, sawmills were run by water power. Water power requires falling water; falling water requires an elevation differential, or "head." Sometimes the necessary head could be obtained from natural waterfalls, but more often it needed to be provided artificially, by a dam. The dams on these logging streams were an insurmountable barrier to upstream migration of stream-spawning fish; all spawning beds above them were cut off. Sometimes large areas of beds below them were cut off, too. This downstream effect was the result of diversion. The dam would be built some distance upstream from the mill, and the water of the river would be diverted into a flume, leaving the river's natural bed—spawning gravels and all—totally dry.

The worst thing, however, was not the streambed scouring, or the bark litter, or the dams. The worst thing was the sawdust.

The mills produced hundreds of thousands of tons of sawdust—mounds of it, acres of it, whole mountains of it. It was a necessary by-product of the milling process, and it was almost impossible to dispose of. Try as they would, nobody could figure out what the hell to do with the stuff. Some of it was used for fuel, but that was messy, and anyway it didn't burn very well because it had a tendency to absorb moisture and to remain damp year-round. Some of it was used for fill, but that was even more unsuccessful than burning it: The sawdust, being organic, would decay rapidly, causing whatever had been built on the fill to sag, heel over, and fall down. In the end, most of that vast production of sawdust was simply dumped. Thus are major environmental disasters born.

The sawmills—as has already been pointed out—were generally located at the mouths of rivers. The mouths of rivers are a coast's prime estuarine areas—its most productive wetland complexes. The sawdust came down on those estuaries like a thick and smothering blanket. Some was dumped in the rivers and washed down to the estuaries, creating a uniform bottom-covering many inches thick over the riverbeds and their adjacent channels and a series of fans reaching far out into the coastal waters. More was dumped directly into the estuaries, which were convenient to the mills, and were "wasted" land where nobody went, and anyway, once the sawdust had decayed and compacted the wetlands would be drylands and maybe people could build things there, so wasn't dumping sawdust there a public service? However it got there, the sawdust, once in the estuaries, was enormously destructive. It duplicated the action of the bark detritus from the log booms, but in a much more efficient manner. The spawning gravels and the food-rich bottom muck were not only fouled but obliterated. The sawdust decayed faster than the bark, using more dissolved oxygen more rapidly; the bottom-dwellers that had not been directly smothered suffocated. Vast areas of once-productive wetlands became deserts where nothing moved. The fish avoided them. That meant they had no spawning and feeding grounds. The whole food chain of the Fifth Coast waters shivered and began to fall apart.

By the late nineteenth century the damage was widespread, severe, and in some places irreversible. The Atlantic salmon was gone from Lake Ontario—its only ancestral Great Lakes home—and whitefish and chub populations were in a precipitous decline. The whitefish could find offshore breeding grounds in the more irregular basins of Superior, Huron, and Michigan, so it survived longer there, but the chub nearly disappeared from these upper Lakes.

In Erie the blue pike began, about this time, a series of wild population oscillations with a curious twist to them. Nets set for the fish near the Lake bottom—its historic feeding area—failed uniformly to catch much of anything; but nets set twenty feet up would on some occasions yield huge amounts and on other occasions come up totally empty. The blue pike was apparently attempting to con-

vert itself from a bottom feeder to a mid-level feeder. The attempt
was unsuccessful. By 1950 the fish was all but unobservable anywhere
in the Lake, and it is thought today that the Lake Erie race of the blue
pike is extinct.

When the mills closed down in the early years of the twentieth
century and the loggers moved on toward the setting sun, the
denuded timberlands began the slow, difficult process of recovery.
Settlers moved in, planted crops in the sandy, sterilized soil, watched
the crops fail, and moved out again. With the settlers gone, the forest
began to creep back. The pioneering aspen came first, sprouting from
windblown seed or from deep, ancient roots that had managed to
survive the logging and the fires and the subsequent desiccation of
the exposed soil. Aspen will not sprout in shade—even its own—and
it is a mark of the severity of the logging-era depredations that 20
percent of the North Woods region here in the Great Lakes Basin
is currently covered with more or less pure aspen stands.

But not all of it. Where the aspen prepare the way, the pines
follow. Today much of the North Woods is again covered with white
pine, and there has been a moderate renaissance of logging, under
better control than in the past. But the great pine forests, the groves
of ancient trees straight and thick-boled as cathedral spires, are gone
forever. In their place are pulpwood forests—acre upon acre of little
matchstick-thin trees, mowed down in their youth by machines,
chewed up in Kraft plants, and spat out as paper and fiberboard. The
current forests of the Fifth Coast are devoted almost exclusively to
pulpwood production. Here and there a taste of the old timberlands
remains—the Estivant Pines, the Hartwick Pines in the central
Lower Peninsula, the forests of Porcupine Mountains State Park—
but they are tastes only. Elsewhere the timber is a crop, not a forest.
They are not the same thing.

The wetlands have seen the same cycle of recovery as the timberlands, but less successfully. The forces of natural succession have
been active where they could be, but it has not been as high a
proportion as on land. The wetlands were in many cases not just laid
waste but removed—filled in or scoured out to bedrock. The mill
sites—many of them—have hung on as towns and villages, still in the
estuaries, still a disturbing influence. Their harbors continue to be

dredged, though the craft that use them today are more often pleasure boats than lumber schooners; their citizens continue to require places to dump unwanted things—dirt, rock, sand, garbage—and as often as not they continue to dump them into the "useless" wetlands. And even if the wetlands were to recover entirely, the blue pike and the Atlantic salmon and the other doomed species would not return. Extinction is a one-way process. Planting fish might work, but planted stocks from other areas are usually poorly adapted to the microenvironments of their new location, and rarely survive; and the ecological niches of these vanished natives have long since been filled by more adaptable alien species such as carp and smelt and Pacific salmon. The changes brought on by the logging were permanent: Even if we were to turn our backs on the region and walk away forever it would never again be what it was. Time is a one-way stream, and we are left, irredeemably, with what we have done. Tastes we have, but tastes are not nearly enough.

Getting to the Estivant Pines, Rod and I soon discovered, was a little more trouble than the brochures had promised. The broad dry road soon turned into a trail; the trail turned to corduroy, sections of four-inch log roughly a foot and a half long laid side by side for interminable distances through a muskeg swamp and slowly sinking into the muck. Our feet sank with them. Mosquitoes and black flies —the ones the locals refer to as "Canadian soldiers"—circled in droves. A sign nailed to a tree said LEANING GIANT ½ MI, and beneath it some wag had scrawled: ABANDON ALL HOPE, YE WHO ENTER HERE. Finally, after at least forty days and nights in the wilderness with neither a pillar of cloud by day nor a pillar of fire by night to guide us, we came to a sluggish little stream with a narrow log across it. On the far side was a grove of small pines, and rising out of them was a great tree, indisputably leaning, indisputably giant. The goal, at last.

We crossed the footlog, climbed the far bank, and approached the Leaning Giant's seven-foot-thick trunk. We walked around it. Rod snorted. "Some giant," he said. "I wouldn't put it out to pasture with a Douglas fir—it would get eaten alive." I said nothing, but I had been thinking the same thing. But then, Rod and I are from Oregon, and they grow them big out there. This was Michigan, where they only used to grow them big. Think of the entire Fifth Coast, pounded by clear surf, empty of cities and heavy with these pines. Yes, of course it was necessary to cut them down—of course. I live in a wooden house; I burn wood in my fireplace; I write, and read, books printed on paper made from wood pulp. Necessary. Of course. But what of the wild places, the deer and the dragonfly, the deep waters and distant breezes and dark untamable forests we once knew and will never know again?

In 1820, Henry Schoolcraft spoke wonderingly of the "abundance of fish" provided by Saginaw Bay and its tributary waters. By 1845—just ten years after serious logging began in the Saginaw country—that abundance was only a memory. It has never returned. It is almost certain that it never will.

VIII Metals

On arriving at Teal Lake, we found the ore just as he had
described it. There lay the boulders of the trail, made smooth by
the atmosphere, bright and shining, but dark colored, and a
perpendicular bluff fifty feet in height, of pure solid ore, looking
like rock, but not rock. . . . From all that could be seen, it seemed
that the whole elevation for half a mile or more was one solid
mass of iron ore.

Philo M. Everett, in *Michigan Pioneer &*
Historical Collections, vol. 11 (1875)

While some were busily denuding the soil of the Fifth
Coast, others were just as busy with the soil itself—
digging into it, bringing out its minerals, and carting
them off. Like the furs and the trees, the minerals would primarily
be used elsewhere. It had become a pattern. Rip out a resource, ship
it off for someone else's benefit, and call it development—and when
the inevitable payment came due, rip out something else to raise the
cash. The Lakes were a fountainhead of wealth, but that wealth was
paradoxical: It could not seem to be obtained without taking it away.

The mining began almost accidentally. On September 19, 1844,
the distinguished American inventor William Austin Burt—holder
of early patents on the typewriter and developer of the Burt Solar
Compass—was leading a crew of surveyors through the tangled
brush of Michigan's Upper Peninsula near what would someday be
the city of Marquette. The U.S. Surveyor General, who didn't understand anything more about the oak/pine ecotone than anyone else
did, had decreed that Upper Michigan should be opened to settlers:
Therefore it had to be surveyed into township and range and section.

Burt and his crew were running township lines. His Solar Compass, which pointed to true north without the aid of magnets, had gotten him an appointment as Deputy U.S. Surveyor, but the government, in its slow bureaucratic fashion, insisted that he continue to take readings with the traditional magnetized needle instead. That was all right with Burt. He was, in effect, drawing a government salary for field-testing the Solar Compass, and he wasn't going to complain too hard about the preconditions. Anyway, the rest of the crew could watch the magnetic compass. That's what they were paid for.

This morning they had left the southeast corner of Teal Lake, about ten miles west of Marquette Bay, and begun cutting brush south along the line between Range 26 W and Range 27 W, Township 47 N, Michigan Meridian, climbing a steep little hill in the western outskirts of the future town of Negaunee. They had gone less than a mile when the compassman asked Burt to look at the needle on the magnetic compass. Something in the area was perturbing it; it was gyrating wildly, swinging in an arc of 60 to 70 degrees around true north. The further south they went, the worse the gyrations got, until finally the needle was actually pointing south part of the time. There was only one thing that could do that: There had to be a very large body of relatively pure iron ore close by. There was. They were, in fact, standing on it. The hill they were climbing was part of the Marquette Range, the richest iron lode discovered in North America to that time. Burt's survey party was the first to recognize this. There were exclamations of glee as the recognition set in.

There were exclamations of glee from Burt as well, but for an entirely different reason. That night his assistant, Jacob Houghton, wrote a bemused account of the day in the private journal he was keeping:

> I shall never forget the excitement of the old gentleman when view-
> ing the changes of the variation, the needle not actually traversing
> alike in any two places. He kept changing his position to take obser-
> vations, all the time saying, "How could they survey this country
> without my compass? What could be done here without my com-
> pass?" It was the full and complete realization of what he had fore-
> seen when struggling through the first stages of his invention.

Burt may have been more interested in the performance of his new toy than in locating the source of the conventional compass's problems, but the rest of the crew felt differently. Scattering into the brush, they stuffed their pockets with ore samples, bringing out—Houghton remarks—"all that we could carry." Within a year, those samples would set off a major stampede.

The country around Lake Superior is different from that around the other four Great Lakes. Elsewhere along the Fifth Coast the terrain is predominantly sand, clay, and gravel—the materials of glacial drift. Here at Superior it is rock. Here the ancient basalts and conglomerates of the Keweenawan series lap up against the eroded metamorphic stumps of the Penokean Orogeny; here are some of the southernmost exposures of the even more ancient Canadian Shield granites. Polished cliffs and jagged, torn ridges bear the marks of the continental glacier. This is one of the ruggedest, most persistently up-and-down pieces of land on the North American continent. On a map, the word "mountain" affixed to elevations of 1,700 and 1,800 feet above sea level looks faintly ludicrous. On the ground—or high above the ground, rather, gazing down some impossibly steep face into a lake of clearly glacial origin—there is no possible controversy, even among westerners whose mountains begin three times higher than these leave off. These are big mountains. It is only the numbers on the maps that are small.

That these Lake Superior mountains were rich in what the nineteenth-century prospectors euphoniously called "metalliferous minerals" was known long before William Burt and his Solar Compass came along, but until then it had been thought that the principal wealth would turn out to be copper. Ancient mine pits had been spotted by the earliest explorers, who found copper items in use among the Indians. Copper nuggets lay here and there upon the ground for anyone to see. In some places they still do. In 1820, Henry Schoolcraft, "loitering along the shore" of the Keweenaw Peninsula, picked up numerous waterworn pebbles of a stone he determined to be serpentine, enclosing pockets of pure copper of various sizes. In 1983, loitering along the same shore, I found a good-sized chunk of the same stuff. The stone is actually basalt, not serpentine; its dark green color and serpentine-like texture come from the inclusion of a mineral called phrenite. But the metal trapped within it is definitely copper. My stone with its bright little nuggets was still wet from Lake Superior when I picked it up, the roar of the surf in my ears and the wind coming in from Canada across the vast waters. Only a nickel's worth of metal, if that, but no prospector finding a mother lode could have been more elated than I.

My copper find was not quite large enough to be a paperweight. The country has produced much larger. The most famous of these was probably the so-called Ontonagon Boulder, "discovered" by the fur trader Alexander Henry on the upper Ontonagon River in 1766 but known to the Indians much earlier. The Indians had told the Jesuits about it; the Jesuits had passed the story on to the European courts as early as 1660, where it gained much in the telling. The legend was of a mountainous mass of glistening copper resting on the edge of a great fresh-water sea. The reality was a mushroom-shaped hunk of metal coated with green oxide in the dirt-walled gully of a little river in the Michigan outback. It was roughly 40 inches across and 20 high, and it weighed just under two tons. Not a mountain, perhaps, but impressive enough. Henry went home to England and persuaded the King to underwrite a copper-mining venture on the Ontonagon. The year was 1771, and the mountains of Lake Superior were as remote from England as the mountains of the moon. That venture failed; later attempts failed just as miserably. Despite the area's obvious wealth in copper, it was just too far from everything else in the world, and copper alone couldn't bring it any closer.

Copper and iron together, though, were a different matter.

The rush touched off by William Burt's errant compass needle—and by geologist Philo Everett's discovery of a 50-foot cliff face of pure iron ore in the same region the next summer—was fully as intense as anything seen in the more famous California gold rush a few years later. In Chicago and Cleveland and Buffalo and a hundred other cities along the American north coast, men dropped what they were doing, often on the spot, and rushed down to the docks to board ships bound for the Superior region. Some hired on as "landlookers," prospectors in the pay of financiers from New York and Philadelphia, where speculation in iron and copper shares ran high. Others went strictly for themselves; the standard excuse was that they were doing it "for their health." A Pittsburgh pharmacist named John Hays prevailed upon his doctor to send him to the Keweenaw Peninsula "for his health"; traveling on the doctor's money, he teamed up with a ne'er-do-well from Boston named Jim Raymond who happened to own three copper claims on the peninsula. With the doctor as a silent partner, they formed the Pittsburgh & Boston Company and excavated the Cliff Mine, out of which eventually came forty million pounds of copper. Jim Raymond was no longer a ne'er-do-well, and John Hays was very healthy indeed. A Harvard geology professor with the unlikely name of Raphael Pumpelly took his invalid wife to the Superior region "for her health"; prowling about the Wisconsin-Michigan border region, among the worn stumps of the ancient Penokean Mountains, he came across a hilltop where the needle of his dip compass stood on its head and the rocks showed the yellow stains of limonite, an oxide of iron. He took a claim two miles long. It was at the center of what became known as the Gogebic Range. Within forty years the Gogebic had produced more than eighty million tons of ore.

West of the big Lake, in north-central Minnesota's Mesabi Range, geologists like Philo Everett and Raphael Pumpelly said the rock was wrong for iron. Duluth timber cruiser Leonidas Merritt and his six brothers thought otherwise. They dug down under the muskeg swamps of the upper St. Louis River and found the richest lode yet. Eighty years later the ore of the Mesabi was still coming out of the ground at the rate of nearly a million tons per week.

For every Merritt or Pumpelly or Hays who struck it rich, of course, there were tens of thousands of anonymous miners who didn't. They came into the country in masses, most of them woefully unprepared for life in the North and without any knowledge of what they were looking for or where to find it. Attempts were made to pan for gold, California-style, in the glacial-drift gravels of the Lower Peninsula; iron and copper were sought in the Jacobsville Sandstone of the Pictured Rocks, and the Silurian dolomites of the western limb of the Niagaran Cuesta, and in a thousand other unlikely locations. Shafts were sunk into the promising but unproductive copper veins of Isle Royale, not once but dozens of times. One of these shafts produced 250 tons of copper, and two others produced 100 tons each; the others found nothing but low-grade "poor rock." All eventually withdrew. Like tens of thousands of others, their embittered owners gave up on the country. Some left penniless and broken; some stayed on as laborers in the mines of their more fortunate companions; some simply never came out of the dark northern forests. The forests reverted to their primeval silence. The boom was dead.

The mines the boom had located, however, remained very much alive.

It is one thing to locate an ore body; it is another thing to develop it, and quite another thing yet to integrate it into the national economy. The earliest attempts at mining the Lake Superior copper districts ran hard aground on precisely this last point. When Alexander Henry and the King of England set up their mining company in 1771, the nearest location that the copper could conceivably be used was on the Atlantic coast, and the only way to get it there was by canoe and pack train. Under those circumstances, integration was impossible. It was, as one early critic put it, like "lifting a weight on the end of a ten-foot pole." Before any serious mining could take place in the Great Lakes Basin, either the reward for lifting the weight would have to increase or that pole would have to be made considerably shorter.

By the time the mining boom started in the 1840's, both of these goals had been met. The reward had been increased by the finding of rich iron deposits to go with the copper, and by the development of eastern North America into an industrial region that required far more metal than the agrarian seaboard colonies which had existed in Henry's time could possibly have used; and the pole had been shortened by the construction of the Erie Canal, the coming of the railroad, and the ongoing explosion of settlement—not industrialized yet, but industrializable—in the Midwest. The final key was the completion of the Ohio and Erie Canal in 1835 from Lake Erie at Cleveland to the Ohio River at Portsmouth. The Ohio and Erie was an eccentric waterway with a course that seemed to wander randomly about the state of Ohio (the straight-line distance from Cleveland to the Ohio is a bit over 80 miles; the canal managed to extend that to 243), but it provided a cheap way for ore from the Superior district to get together with coal from the mines in the Ohio Valley. The ore came down the Lakes in ships; the coal came up the canal in barges. They met in Cleveland. The steel industry that they spawned has been the major economic force in Cleveland's development to this day.

The mining boom on the Fifth Coast started only a few years after the lumber boom, but it lasted far longer. In a sense it has never ended; there is still a working copper mine at White Pine, near the base of the Keweenaw Peninsula, and in Minnesota the Mesabi Range continues to produce iron ore at a prodigious rate to this day. In many ways the miners have been far less destructive than the loggers. Mining is by nature a point-source activity; ore lodes, even extremely large ones, take up far less of the landscape than forests. Even on the Mesabi, where the mines have been worked almost exclusively by open-pit techniques, the environmental disruption has been less than might be thought. The biggest pit on the Mesabi is the Hull-Rust Mine at Hibbing, called locally the "Grand Canyon of the Midwest"; it is three miles long by a mile wide. Minnesota is 450 miles long and 350 miles wide. The Hull-Rust has had about as much total effect on the state as a flea bite on an elephant. If that were all there was to the damage of mining, no one could possibly complain.

But that is not all there is. The mineral industry does not include just the mine; it includes the transportation corridors and the smelters as well, and from these the environmental effects have been enormous.

Steel manufacturing is a complicated process. The pig iron to make it does not occur naturally; it must be refined from crushed ore by heating it to the neighborhood of 3000°F in the presence of coke and limestone flux. The coke is itself the product of a coal-refining process that has as potentially dangerous by-products ammonia, coal tar, and methane gas; the limestone must be quarried, usually from the Great Lakes region and often at more expense to its immediate surroundings than the ore itself. (U.S. Steel's Rogers City Quarry, for example—on the northeast coast of Michigan's Lower Peninsula, near Hammond Bay—covers nearly 100 square miles and is the largest limestone-quarrying operation in the world.) More limestone goes into the reprocessing of pig iron into steel; so do significant quantities of fluorite, mined principally along the lower Ohio River and brought up to the mills by train and barge. To make the alloy steels utilized by modern industry, molybdenum, chromium, vanadium, nickel, and other metals must be used; these also require mining and smelting, and many of them are poisonous in the trace amounts that even a carefully controlled smelting operation releases into the environment. "Pickling" the steel, a tempering process, uses significant amounts of cyanide.

All of these things have a tendency to find their way into the water. The steel industry uses massive amounts of water, most of it in the process known as "quenching" where the molten steel, at a precisely determined temperature, is quick-cooled by water sprays in a "quenching tower." For this reason, and for ease of transportation, steel plants are almost always located along large bodies of water. Returned quenching water, leakage of pickling water, and leachate from the heaps of impurities ("slag") removed during both iron and steel processing, all carry contaminants into the water. The burning of coke in the iron-refining portion of the cycle, and the burning of coal to create the vast amounts of energy needed to maintain those exceedingly high temperatures, create airborne pollutants—sulfur compounds, nitrites, fly ash—and these and the water-borne pollutants make an individual plant's impact felt over a broad area. A tour of a nightmare location such as the Cleveland Flats near Lake Erie or the Windermere Basin section of Ontario's Hamilton Harbour will demonstrate dramatically just how great that impact can be.

Added to the difficulties of ore processing has recently come another: preprocessing. The pure magnetite and hematite ores—the so-called Bessemer ores that the early miners were primarily looking for—have long since been used up, and the mines of Lake Superior are now producing primarily a low-grade ore known as "taconite," in which tiny grains of magnetite and hematite are carried in a matrix of impure quartz. Taconite ores need to be greatly concentrated before they can be used in a blast furnace, and this "beneficiating," as it is called, is normally done before the ore is shipped from the iron range to the plant. The desired result of ore beneficiating is taconite pellets, small round artificial pebbles that look like dusty black marbles. The unavoidable side effect is huge amounts of concentrated impurities, or slag. The dumping of this slag has resulted in some immense water-quality problems. Taconite slag dumped into Lake Superior at Twin Harbors, Minnesota, by the Western Reserve Mining Company between 1955 and 1980, for instance, carried significant amounts of asbestos. The floor of the entire western arm of Lake

Superior is now coated with a carpet of carcinogenic asbestos fibers, which have found their way into the water intakes of the city of Duluth, sixty miles from Twin Harbors, forcing the installation of expensive filtering equipment. The mine is "down" now—not working—and the dumping has stopped. But the effects are still being felt. They will continue to be felt for many years, perhaps even for millennia.

Copper smelting did not originally have as many deleterious effects as did the processing of iron ore. In the first place, it is conducted on a smaller scale; and in the second place, Lake Superior copper has historically occurred in such a pure form that it did not require the thoroughgoing refinement typical of steelmaking. Old accounts tell of dockloads of masses of native copper the size of small automobiles—up to 100 tons each, giant brothers of the two-ton Ontonagon Boulder—waiting patiently to be loaded onto ships calling at Copper Harbor, at the tip of the Keweenaw Peninsula; they had been cracked from the rock matrix ("barrel-work") that surrounded them in a spectacularly upscaled version of the Indian hot-and-cold mining technique. Huge bonfires of logs would be built against an ore face, stoked until everything was red-hot, and then quenched suddenly by the application of massive amounts of water. But these relatively nonpolluting mass workings did not last forever. By the turn of the century, native copper was occurring typically in small nodules scattered through the matrix rock, rather like the piece I picked from the Lake Superior surf on the north shore of the Keweenaw; these required crushing followed by washing with a solvent—often sulfuric acid—to dissolve the barrel-work and flush it away. Usually the flushing led it, intentionally or not, into a watercourse. Copper-country waters have suffered severely as a result.

Perhaps the worst-hit has been Torch Lake, located at the base of an escarpment of copper-bearing conglomerate a few miles east of the town of Houghton in the central part of the Keweenaw Peninsula. Though separately named, Torch Lake is actually an isolated embayment of Lake Superior; it is connected to the big Lake by a sequence of two straits, a narrow bight known as "The Cuts" between Torch Lake and nearby Portage Lake (also actually a bay) and a broader passage called "Portage River" leading from Portage Lake into Keweenaw Bay. Over 100 years of operation at the nearby Calumet and Hecla Mine and its associated smelter complex between 1855 and 1968 have left Torch Lake probably beyond hope of recovery. Its banks today are barren and lifeless; its waters, shoaled and shallowed by mine wastes, are a dull reddish color. The lake's condition has been graphically described by Kansas City financial consultant Leonard Asselin, who has spent his summers there since he was a child in the late 1940's. As Asselin wrote to me angrily not long ago, in a letter that is worth quoting extensively:

> For over a century the Calumet and Hecla mined and smelted copper in the area, loading ore boats in Torch Lake, and dumping the chemicals and slag into the lake. The large ore boats came to Lake Linden [a city on Torch Lake], and I remember watching the crews hose out the holds that were full of coal dust. (My grandfather, a saloon keeper in Hubbell, knew the captains, and used to take me on the tied up ore boats.) God knows what else they dumped into the lake. . . . Along with the waste from the smelting process came the wastes of a whole town. . . . So here you have what was once a beautiful lake, for all intents landlocked, and what does anybody expect after all those years? I recall my grandfather telling me once in boom times how somebody was going to pay—hell, I was only 16 and didn't have the foresight. Now the soul of this area around Torch Lake is gone and so is most of the town. The factories are decaying—left as they were the day they closed—and the copper company sold the property (they owned damn near everything) to a big oil company. It looks like a war—and nobody had the ethics to clean up. Ignorance and neglect put it where it is—intellect, responsibility, and work will clean it up in time. The money has to come from the perpetrators—reality dictates that it won't.

Along with iron and copper, other mining operations have taken their toll of the Great Lakes. Limestone is quarried for building material as well as for steel flux; at one time there were eight major quarries on Wisconsin's Door Peninsula alone, and sunken "stone boats"—the barges that carried the stone to market—continued to clog the Door's major shipping channel at Sturgeon Bay until well into this century. Sandstone, especially that from the Bayfield Peninsula west of Ashland, Wisconsin, has also historically been in demand for building. At times, even the sands of the shore have been extensively mined. Whole trainloads of sand went west from the Indiana Dunes to Chicago for shore fill in the 1920's; much of the hundred-mile dune belt on the east shore of Lake Michigan has been bulldozed and shoveled out for the manufacture of casting molds by companies such as Martin Marietta and the Uninim Corporation. As late as the spring of 1984 a major battle was raging near the Michigan-Indiana state line over Uninim's proposed mining of the ecologically unique Bridgman Dunes; critics claimed that Uninim had the option of mining other sand sites, while, as zoologist Matthew M. Douglas put it, "if the dunes are mined, nothing short of another full-blown ice age can ever re-create them." It is too early to tell, as this is being written, which side will win.

Nickel mining in Canada's Sudbury Basin has been a special case.

No one is quite sure how this small, torn basin in the midst of the Canadian Shield came to be; perhaps it was volcanic activity, or perhaps it was an ancient meteor impact. Whatever the cause, it left a massive, incredibly nickel-rich deposit beneath the floor of a geologically inexplicable depression 38 miles long and 17 wide near the headwaters of the Spanish River—a northern tributary of Lake Huron. Nickel mining here began as early as 1883; since 1929, when several separate mining companies in the area merged to form the International Nickel Corporation (INCO), that mining has been on an extremely large scale. As of 1980, it was producing 40 percent of the Western world's production of this strategic material.

Nickel mining in the Sudbury Basin has primarily been carried on underground, and except for the inevitable pollution from rainfall leaching through the mine tailings it has been a relatively clean operation. The smelting and milling accompanying it, alas, have not. INCO currently operates four mills and two smelters in Sudbury, and the sulfide fumes from them have killed virtually every plant within twenty miles. The overwhelming impression a visitor gets from Sudbury is one of desolation. This is what J. R. R. Tolkien's Land of Mordor must look like. The black slag heaps from the mills and smelters are piled on and around the naked black rock of the Canadian Shield; the typical shield ponds scattered here and there look blasted and wasted and forlorn. Over everything looms Superstack, the largest smokestack in the world. It is 1,250 feet high—taller than the Empire State Building—and was designed to inject the smelter fumes into the upper atmosphere, where the winds could take them away. Perhaps, it was thought, vegetation would then return to Sudbury. It has worked, too, after a fashion; a few struggling trees and hardy grasses may now be seen, carefully pampered, in isolated spots within the town. But the price has been immense. The areas downwind from Sudbury—including the scenic lakes of Killarney Provincial Park on the north shore of Lake Huron—are now subject to severe acid precipitation. The sulfides that once would have destroyed the grasses of Sudbury are now literally raining destruction on much of the rest of the province. This is the price that is paid for the nickel-steel blade on your carving knife, the nickel-steel edge on your razor, and the masses of nickel-steel armor that clothe our tanks so that the nickel-steel projectiles sent by the enemy cannot pierce them. Thus does logic spiral into insanity.

Mining is currently so integral to the economy of the Fifth Coast that it is difficult to criticize it. It is the mineral wealth of Superior, after all, that drives the steel mills of Cleveland and Gary and Hamilton; and it is the steel mills of Cleveland and Gary and Hamilton that produce the raw materials for the automobile industry of Detroit and Windsor, and the appliance industry of Kenosha, and the outboard-motor factory at Waukegan, and a thousand other major industries below The Line, tied to the lower Lakes or grouped around the south end of Lake Michigan like wolves around a dying caribou. The mines and the mills and the factories and the power plants are all intimately connected with each other: Not one of them could exist without all of the others. In a very real sense, the Great Lakes Basin is a one-industry town. The Basin has always been that way. First the industry was furs, then the furs gave out. Next it was lumber, until the trees gave out. Now it is mining and manufacturing, and this, too, is in danger of giving out. It is difficult to say what will replace it, but whatever it is will almost certainly again be Basin-wide. This conclusion is drawn from a little-understood fact of Fifth Coast life: All these "primary" industries are actually secondary. They are built upon a base industry: waterborne transportation. This has always been true. It was the shipping lanes of the Great Lakes that provided the avenues for the furs of Upper Canada to get to France and England; it was the shipping lanes of the Great Lakes that allowed Michigan timber access to markets in New York and Chicago and the Great Plains. Now it is the shipping lanes of the Great Lakes that tie together the mines of Minnesota and the mills of Gary and the factories of Detroit. Because of shipping, the Great Lakes Basin has a single, unified economy. But, as usual, a price must be paid for value received; and in the case of shipping on the Great Lakes, that price—to a much greater extent than most people allow themselves to realize—has been levied upon the Lakes themselves.

IX Ships

Once Man starts to muck up a system, you know, it gets more and more complicated.

Jane Elder, Sierra Club Staff for Midwest and Great Lakes issues (personal conversation)

I n the beginning was the canoe. A frame of bent cedar was lashed together by spruce roots and covered with birchbark; the birchbark was sewed together with more spruce roots and caulked with pine gum. Up to 40 feet long and 5 feet across the beam, but drawing only a few inches of water, a large freight canoe had a payload of several tons, was stable and easily manageable on big water, and would go—propelled by the red-painted ash paddles of eight or ten brawny voyageurs—like the hammers of hell. It was a marvel of what is known today as "appropriate technology." It skimmed over the water, the water closed behind it; there was no track of its passage, no smoke, oil, or other emissions, no environmental effect whatsoever. Because of its shallow draft, all stream mouths on the Great Lakes were open to it without dredging. Developed on the Lakes, for the Lakes, by Lakes residents, it was in most ways the perfect vehicle for them, and for many centuries no other water craft was needed.

The canoe did, however, have two major drawbacks. It was open; it had no cabin to protect delicate goods or to shield passengers from the weather or the flying spray from waves breaking over the bow. And it was strictly limited in its ability to grow. Extended too far, that marvelously strong and flexible cedar frame could not keep its rigidity. Forty feet from bow to stern was the practical maximum.

The development of large-scale commerce on the Lakes would require much more than that.

The first attempt to bring oceangoing ship technology to the great freshwater oceans off the Fifth Coast was a very early one. In 1674 the Governor of New France, a gentleman with the grandiose name of Louis de Buade, Comte de Palluau et de Frontenac, was building a fort and fur-trading station—named, with great and fitting modesty, after himself—on a site near the present city of Kingston, Ontario, where somewhere among the intricate waterways of the Thousand Islands the Great Lakes imperceptibly become the St. Lawrence River. His assistant in this venture was a man named Robert Cavelier, a brash young trader with a restless foot who held a royal land grant near the village of Montreal. Cavelier was a gifted orator and debater (had he lived today, he would undoubtedly have become a lobbyist); and so when King Louis XIV demanded an accounting of the fort from Frontenac—who was operating without benefit of a license and was technically, therefore, violating the law—the multitudinously named Count sent Cavelier to France to represent him. The Sun King seems to have been deeply impressed. The next year, his mission accomplished, Cavelier returned to Canada with a patent of nobility of his own and plans for a venture almost as grandiose as his employer's name: He would travel west through the Lakes and south down the newly discovered Mississippi River, establishing forts and claiming that vast tract of inland North America for France. All this would be done in the King's name and his own, his new one, freshly granted with his noble title. He was no longer just Robert Cavelier: He was Robert Cavelier, Sieur de La Salle.

Contemporary reports picture the new Sieur de La Salle as an arrogant and bull-headed individual, a fop and a martinet who wore, even in the wilderness, a scarlet cloak trimmed with gold lace, a man who, in the words of his friend and longtime associate Louis Hennepin, "never took any one's advice." It could not be expected that such a man would be content with the canoe—technology, after all, developed by mere Indians—and La Salle wasn't. Between 1675 and 1678 he built three European-style barques of roughly ten tons burden each to sail the waters of Lake Ontario. These were no larger than the largest canoes, but greater things were in store. In 1679, ready at last to begin his bold venture to the west, La Salle led an expedition south from Ontario along the Niagara River, climbing the escarpment beside the thunder of the huge Falls—which Hennepin, leading an advance party, became the first European to see—and coming out at last to the shore of Lake Erie at the present site of Buffalo. Wide blue waters stretched forth beyond sight to the west, connecting to still greater waters, sailing room for a thousand miles. La Salle established a shipyard.

In two months the ship was complete. Sixty-five feet long, of forty-five tons burden, she carried two brigantine-rigged masts, five cannon, and a crew of thirty-two. La Salle christened her the *Griffon* —this mythical beast was prominently featured in Count Frontenac's family coat of arms, and the Count was still footing the bills—and set sail to the west.

Slightly over a month later, having weathered a storm on Lake Huron and tarried for a while at St. Ignace, where Father Jacques Marquette had established a mission some years before—and where he was now buried, beneath the altar of the Mission church—the *Griffon* glided across northern Lake Michigan and nosed her way into Green Bay. Forty-five years had passed since Nicolet came that way, and no one expected to find China there anymore, so there were no mandarin's robes on board; La Salle's scarlet cloak would have to do. He landed. From here the journey would have to be on foot or by canoe; they could not very well drag the *Griffon* over the portages to the Mississippi. They loaded her with furs (Radisson and Groseilliers had proved the value of that) and headed her back for Niagara.

She was never seen again. Somewhere along the several thousand miles of coastline between Green Bay and Niagara—the precise spot has never been established—the *Griffon* sailed into a Great Lakes storm and went down with all hands. The first large ship on the Fifth Coast was also the first shipwreck. It would be eighty years before anyone would make a second attempt.

After that second ship, however—the sloop *Oswego*, built by the British Navy for service on Lake Ontario in 1755—things went much more rapidly. The naval fleets that plied the Lakes during the Revolution and the War of 1812 were accompanied, and quickly outnumbered, by merchanters. By 1820 sail was fairly commonplace on the Lakes, and the 132-foot, 220-ton *Walk-in-the-Water* had established regular steamship service between Buffalo and Detroit down the length of Lake Erie, calling at Erie, Cleveland, and Portland (now Sandusky) along the way. The emigrant boom of the next few decades was a boom in shipping as well. The *Walk-in-the-Water* foundered on a Lake Erie sandbar in 1821, leaving only her engine salvageable (that was the engine that was eventually used to run Harvey Williams's premiere sawmill at Saginaw Bay), but she was replaced by two others within the next two years; and those two, the *Superior* and the *Henry Clay*, were just the start. By 1834 there were forty-eight steamboats of up to 750 tons burden each plying between Buffalo and Detroit, and a few tentative stabs had been made toward extending service through Huron and Michigan to the little village of Chicago. Eleven years later, in 1845, the number of steamboats had increased to ninety and the so-called propellers—driven by screws instead of by paddle wheels—had begun to make their appearance. Approximately 200,000 passengers crossed the upper Lakes that year bound for Chicago, Milwaukee, and other western ports. Tourist excursions by steamboat to Green Bay and other points of interest in the near North had become fashionable: wealthy New Yorkers engaged in Great Circle tours—down to New Orleans by coastal schooner, up the Mississippi by steamboat, a short rail or stage transfer to the Lakes at Chicago, down the Lakes by luxury liner to Buffalo, and thence by train or Erie Canal packet boat to the Hudson and home. It had been just twenty-five years since the Cass expedition had found most of the Lakes a howling wilderness. Now they were seeing women in evening gowns and men in tails on promenade decks lined with plush cushions. Henry Schoolcraft, now the Indian Agent at Mackinac, quit his post and went home in disgust to write his memoirs. Civilization, he thought, had taken over far too completely.

Passenger traffic was primarily by steamboat, but sail still dominated on the Lakes; nearly all freight shipments continued to go that way. Wind was cheap, and a hold full of freight didn't get impatient and start pacing the deck if it happened to be becalmed for five days.

In 1856 there were 118 propellers and 120 paddle-wheel steamers registered with the federal government for the Lakes trade; that same year there were 1,149 sailing-ship registries, a sail advantage of better than four to one. By that time the Fifth Coast had evolved its own type of wind-powered vessel, the Great Lakes clipper schooner. The first of these, the *Challenge*, was built at Manitowoc, Wisconsin, in 1852 by an expatriate Canadian shipbuilder named William Wallace Bates; she was similar to a salt-water clipper, but she incorporated several design changes aimed at accommodating some of the peculiar limitations of Fifth Coast sailing. Great Lakes winds tend to be gustier than those on the ocean; for this reason the *Challenge*'s foremast was made noticeably shorter than her mainmast (on ocean clippers they were usually the same height). Speed and maneuverability were increased by placing the point of greatest hull width aft of midships—the reverse of the ocean clipper's "bulbous foreship" design. Bates's greatest innovation, though, had to do with keel depth. A deep-draft boat is needed for stability in the big water of an ocean or a Great Lake, but Fifth Coast ports, almost uniformly, were plagued by shallow sailing conditions—bars, sandbanks, and wide, shoally bottoms—and there, a shallow-draft boat was essential. The *Challenge* managed, brilliantly, to be both. She drew only six feet of water in port; but when she got into deep water she could lower a hinged centerboard that gave her another ten feet of effective keel depth. On a boat of only 125 feet LOA (length over all), that was quite enough. The *Challenge* managed to be among both the most stable and the most maneuverable—in the yachting world's excellent term, the most yare—sailing vessels ever built.

She was also among the most copied. Centerboard clipper schooners became the norm for Great Lakes shipping, and William Wallace Bates became, successively, U.S. Naval Commissioner and founding president of the American Shipbuilding Society. His competitors knew a good thing when they saw it.

The Great Lakes clipper schooner design was successful enough to extend the reign of sail on the Lakes for another forty years, into the 1890's, but its days were numbered. Wooden sailing ships could be built considerably larger than canoes, but they too had a maximum beyond which they could not grow. Cargoes did not. Cargoes were limited only by the market, and as industry exploded on the Lakes in the late nineteenth century, the demand for larger cargoes exploded, too. The wooden sailing ships could not keep pace.

The steel industry was particularly demanding. The mines were in Minnesota and upper Michigan and Wisconsin; the mills were on Lake Erie and Lake Ontario and grouped around the southern end of Lake Michigan, near the coal sources and the markets but far from the mines. The ore had to be moved along the water, and it had to be moved rapidly, in massive amounts. The first ore shipments from Superior were loads of 400 to 500 tons that were loaded and unloaded by wheelbarrow. When the schooner *Pelican* took on a record 1,050 tons at Marquette in 1873, there were critics who said she would (1) founder under the load or (2) prove uneconomical to operate or (3) both. But the record stood for only a few months. By 1897 a single steel port, Cleveland, was requiring nearly three million tons of ore per year. That kind of volume could not be loaded and unloaded by wheelbarrow, and it could not come in piddling little 1,000-ton loads. Burden would have to be expanded to 2,000 tons, 4,000 tons, or more. The wooden ships couldn't do it.

They tried. A massive, five-masted schooner, the *David Dows*, was built at Toledo in 1881. She was 265 feet long and could carry a little over 1,400 tons of cargo. She was also a sailor's nightmare: unwieldy, ponderous under way, slow to answer the helm, and virtually unmanageable. In 1882, after less than a year in service, she was caught in a relatively minor Great Lakes storm, lost a mast, and came close to foundering. Her owners had her towed in and converted to a barge. Another answer to the problem of large loads would have to be found.

It was. The best way to move iron ore, it turned out, was going to be in iron ships.

The first bulk-cargo iron ship, the *Onoko*, came down the ways at Cleveland the same year the *David Dows* was built. She was forty feet longer than the *Dows* and would carry more than twice as much cargo—and, notwithstanding that she was built like a canal boat, that is, square and squat, she would also handle well. That is the advantage of propellers over sails. Soon boats of the *Onoko* type were the standard Lakes freight vessels. A few schooners hung on—the old *Challenge* remained in service until 1910, and there was still at least one clipper schooner carrying freight on Lake Michigan as late as

1929—but the days of sail were over. The old ships became barges, their masts shortened and cabins removed, taken in tow three or more at a time behind power tugs. Then even that ended. A new type of barge, the steel-hulled Whaleback, made its debut at Duluth. Iron, steam, and diesel had won a complete victory.

With construction material and motive power firmly established, Lakes ships began—around 1885—a period of intense growth and evolution. The 287-foot *Onoko* was followed four years later by the 310-foot *Spokane* and, eight years after that, by two 400-footers, the *Victory* and the *Zenith*. The explosion of ship size slowed down somewhat in the 1890's with an abortive design side trip, the ugly, inefficient, but oddly appealing Whaleback—a descendant of the Whaleback barge—but only forty-one of these round-hulled, pig-nosed bulk carriers were built before it was discovered that their arched hull tops limited effective vessel width to 40 feet and therefore length to roughly 400 (maximum length being determined, approximately, by ten times hull width). Ship designers kissed the Whaleback goodbye and went back to straight-sided vessels, and lengths began to grow once more. In 1900 the *John W. Gates* and her three sister ships of the Wolvin Steamship Line reached 498 feet; in 1904 came the 560-foot *Augustus B. Wolvin,* and in 1905 the 600-foot *J. Pierpont Morgan.* Today there are approximately 300 "Lakers" of lengths ranging from 650 to 730 feet and cargo capacities of more than 20,000 tons cruising the deep waters off the Fifth Coast; the biggest ships have reached 1,000 feet and 60,000 tons. Ship design has become standardized, with the wheelhouse in front, the engines and crew's quarters in the rear, and more than an acre of deck between. Prowling the decks like long-legged grasshoppers are steel gantry cranes called "self-unloaders"; these enable a ship to discharge its cargo in any port on the Lakes, whether or not it has mechanized loading facilities, at a rate that approaches 5,000 tons per hour—a far cry from shovels and wheelbarrows. It is worth noting that the first "large" ship on the Lakes, La Salle's *Griffon,* could literally be picked up by a large modern self-unloader, turned sideways, and plunked down through one of its voluminous hatches with room to spare on all sides.

From an environmental standpoint, the wooden sailing vessels were little more hazardous than the canoes that had preceded them.

Wind was a clean, abundant, renewable power source. It produced no wastes; it depleted no resources. No lands were torn up to obtain it. The ships slipped through the water quietly and cleanly, leaving no trace of their passage. The water—even in the harbors—stayed fresh and clean.

The steamboats, and the diesels that followed them, were considerably worse. Stacks belched black smoke and foul-smelling fumes; fuel spills created slicks and skims of coal dust on harbor surfaces. The harbor waters became foul and opaque. Since the harbors were usually reclaimed from wetlands, with more wetlands nearby, the wetland waters became opaque, too. Skims of coal dust found their way into everything. Woodcutters supplying fuel for steamboats denuded large areas of land, including much the loggers had passed over as unworthy: If you're only going to burn it, it doesn't matter much how strong it is or what it looks like. Islands handy to the steamboat lanes were the most endangered. Most of the original land cover of the Bass Islands of Erie, the Beaver and Manitou Islands of Michigan, and the Apostle Islands of Superior went that way—cut down, piled on cordwood docks, and sold to the first steamer that came along with an empty fuel bin.

As the ships grew larger and their cargoes became more sophisticated, the environmental hazards from operating them increased. The deeper-draft vessels ran closer to the bottoms of the channels, stirring up the muck and eliminating the bottom communities. Greater size and greater numbers meant greater emissions, and the emissions themselves increased in toxicity. Shipping channels and harbors began to turn into poisoned deserts. Waves kicked up by passage of the huge hulls threatened shore stability, increasing erosion and causing considerable property damage. Cargo and fuel spillage, though never common, became a far more serious problem when it did happen. Spilled cordwood floats harmlessly to shore, spilled ore sinks, spilled grain decomposes, but spilled chemicals dissolve in the water and enter the food chain, and spilled fuel oil forms murderous slicks that destroy aquatic life. When the schooner *Rouse Simmons* went down off Sheboygan, Wisconsin, in 1913, her load of Christmas trees caused hardly an environmental ripple. When the freighter *Nordmeer* grounded off Alpena, Michigan, in 1966, her 47,000 gallons of fuel oil were quite another story.

A far greater hazard to the Lakes than the ships and their cargoes, however—even the relatively dirty steamboats and diesels and the potentially disastrous chemical tankers—were the navigation works that accompanied them. I have spoken elsewhere about the hazards associated with harbor construction and maintenance—the dredging, with its disruption of natural current flows, destruction of bottom-dwelling life forms, and accumulation of dredge spoil that must be dumped somewhere; the breakwaters and their effect on shore drift; the elimination of valuable wetlands; the concentration of pollutants in sensitive areas; and so on, into the dark, uncomfortable night. Here I want to concentrate on a related and perhaps even more serious problem. That problem is canals.

X Canals

In the early evening of November 4, 1825, a strange little ceremony took place on board the vessel *Seneca Chief*, anchored in the middle of New York Harbor. The Governor of New York, De Witt Clinton—decked out in top hat and tails and attended by a party of equally distinguished looking dignitaries—stepped to the rail, made a short, solemn speech, and, grasping a barrel full of water in both hands, tipped it over and poured about half its contents down the side of the boat. Cheers erupted all around. An odd reaction, indeed, to the spilling of ordinary water, but the water in that barrel, as it happened, was not quite ordinary. It was water from Lake Erie, and it had come all the way to New York Harbor on board the *Chief* with the Governor and his party. The *Chief* was a canal boat. The Erie Canal, with this symbolic "marriage of the waters," was officially open and ready for business.

The Erie Canal was the greatest engineering feat of its day, comparable in our own time only to such monumental tasks as building the Interstate highway system or placing a man on the moon. Forty feet wide and four feet deep, it stretched 363 miles from Albany to Buffalo across the northern and western parts of the state of New York. Eighty-three stone locks with a combined lift of 662 feet raised and lowered boats over the pass at Utica and up and down the Niagara Escarpment at Lockport. The costs were enormous: ten million man-hours of pick-and-shovel labor, eleven million dollars, more than one hundred lives. The wags called it "Clinton's Folly," but it immediately lowered the cost of transporting a ton of merchandise from Lake Erie to New York by nearly 97 percent, from $120 to $4. By 1836, packet boats were leaving Albany for the Lakes at the rate of roughly one per hour around the clock. Grain was coming down from Chicago and the Ohio Valley; emigrants were going up to populate Michigan and Wisconsin and Illinois and Ohio. Passengers traveled from Albany to Buffalo at the sedate speed of three miles per hour, making the trip in five days at a total cost of $14.52, including meals. Clinton's Folly had proved very wise indeed: The canal had become what one effusive mid-nineteenth-century writer called "a gift of the gods. . . . nothing more nor less than a great sluice of wealth."

There was, however—as far as shipping along the Fifth Coast was concerned—a major trap across this great sluice of wealth—in fact, many traps. Commerce, unfortunately, had to get across the canal as well as along it, and so there were, over the 363-mile length of the waterway, numerous bridges. Only a few were drawbridges; most were made of stone or solid wooden beams, fixed and immutable as time itself. From these came the Erie Canal song learned by generations of American schoolchildren: "Low bridge, everybody down." From them also came trouble—deep, deep trouble—for sailing vessels. Their masts wouldn't fit under the bridges. Only the dumpy, mastless canal boats—pulled by horses or oxen "treading dirt" along the canalside towpaths—could negotiate the full length of the canal. A few Lakes schooners each year pulled into Buffalo, unstepped their masts and lashed them along the decks, and so passed down the canal and under the bridges to the sea; but they were rare. The Erie was a barge canal. For Lakes shipping to develop to its full potential would require—not barge canals—but ship canals.

They were not long in coming. Even as Governor Clinton poured his barrel of Lake Erie water into New York Harbor, work was proceeding on a Canadian project a few miles beyond the Erie's western terminus at Buffalo that would go much further toward connecting the Lakes to the Atlantic than merely polluting the latter with a little Lake Erie water ever could. It was called the Welland Canal, and it would be responsible—even more than the Erie—for changing the face of Lakes commerce forever.

. . .

The way to go is north and west, out of Niagara Falls, Ontario, along the Queen Elizabeth II freeway toward St. Catharines. Passing through the rural district around Stamford, you drop over the Escarpment in a long sweeping curve and enter the orchard country of the Niagaran Fruit Belt. At Exit 38, six miles from the river, you leave the freeway and head southwest along Glendale Avenue. In less than a mile you come to a green steel lift bridge. If you are lucky, the bridge will be up, and passing through it, moving at the sedate speed of six knots, will be one of the immense deepwater vessels of the Canada Steamship Fleet. You have arrived at the Welland Canal.

The Welland Canal, like the Erie, is one of the great engineering feats of the world. Twenty-seven miles long and more than 300 feet wide, it flows northward across the isthmus between Lake Erie and Lake Ontario like a second Niagara River. Seven giant locks lift or lower ships a total of 327 feet, bypassing the great Falls and making waterborne commerce possible between Ontario and the four upper Lakes. The locks can handle ships up to 730 feet long and 75 feet wide, drawing as much as 27 feet of water; their average lift is nearly 50 feet. Three of them—locks 4, 5, and 6, the so-called flight locks, just north of the village of Thorold—are twinned to allow passage of two ships at once, and are placed headgate to headgate to carry the canal directly up the face of the Escarpment. Among Fifth Coast skippers this is known as "climbing the mountain," and when an oceangoing ship considerably longer than two football fields placed end-to-end goes mountain-climbing, it is a spectacular and unforgettable sight.

There have been, through history, four Welland Canals. The first was opened in 1829; it was the brainchild of a St. Catharines businessman and veteran of the War of 1812—on the British side—named William H. Merritt. From his father, a New York Loyalist who had fled to Canada shortly after the close of the Revolution, Merritt had inherited a strong anti–United States bias. He had watched the Erie Canal being constructed across the border to the south, and he knew that it would be a Lakes-to-ocean route for any vessel capable of fitting through its locks and under its bridges. Canada, he said, would need a similar route, or commerce on the upper Lakes would be dominated by the upstart Republic to the south. Anyway, he needed a reliable water source for a gristmill he was building in St. Catharines. A little water out of the canal would do the trick nicely, and would never be missed. . . .

Grist (political or otherwise) aside, the Welland Canal was a good idea, and it remains one today. It solves what was for early Great Lakes mariners a major logistical problem. The three middle Lakes —Michigan, Huron, and Erie—form a single, uninterrupted maritime highway nearly 900 miles long stretching unbroken from Chicago to Buffalo. Michigan and Huron, connected to each other through the 300-foot-deep Strait of Mackinac, share a common surface level and an interconnected set of circulation patterns, and are so closely tied together that most hydrologists consider them a single body of water. Erie and Huron are nearly as well connected; the elevation difference between them is so little that no locks are needed. The two Lakes affect each other's levels. The channel between them is nearly thirty feet deep; their surface levels are just eight feet apart. A fish going upstream from Erie into Huron could actually end up swimming downhill to get there.

No such fortunate connections exist between the three central Lakes and the two at the ends of the chain. Superior lies twenty-four feet above Huron and falls into it via a twenty-foot rapid at Sault Ste. Marie that was, in its original form, barely navigable by canoes and totally closed to anything larger: Ontario lies more than 300 feet lower than Erie and is separated from it by Niagara Falls, which— needless to say—is not navigable by anything. (A few sailing vessels loaded with collections of live wild animals were sent over Niagara as stunts in the early nineteenth century before decency put an end to this form of "entertainment." Recognizable pieces of them were rarely recovered downstream.) In order for the Lakes to live up completely to their navigational potential, a single sea off a true Fifth Coast, the two outer Lakes had to be integrated into the three-Lake inner system. Nature hadn't provided that integration, but humans could. For Lake Ontario, the Welland Canal was the way.

The Welland was an immediate success—so much so that modifications were immediately begun to make it even better. At the time of the 1829 opening there were thirty-nine locks in the canal, which followed a sinuous route somewhat to the west of the present one; the upper end was located, not on Lake Erie, but on the little Welland River. Ships would pass up through the canal, descend the Welland to its mouth on the upper Niagara, and make their way up the Niagara to the upper Lake—a difficult process that made great use of what the old Lakes sailors called the "ash breeze" and the "horned breeze," that is, oars and towing oxen. This detour, however, was strictly temporary. In 1833, just four years after its opening, the riverine portion of the route was replaced by an extra length of canal extending to Lake Erie at Port Colborne; and twelve years after that, a complete rebuilding brought into existence the "second Welland Canal," broader and deeper than the first, with 27 stone locks replacing the original 39 wooden ones. Two more total rebuilds and nearly 100 years later, in 1931, the "fourth Welland Canal" was dedicated: It remains, with minor alterations, the canal in use today. The original 110-foot lock length was increased by those 1931 alterations to a bit over 800; the sill depth went from eight feet to twenty-two (it is now twenty-seven). Ships leaving Chicago or Cleveland or Goderich could finally expect full access to Toronto or Hamilton or Oswego or any other port on Lake Ontario. The four bottom Lakes had been successfully integrated into a single system.

While this activity was going forward on the Niagaran Isthmus, similar things were taking place 600 miles to the northwest at Sault Ste. Marie. Here at "the Soo" the task was considerably easier: There was no mountain to climb, only a broad mile of white water and a lift of a bit more than twenty feet. That took no particular engineering skill to bypass—only determination—and so it is not too surprising to find that it was done very early. The first Soo Lock was built by the North West Company in 1797, on the Canadian side, well before William Merritt conceived the idea of the Welland Canal; it was thirty-eight feet long and would hold one normal-sized Montreal canoe. That was obviously not adequate for much in the way of large-scale commerce, and it became even less so during the War of 1812, when it was reduced to unusable rubble by a team of American saboteurs (just what warships they expected to pass through, it has never been quite clear). It was not rebuilt. After the war, gear was portaged around the rapids by wagon road; ships—steamships and schooners alike—went the same route, hauled out and dragged up on rollers to be relaunched on the far side of the obstacle. Most of the little Superior fleet of the early nineteenth century had been through that experience; very few of them had actually been built on Superior. There was a shipyard at Point Aux Pines, just above the Soo, in the early days, but it had proved unprofitable. By 1820, when the Cass expedition passed that way, it was already in ruins.

The copper and iron discoveries in the Superior mining districts altered that bucolic little picture considerably. Traffic increased hugely; it was evident very rapidly that there would have to be something more efficient than a portage to carry goods around the Soo. By 1855 that "something more efficient" had been built. It was called the State Lock, and it would handle ships up to 60 feet wide and a bit over 300 feet long, with a draft of up to 12 feet. Two ships, the steamers *Illinois* and *Baltimore*, locked through the State Lock on its very first day of operation, and it was all uphill from there. By 1876, twenty years after its construction, the lock was handling a million tons of cargo a year and work had begun on a new and larger lock to the south, the Weitzel Lock, 515 feet long and 80 feet wide; within another twenty years the State Lock (referred to by then as the "Old State Lock") had been torn up and replaced by a lock called the Poe —800 feet long, 100 feet wide, and 19.5 feet deep—the self-proclaimed "largest lock in the world." That designation lasted less than a year. Late in 1896 the Canadians dedicated a lock 100 feet longer and 8 inches deeper than the Poe on their side of the river. With the Poe and the Weitzel still in operation, that meant three ships could lock past the Soo Falls simultaneously. They often did. Nearly 19 million tons of freight was carried past the Soo that year: The integration of all five Lakes into one system had been accomplished.

Today there are five parallel locks at the Soo—four on the American side and one on the Canadian. Two of the locks, the Davis and the Sabin, are 1,350 feet long by 85 feet wide and can handle two 600-foot bulk carriers at once; a third, the rebuilt Poe, stretches 1,200 feet by 110 feet and is capable of passing the new 1,000-footers, which —at 105 feet across the beam—are too wide for the Davis and the Sabin. Thirteen thousand vessels of varying sizes carrying an aggregate of more than 80 million tons of cargo pass through the five locks each year—more ships, and more tonnage, than use the Panama and Suez Canals combined. The passage between Lake Superior and Lake Huron has become the most-used waterway in the world.

·   ·   ·

There are other canals on the Lakes—roughly 1,200 miles of them, all told. The old Erie Canal is still operating, rebuilt substantially and now called the New York State Barge Canal: The Illinois Canal and the Erie and Ohio are dead, but the old Chicago Sanitary and Ship Canal—the reversed Chicago River—still carries a considerable amount of traffic between Chicago and the Mississippi. In Canada the Trent-Humber Waterway connects Lake Huron to Lake Ontario via an old upper-Lakes outlet channel through Lake Simcoe and Sturgeon and Rice Lakes to the Bay of Quinte; and the Rideau Canal—built as a military precaution after the War of 1812, when feelings still ran high along the United States border and there was fear that the St. Lawrence, with its American bank, could be closed to Canadian shipping—still connects Ottawa to Kingston through the quiet Rideau River Valley a few miles north of the big river. There is a canal through the Keweenaw Peninsula at Portage Lake, and another through the Door Peninsula at Sturgeon Bay. There is also persistent talk about a canal to be blasted through Michigan's Upper Peninsula from Au Train to Escanaba, connecting Lake Superior directly to Lake Michigan, but so far it has remained only talk.

The success of the canals has been reflected in the design of the ships that use the Great Lakes. A modern Laker is a heavily specialized craft, as thoroughly designed for the engineered Lakes of the modern era as William Bates's clipper schooner was for the relatively natural conditions the Lakes still exhibited in the mid-nineteenth century. Watching a ship like the Canada Steamship Lines' bulk carrier *H. M. Griffith* lock through the Welland Canal, one cannot help getting the impression that the ship fits the lock like—well, like a key. That impression is not wrong: It is precisely the dimensions of the locks that have determined the dimensions of most modern freighters. The maximum length for a ship that is going to pass through the Welland Canal is 730 feet; the maximum width is 75 feet, six inches; and the maximum draft is 27 feet. There are an amazing number of Lakers of exactly those dimensions running around the Great Lakes these days. Slab-sided, square on the ends, and flat across the deck, Lakers look like inverted molds of the locks they use. "Bow thrusters," small propellers mounted crosswise in the vessels' bows, allow extreme maneuverability in the tight confines of locks and canals. This is called Making the Most of Available Space. As Larry

Van Dusen of Duluth-Superior Excursions once put it, "To the sailor's eye they are an ugly sight, to the accountant's eye they are beautiful indeed."

(That accountant is probably going to work for a very large firm. In the days of the clipper schooner, it was possible for a captain to own his own ship and operate independently, cruising the length of the Fifth Coast and calling at harbors as he saw fit, contracting to carry cargo at whatever rate he could get. But those days are long gone. It takes an immense amount of capital to build and operate a ship a fifth of a mile long. Today's Lakers are almost exclusively owned by major corporations, often with a considerable stake in Great Lakes cargoes—companies like U.S. Steel or Detroit Edison or the Cleveland Cliffs Mining Corporation. This has diversified the companies in question, but it has had the reverse effect on the Great Lakes economy as a whole. Lakes shipping today is a highly unified, concentrated activity, contributing greatly to the transformation of the Lakes basin into a vast one-industry town. Nearly all economic eggs here are in the single basket of heavy industry, and as heavy industry faces an uncertain future in the last decades of the twentieth century, the Lakes' future is also uncertain. The risks of corporate failure have been magnified enormously: If a shipowner/captain with a 100-foot schooner went bankrupt, it was not likely to affect much of anything else, but if a shipping conglomerate owning thirty 600-footers turns belly-up, the shock waves through the economy will be felt for years. The widespread depression that has recently hit the Great Lakes Basin has been at least partly brought on by these twin misjudgments—heavy dependence on a single industry and concentration of that industry in the hands of a relatively few firms—and it is thus largely self-inflicted. This makes it no less serious to those suffering from it, of course, but knowing the causes may at least help show us part of what needs to be done to get out of it.)

Environmentally, the canals and the ships that have been designed for them have had a series of effects quite similar to those already detailed for harbor improvement projects. The disposal of dredge spoil has filled wetlands and other Lake-edge environments, often with material polluted by leakage of oil and liquid cargoes from the passing ships. Where the ships must pass close to shore, their wakes have accelerated the Lakes' already severe erosion problems; one recent study by the Army Corps of Engineers found nearly one-third of the Great Lakes shoreline in the United States subject to erosion problems of varying degrees, most of that on the land nearest the shipping lanes. The St. Marys, St. Clair, and Detroit rivers are more canal than river these days—dredged, blasted, and channelized to within an inch of their lives. There used to be a rapid at the head of the St. Clair, where Lake Huron spilled over its sill of Antrim shale; there was a limestone reef near the mouth of the St. Marys, and a rapid a few miles up at the southern end of the Neebish Channel. Lake St. Clair was so shallow that it was known among mariners as the "St. Clair Flats." All these are gone now, turned into shipping channels with a uniform twenty-seven-foot depth. Dredging, and the effects of the passage of the immense hulls of the Lakers a few inches above the bottom, have virtually eliminated bottom-dwelling life in the canals and the channelized rivers; it has also seriously affected bottom life in large portions of some of the Lakes, notably Erie, much of which is only thirty feet deep—just three feet deeper than the draft of the standard Laker. In the rivers, the almost constant erosion from the wakes of passing ships has destroyed the riparian vegetation along the banks, and that, in turn, has meant the end of the riparian animals. The rivers are gone; the shipping channels that have replaced them today are safe, blue, attractive, efficient —and sterile.

The greatest effect of the navigational improvements in the Lakes, though, has been one that was totally unexpected: a drastic and virtually complete change in the types of fish inhabiting Lakes waters. Fifth Coast navigation works have led, unintentionally but directly, to the collapse of Fifth Coast fisheries. The key event in this collapse took place in 1881, but it only lit what turned out to be a very long fuse; it wasn't until the early 1950's that the bomb the fuse was attached to finally went off with an explosion loud enough to awaken the Lakes dwellers and the politicians that represent them, and by that time the makeup of Great Lakes biota had already changed— drastically, irrevocably, and for all time.

XI Fish

W hat happened in 1881 was really quite simple. In the process of reconstructing the southern reaches of the Third
Welland Canal, Canadian engineers changed its water
supply pattern. To ships using the canal, this change was of little or
no importance. To fish—especially anadromous fish, those that live
in oceans or large lakes but spawn in rivers—it was of very great
importance indeed.

The First and Second Canals had been slightly humped in the
middle, rising gently out of Lake Erie to a point called the Deep Cut
near the town of Welland and falling again from there to the lip of
the escarpment and the multiple locks that lowered ships down to the
level of Lake Ontario. Water couldn't flow uphill from Erie: It had
to be fed in from some source higher than the water level in the Deep
Cut. A diversion-works on the nearby Grand River at Dunnville did
the trick, shunting most of the river into a twenty-five-mile-long
"feeder canal" that entered the main canal at its highest point, just
south of Welland. There the stream divided, the water in the southern section of the canal flowing south to Lake Erie and that in the
northern section flowing north through the locks and down the
escarpment to Lake Ontario. This meant that a fish from Lake Ontario, swimming upstream through the canal in its instinct-driven
search for the headwaters, would suddenly—at Welland—find itself
swimming downstream instead. Instinct would complain vocifer-

ously; the fish would turn aside, passing through the feeder canal into the Grand River and never reaching Lake Erie at all.

The 1881 construction work changed that pattern. The engineers of the Third Canal deepened the Deep Cut to the point where it was lower than Lake Erie, allowing water to flow directly from Erie to Ontario through the canal for the first time. The feeder from the Grand was no longer needed. It kept running for a time, providing a secondary supply with enough of an attraction current that headwaters-hunting fish apparently kept using it in preference to the main canal, but in 1919, during construction of the Fourth Canal, it was cut off entirely. Now Lake Erie—and only Lake Erie—was upstream from Lake Ontario through the Welland, and the fish that had been running up the Welland to spawn in the headwaters of the Grand had no place to go but into the upper Lake.

One of the fish that had been using the Welland as a path into the Grand was an elongated, jawless species of extremely ancient lineage called the sea lamprey. In 1921, two years after Lake Erie became, finally and irrevocably, the canal's entire water supply, the first sea lamprey was discovered in its waters. No one knew it yet, but the upper Lakes fisheries were about to undergo one of the most drastic resource declines in history.

The sea lamprey (*Petromyzon marinus*) is one of the world's ugliest fishes. Eighteen to twenty inches long but only two to three inches through, it is eel-like in appearance but without an eel's grace. The fins are reduced to tiny appendages, mostly near the tail; the gill slits are absent, replaced by a series of porthole-like vents reminiscent of those of an ancient Buick. The most striking feature is the mouth. Large, round, and undercut, with several rows of sharp inward-pointing teeth, it is provided with a tongue the texture of a carpenter's file and surrounded by a disc of fleshy muscle that looks—and acts—like a powerful suction cup. That suction-cup mouth can be used to move stones during nest-building or to inch the fish along rock faces against the current of the rapids in its spawning streams. Its principal use, though, is in feeding. The lamprey is a parasitic predator on large game fish. Its technique is to approach its prey broadside, latch on with that immense living suction cup, rasp a hole

in the larger fish's flesh with its tongue, and gorge itself on blood and
other bodily fluids. Its saliva contains an anticoagulant called
lamphredin that keeps the blood flowing until the lamprey lets go.
Usually by the time this happens, the victim is seriously disabled;
often it is dead.

Lampreys are normally salt-water dwellers, but they are anadromous, and like most anadromous fish they are perfectly capable of
living their entire lives in fresh water if the size of the body of fresh
water is sufficient to provide them with enough prey. The great fresh
water oceans off the Fifth Coast are more than ample. The historic
Great Lakes outlet channel down the St. Lawrence was apparently
too full of rapids to allow any lampreys to use it as a passageway into
the Lakes (there is some question about this), but human engineers
helpfully took care of that little problem. Completion of the Erie
Canal in 1825 meant that a bypass had been created around the St.
Lawrence, providing a link to the Atlantic via the easier waters of the
Hudson/Mohawk system instead. The lampreys were not long in
finding it. The first sea lamprey was positively identified in Lake
Ontario in 1835.

By the mid-nineteenth century, lampreys were well established
in Ontario and the nearby Finger Lakes. There, for the time being,
they stopped. They couldn't pass Niagara Falls, and since both the
Erie Canal and the Welland Canal were fed by higher-elevation
feeder streams instead of being directly watered from Lake Erie, the
lampreys' ancient anadromous instinct to move upstream—always
upstream—led them through the canals into the feeder streams instead of the upper Lakes. Anyway, their foothold in Lake Ontario
during those early years was, at best, tenuous. The Lake itself had
close to ideal conditions for them, but its tributary streams did not.
Lampreys require clear streams with temperatures of 60°F or higher
to spawn, and though the deep, tree-shaded presettlement Lake Ontario tributaries almost always met the first of these conditions, they
rarely met the second. So the lampreys lived in Lake Ontario—in a
sense, they thrived there—but they did not overrun it. There was
little reproductive energy left to colonize on upstream into Lake Erie
and beyond.

The settlement of the Fifth Coast, and the associated clearing and
cultivation of land along Great Lakes rivers, changed all that. By the

end of the nineteenth century, stream temperatures had risen significantly throughout the Ontario basin, and the lamprey had an enormously expanded number of spawning areas to choose from. Its population shot up. At the same time, the three principal food fish of Lake Ontario—the Atlantic salmon, the Lake whitefish, and the Lake trout, all of which reproduce at lower stream temperatures than the lamprey does—found their own choice of spawning streams shrinking. That, combined with overfishing by humans and predation from the growing lamprey populations, did them in. By 1900 the Ontario population of the Atlantic salmon was extinct, and trout and whitefish numbers in the Lake were rapidly declining—a decline that has been only modestly reversed to this day.

The lampreys now had a growing population and a declining food source—the classic conditions for the colonization of new areas. All they needed was a place to colonize, and the engineers of the Third Welland Canal gave them that. Suddenly a lamprey-path had been provided into the fertile fields of the upper Lakes. It was as though a gate had been opened between a pasture containing sheep and another containing wolves. It would take time, but the upper Lakes' fisheries were, by the opening of that gate, effectively doomed.

It would probably be wise to digress here long enough to provide a brief outline of the pre-lamprey fish populations of the Great Lakes, so that the effects of the arrival of these voracious animated suction cups can be better understood.

There were approximately 150 separate species of fish in Fifth Coast waters when the first Europeans arrived, ranging in size from sticklebacks and sculpin only a few inches long to the enormous Lake sturgeon, up to nine feet in length and weighing in at close to 400 pounds. There were burbot, or lawyers, with livers like those of cod and flesh like that of lobster; there were chubs and bloaters from the profundal zone, deep in the offshore waters; there were Lake herring, or cisco, foot-long plankton eaters that schooled in huge numbers in the autumn shallows. There were blue pike and yellow perch and pickerel and a hundred more—living together, preying and being preyed upon, essential links in an interlocked, intricate system that had been evolving gradually into place for nearly 10,000 years.

At the top of this great chain of life stood three magnificent predator species. The first of these, the Atlantic salmon, was limited to Lake Ontario by Niagara Falls; the other two were found in all five Lakes, and were the base upon which the hugely profitable Great Lakes fishery would eventually be built. There is still a remnant fishery on them today: Rod Badger and I reaped some of the benefits of it in that little general store beneath the Grand Sable Banks at Grand Marais. One is a salmonid, the Lake trout *(Salvelinus namaycush)*. The other is a coregonid—the Indians' *ticaming*, the ichthyologists' *Coregonus clupeaformis*. The gourmet's delight. The Lake whitefish.

The productivity of these cold northern waters astounded their first visitors. "Stores of fishes, sturgeons of vast bigness, and Pycks seven feet long," wrote the effusive Pierre Radisson of Lake Superior's Chequamegon Bay in 1658; "a months subsistence for a regiment, could have been taken in a few hours time," declared an awed Alexander Henry at the Indian fishery near Fourteen Mile Point, some eighty miles east of Chequamegon, 100 years later. Sturgeon were so common over the bar off the tip of Point Pelee in Lake Erie, according to one early account, that fishermen "standing in a flat bottomed boat killed numbers of them by hitting them on the head with an axe." The Chippewa of the Ontonagon River band lived almost completely on sturgeon, which they caught by spearing them from a weir near the river's mouth; 200 miles to the east, those from the Sault Ste. Marie band were living largely on whitefish, taking huge amounts with canoe and dipnet below the great rapids. The Ottowa of the Au Sable valley ate fair numbers of grayling (the nearest grayling is now in the Northwest Territories). The Huron and the Iroquois heavily utilized the salmon of Ontario.

Early European settlers also found fishing attractive. There was a commercial fishery of sorts on Lake Erie as early as 1795, and the American Fur Company was running a whitefish operation on Lake Superior by the 1830's, salting its catch and packing them in barrels for the New York market. The industry had expanded greatly by the beginning of the twentieth century. More than a million annual pounds of Lake trout, and nearly two million annual pounds of whitefish, were coming out of Lake Ontario—the least productive of the Great Lakes—as far back as 1879. Shallow, warm Erie was much better: In 1900 alone, Erie's total fish production—trout, whitefish, chub, blue pike, Lake herring, sturgeon, and small amounts of other fish—came to over thirty-three million pounds. This was considered a poor year. Huron produced 7.4 million annual pounds of a single species, Lake trout, in the 1890's; Michigan had an annual trout catch of more than three million pounds a year during that same period. Superior's waters were the best habitat for the cold-loving whitefish. Standing in a canoe with a dipnet, a single fisherman could catch more than 1,000 four- to five-pound fish in a single day. In 1885 the Superior whitefish harvest topped five million pounds; in 1903, it hit eight million. By this time, Lakes fishing was big business. Hundreds of fishing ports had sprung up along the Fifth Coast; specialized gear was developed, specialized boats were adopted, and the Great Lakes became, for a time, one of the continent's premier commercial fishing grounds.

By the 1920's, when the lamprey reached Lake Erie, certain man-caused elements of instability had already made their way into this rosy picture. The familiar pattern of resource mining had set in; like the furs and the trees and the minerals, the fish were being taken from the basin for use elsewhere at a greater rate than could be sustained by natural production. In the case of the fisheries, though, resource depletion was somewhat harder to see than it was with the others. It was hidden in the catch statistics. Overall, the catch remained nearly constant; it was only the species mix that changed.

The total Lake Superior fishery, for example, was a remarkably stable 12.5 million pounds per year throughout the period from 1880 to 1920. But beneath the surface of that apparent stability lurked a slowly unbalancing ecosystem. The principal commercial target during the early part of the period was whitefish. By 1910, whitefish numbers had decreased in the Lake to the point where the fishery could no longer be sustained on them, and the fishermen turned to Lake trout; and ten years after that the Lake trout populations were as depressed as the whitefish populations, and Lake herring had become the prime commercial target. The desirable species were being picked off one by one; the delicately tuned proportional relationships among species worked out by the slow turning of natural process over the last 10,000 years were coming unglued.

A further destabilizing factor was provided by a pair of introduced species, the domestic carp *(Cyprinus carpio)* and the rainbow smelt *(Osmerus mordax).*

The smelt was an anadromous salt-water fish, a resident of both the Atlantic and Pacific oceans which happened to be a favorite food of salmon; and so when a series of somewhat quixotic attempts were made in the late nineteenth and early twentieth centuries to mitigate the loss of Atlantic salmon in Lake Ontario by planting Japanese salmon in Lake Michigan, smelt were thoughtfully planted along with them. The salmon failed; the smelt thrived. First introduced to Michigan waters in Crystal Lake, an isolated Lake Michigan embayment near Sleeping Bear Dunes, in 1912, the fish rapidly made its way into the main Lake. By 1925 it was in Lake Huron; five years later the first individuals were sighted in Lake Superior, and two years after that they started entering fishermen's nets in Lake Erie. The population soon grew to immense proportions. A modest commercial harvest of 86,000 pounds was taken from Lake Michigan in 1931; less than ten years later, the catch had grown to more than four million pounds and showed no signs of slowing down. Huge spawning runs entered streams all around the Lakes, to be taken by sportsmen dipnetting from banks and bridges at a rate that has been estimated at ten million pounds annually. The town of Menominee, Michigan, on the west shore of Green Bay, instituted an annual "smelt carnival" to celebrate the run, featuring—among other things—a wrestling match conducted in a foot of dead smelt (spectators, as environmental writer Tom Kuchenberg once put it delicately, "tended to cluster on the upwind side of the ring"). The population collapsed precipitously in 1944—the commercial harvest declined to 5,000 pounds—but it rebounded almost as rapidly, and was back up in the millions by the 1950's. Today this alien salt-water species is one of the most important commercial fish in the Lakes, leading the harvest figures for Lake Superior and Lake Erie and running fourth in Lake Michigan. Its abundance is undoubtedly a factor in the decline of Lake herring and Lake whitefish, which feed on many of the same species: When the great collapse in smelt populations came in 1944, Lake Huron recorded the largest increase in yearling whitefish numbers in history.

The carp is another problem altogether. A fresh-water species from Asia that has been cultured in European fish ponds for centuries, it was brought to the New World by the great wave of mid-nineteenth-century cross-Atlantic immigrants, to be raised on farms like cattle. But ponds are much more difficult to fence than pastures, and the carp rapidly escaped. They were in the Lakes by 1893, and they have been there ever since, apparently slipping quietly into the ecological niche once occupied by the sturgeon—but with one destructive difference. A large bottom feeder, the carp has a fondness for the roots of aquatic vegetation, and in the process of digging them out it stirs up vast quantities of sediments, resuspending them in the water as miniature mudstorms along the Lakebeds. This is more than just an aesthetic irritation: There is strong evidence that it interferes with the spawning and feeding behavior of the whitefish. The carp does not compete with the whitefish for food, but it is almost certainly keeping whitefish populations depressed anyway.

Into this destabilized and artificially unbalanced environment the sea lampreys fell like wolves on the fold. Moving slowly through the inhospitable (to lampreys) waters of Lake Erie, they arrived in Lake Huron in 1933 and in Lake Michigan in 1936. Here their numbers exploded. By 1948, fishermen along the Michigan and Wisconsin coasts were reporting localized populations so large they roiled the surface of the water as they swam about. Fishing boats sent out to check the nets came back trailing clinging lampreys like the tentacles of giant sea anemones. They also came back with empty holds. Some nets were raised full of dead fish—the lampreys had apparently discovered that the fish in the nets were easy prey, unable to move enough to get away from them. Other nets simply came up empty. As time went on, the empty ones began to predominate. The 1943 Lake Michigan trout catch was nearly seven million pounds; ten years later, it was under 4,000 pounds and still shrinking. Huron's catch declined in similar fashion, dropping from nearly 3.7 million pounds in 1940 to under 1,000 in 1960.

The Lake whitefish decline was not quite that bad, but it was bad enough. In 1948, the whitefish catch in the five connected Lakes was twelve million pounds; eight years later it had dropped by more than 90 percent, to less than one million. Most of that was coming from a single Lake, Superior, where the lampreys had not taken over quite as thoroughly as elsewhere.

Surprisingly, perhaps, the overall catch figures for Great Lakes fisheries through this period remained relatively constant, between 60 and 80 million pounds per year. Their value, however, dropped precipitously. Commercial fishing operations brought in $14 million in 1946. Less than twenty years later, fishing revenues had declined by nearly 66 percent, to $5 million. The reason was simple: With the trout and whitefish gone, and the herring declining, the fishermen were falling back on less desirable species such as smelt and lawyer and perch. These met catch quotas but not expenses. All along the Fifth Coast, bankruptcy lawyers (human variety) did a fine business.

The loss of the whitefish and trout was more than just an economic disaster for the fishing industry: It was an ecological disaster as well. It had a further destabilizing effect on an ecosystem already reeling from the effects of 200 years of human interference, driving it over the brink from instability to total disorder. Whitefish and trout had been the top predators—the peak of the food chain, the principal controls on the prey species beneath them. Now they were no longer there, and the controls had been switched to "off." Prey fish populations exploded.

One of those prey fish was a little-known (at that time) ocean species that had come in, like the lamprey, through the Welland Canal. Its name was the alewife. It was not destined to remain little-known for long.

The alewife *(Alosa pseudoharengus)* is an unobtrusive, innocuous little thing that closely resembles a small silvery shad. A member of the herring family, it is a native of the North Atlantic, where it schools in great numbers off Newfoundland and Maine. Unlike other marine invaders of the Great Lakes such as the smelt and the lamprey, the alewife is not primarily an anadromous species; it spawns principally in nearshore and offshore shallows, only occasionally making spawning runs up rivers. It tolerates fresh water but does not exactly thrive there. In its salt-water form in the North Atlantic, it grows to ten or twelve inches in length and is meaty enough to be prized as a food fish; in the Great Lakes it is stunted and skinny, peaking out at barely four inches long and of not much use for anything except pet food or fertilizer. Its liver and kidneys are apparently affected by the difference in osmotic balance and iodine content between salt water and fresh, making it subject to periodic dieoffs of a massive nature. It is not a dangerous fish like the lamprey or an obnoxious one like the carp: It attacks no food fish and muddies no waters. It does little of anything but eat and breed. Those two things, however, it does very well indeed, and in the absence of controlling predators, eating and breeding are quite bad enough. The first alewife wasn't observed in Lake Michigan until 1949. Just fifteen years later, over 90 percent of the fish in the Lake by weight—by *weight*—were alewives.

Its vast numbers make the alewife at least as much of a pest as the lamprey. It competes with more desirable fish for food, literally eating species like the Lake herring and the chub out of house and home and seriously threatening the whitefish, which as a juvenile hunts the same zooplanktonic food in the same habitats. It fills nets set for other species. During the spring dieoff—a nearly annual event since 1967 —great numbers of alewife bodies litter the shallows and wash up on the beaches, clogging water intakes and smelling to high heaven. Dead alewives, unfortunately, are almost impossible to get rid of. In 1983, the dieoff occurred in early February. As late as July of that year, when I stopped at a roadside park near Petoskey, Michigan, the beach was still strewn with dried, blackened, parchment-like alewives.

The twin invasions of the lamprey and the alewife completed the job that overfishing, spawning-stream and wetland destruction, and the introduction of smelt and carp had begun: They removed the last vestiges of the pre-European-contact Great Lakes ecology, ushering in a period of massive instability that has persisted ever since. They sent some species reeling to extinction; of the seven species of chub that once inhabited the Lakes, for example, only one remains today. The blue pike and the Lake trout have disappeared entirely from Lake Erie, where they were once abundant; the Lake herring is gone from Ontario, where the harvest once approached fifteen million pounds. The total number of species has been reduced and the balance among them has been drastically altered. Fish unknown in the Lakes before humanity started fooling around with them—alewives, carp, smelt, lampreys—have become the most abundant species. The sport fishery today is based almost entirely on hatchery-raised Coho and Chinook salmon and the related Steelhead trout, all salmonids native to the Pacific Ocean which apparently cannot breed in the

Great Lakes. The Lakes have become one vast artificial fish farm. That is, perhaps, better than one vast emptiness, but it is not exactly the ecological role one would expect to see for the greatest body of fresh water on earth.

By the early 1960's, some measure of human control had finally begun to be exerted over the runaway lamprey population. A chemical poison called TFM had been developed that was selectively toxic to lamprey larvae, without—it was believed—severely harming other forms of aquatic life, and plans had been laid to treat every lamprey spawning stream in the upper Great Lakes Basin with it. Before those plans could be carried out, however, a new crisis had developed to take the public's attention away from lampreys. Another extinction was apparently about to occur, and this time the victim was not just a fish. This time the organism floundering toward disaster—about to be declared officially and irrevocably dead—was Lake Erie.

XII Algae

In retrospect, it is difficult to claim that we weren't warned. Lake Erie had been acting funny for a long time.

Wild rice and other aquatic plants, recorded as "very abundant" over several thousand acres of Sandusky and Maumee Bays in the early nineteenth century, were long gone by the early twentieth. Complaints about beaches being fouled by drifts of smelly seaweed began surfacing as early as the 1930's, and in the summer of 1933 much of the western end of the Lake briefly turned such a bright green that Dr. Clarence Taft of Ohio State University, observing the phenomenon from the University's Franz Theodore Stone Laboratory on South Bass Island, noted that the water "looked as if it were coated with green paint." During the 1940's and 1950's, many beaches around the Lake had to be closed as health hazards; the city of Cleveland was forced to move the main intake for its water system from half a mile offshore to five miles out during the same period. The reason: "dangerously high counts of fecal coliform bacteria." That is just a nice way of saying too much shit. The Lake's shore waters were, in many places, well on their way to becoming the functional equivalent of a septic tank.

Down at the Lake's outlet, the most famous tourist attraction in North America—the great Falls of Niagara—began, sometime in the 1950's, to literally stink out loud. The water flowing over the brink was marred by broad, conspicuous brown streaks: The little *Maid of the Mist*, the boat that takes brave (or foolhardy) tourists through the oceanic turbulence of the plunge basin to the base of the enormous cataract, had to make its way through miasmic, sludge-coated waters and mounds of discolored detergent foam up to eight feet high. It looked like a sewer; it smelled like a sewer; for all practical purposes, it *was* a sewer. Not coincidentally, it was at about this time that Niagara began to lose its reputation as a honeymooners' heaven.

All these things, as I said, should have warned us, but we were curiously unwarnable. The Lake was just too damned big to be worried about. How could a body of water the size of a small ocean be seriously polluted by anything as tiny and insignificant as human beings? Local problems, yes: We had those, in spades. Perhaps something should be done about them. But Lakewide deterioration? Don't be ridiculous. Must be some mistake.

The first crack in this comfortably smug belief in the invincibility of size came in the summer of 1953. That was when limnologist Wilson Britt, taking routine bottom samples in the west end of the Lake, came up with some less-than-routine results: The nymphs were gone.

Nymphs—mayfly larvae, the immature forms of various insect species of the genus *Hexagenia*—had been the predominant bottom-dwelling animal in all previous studies of the Lake. Now, suddenly, there were virtually none. Where they had formerly numbered between 400 and 1,000 per square meter, Britt found populations ranging from 40 or 50 down to zero. In their place were oligochaetes—creatures adapted to an oxygen-poor environment, creatures not previously found in significant numbers in any of the Great Lakes. There had been, in fact, what might be termed an oligochaete explosion. Within a few years, bottom samplers were pulling up sediments with as many as 50,000 specimens per square meter of these primitive, segmented annelids—commonly known as "sludge worms"—off the mouth of the Detroit River.

Five years after Britt's work, another limnologist, Dr. Alfred M. Beeton of the U.S. Bureau of Commercial Fisheries, came up with an even more shocking set of experimental findings. He had been studying dissolved oxygen levels in the central part of the Lake, and what he had found was an anoxic desert—a 2,600-square-mile area where the bottom waters had no oxygen in them at all! Putting that data together with Britt's oligochaetes and Taft's paint-green waters and all those closed beaches, Beeton came to a startling conclusion. Lake Erie—not just parts of it, but the whole Lake—was undergoing massive, wholesale ecological deterioration. Its trophic state was shifting; it was becoming, as environmental writer Gene Marine would put it a few years later, "as eutrophic as hell."

In 1961, three years after his field work and at the height of the war on the lampreys, Beeton published his findings in the *Transactions of the American Fisheries Society*. The article was called "Environmental Changes in Lake Erie," and it dealt largely with eutrophication. The science writers of the popular press got hold of the article, changed the key word "eutrophication" to what they thought would be its more easily grasped equivalent—"accelerated old age" —and broadcast it widely about. And that is how it came to the attention of the public at large that one of the Great Lakes was dying.

If you try to talk to a limnologist today about the death of Lake Erie, you are likely to be greeted with a derisive snort. The word "eutrophic," he will point out, does not mean "dying" at all; in fact, it means quite the opposite. A eutrophic lake is not dead but alive— far too alive for its own good. Your limnologist will probably give you a quick lesson in the modern meaning of trophic levels, taking a good sidewise slap or two along the way at journalists who abuse biological terms without knowing what the hell they are talking about. Very well: Limnologists clearly know more about limnology than journalists do, and a eutrophic lake is not, strictly speaking, a dying one. But before accepting that judgment of term-abuse fully, consider these two facts. One: In the 1960's, the word "dying" for Lake Erie was—proper translation of "eutrophic" or not—uncomfortably accurate. And two: In those days, when it came to trophic levels and their meanings, limnologists didn't really know what the hell they were talking about, either.

Trophic levels are classifications used in the biological sciences to describe the amount of nutrients (Greek *trephein*, nourishment) in the water of a lake or a stream. There are four of them: oligotrophic (poorly nourished), mesotrophic (moderately nourished), eutrophic (well nourished), and dystrophic (unnourished). Developed by the German biologist C. A. Weber around 1907 as a means of classifying freshwater bogs, the trophic-level system was first applied to lakes by Weber's countryman, the brilliant pioneer limnologist Einar Naumann, in 1919. It has been safely ensconced in limnology ever since.

It has not, however, always referred to precisely the same thing. Naumann and other early users of the terminology thought that trophic levels were part of a time-oriented system. All lakes, they taught, began in the oligotrophic state. As time went on and their beds filled in with sediments, they gradually gained more nutrients, undergoing a slow transformation through mesotrophic to eutrophic. Oligotrophic lakes were deep and cold, with little accumulated sediment and virtually sterile waters; eutrophic lakes were shallow and warm, full of sediment and water weeds, their waters a thin organic "soup" of microscopic life forms. There was more dissolved oxygen in an oligotrophic lake than in a eutrophic one, because there were fewer living things to use it—in technical terms, because the biological oxygen demand (BOD) was lower. BOD was a principal measure of a lake's trophism: The more BOD, the higher the trophic level.

If the BOD got too high, of course, all the oxygen in the water would be used up and everything would die. That was a dystrophic lake. (Oxygen isn't exactly a nutrient, but you get the idea.) Dystrophism normally didn't happen until a lake was well on its way to filling in with sediments to the point where it was more swamp or bog than lake.

Because the trophic-level system was thought to be time-oriented —dependent on sediment accumulation and the slow change of water chemistry—it followed that the shift from oligotrophic to eutrophic and beyond that to dystrophic would take far longer in a large lake than in a small one. This was, in fact, observable. Farmers' ponds became eutrophic much more rapidly than full-size lakes; small lakes became eutrophic more rapidly than large ones. Super-large lakes such as the Great Lakes should therefore take essentially forever. "Biotic [trophic-level] succession is scarcely discernible . . . in very large or very deep lakes," wrote University of Illinois zoologist Charles Kendeigh confidently in his classic textbook, *Animal Ecology*. "The Great Lakes, for instance, will endure until erosion lowers their outlets." That was in 1961—the same year that Alfred Beeton published his paper on what was happening to Lake Erie and knocked the whole idea of trophic-level succession into a cocked hat.

Today's limnologists do not speak much of trophic-level succession. The current belief is that trophic levels are not time-dependent but morphometric and watershed-dependent—which means that it is the shape ("morphometry") of a lake and the nutrients available in the runoff reaching it that are the prime factors in determining its trophic state. Age does enter, but only as a secondary factor. As the processes of erosion fill in a lake's bed and lower its outlet, it becomes shallower, and this change in its morphometry can lead to a change in its trophic level if the watershed has enough nutrients available to cause the change. The bottom line is the nutrients. Because of this, it is now believed that a lake's trophic level is determined almost as soon as it is created, and that it remains at this level for nearly the entire span of its existence. The concept of slow trophic-level succession—of "aging" and "dying"—are as defunct as Lake Erie almost became because we once accepted them.

And make no mistake about it: We did almost destroy Lake Erie. We didn't "artificially age" it; we didn't, as one overzealous commentator suggested at the height of the crisis, put it in any real danger of becoming "a noxious swamp." But we did alter its trophic state. And we did very nearly kill it.

It is extremely important to understand this fact—if only because, should we fail to understand it, the whole situation is very likely to happen again.

The best way to get from Windsor, Ontario, to the southernmost point of mainland Canada is to take King's Highway 3, heading southeast from the Ambassador Bridge through the edge of the city and out into rural Essex County. This is the region Canadians call the Sun Parlour—a flat green land, tidy, rich, and intensely cultivated. Seventy percent of Canada's commercial garden-vegetable crop is grown here; there are also tobacco fields, tropical greenhouses, and orchards. Roadside stands offer fresh produce. At Leamington, the self-proclaimed Tomato Capital of the World, you leave Highway 3 and head south, following the signs to Point Pelee National Park. In six miles, you pass the park boundary; in another five, you reach the interpretive center. Here, during the summer months, you leave your car and transfer to the Balade, a sort of motorless trolley on rubber tires drawn behind a propane-powered pickup. Ten minutes later you are deposited in front of the bathhouse on East Point Beach. From here the journey will be on foot.

It is not far, now—only a few hundred yards. In the beginning the trail lies in deep woods, dark-canopied and festooned with trailing vines; but soon it breaks out on the edge of the beach, and you can see the surf you have been hearing since you left the Balade. The beach is lonely—most of your fellow-passengers have stayed back around the bathhouse—and the great restless animal that is Lake Erie is rushing at it in series after series of two-foot breakers, pounding it as if frustrated at its inability to climb any further, then sliding resignedly back into its bed. Overhead a gull cries. The last few feet of your journey are on the sand itself, out the long curving spit that park personnel refer to as the Tip. The breakers are rushing at you from both sides, now, and beyond the last little bit of land, out there over the Point Pelee Bar, they are crashing into each other in a surging white maelstrom that completely justifies the bilingual sign you passed a few steps back:

DANGEROUS CURRENTS

COURANTS DANGEREUX

NO SWIMMING OR WADING

IL EST DEFENDU DE SE BAIGNER

OU DE S'AVENTURER DANS L'EAU

You are standing on a piece of Canada, now, that is farther south than all of the French Riviera; farther south than much of Spain; farther south than parts of California and Utah and Nevada. Off to the southwest, beyond the distant shapes of the freighters making their way gingerly through Pelee Passage, there is the low, vague bulk of Pelee Island; otherwise all is water and sky and the blurred blue far-off line where they seem to touch. You might be back with Louis Joliet, discovering the place for the first time; but you are not, and in the early 1960's you would have known it. It was here on Point Pelee that Erie's eutrophication problems reached their most obnoxious level. Even today the problems—the green water, the fouled, putrescent beaches—occasionally recur.

Among the Great Lakes, Erie stands out as a ringer. It looks like the others, but beneath the surface it is quite different. It is older; it was formed early, almost as soon as the glaciers left, and it has not changed shape significantly for nearly 12,000 years. It is more southerly than the other Lakes, and is surrounded by a relatively large watershed developed not on rock like Superior's and northern Huron's or on gravelly glacial outwash like Michigan's, but on earth, the good black earth of Ohio and Indiana and southern Ontario. It lies far to the south of the taiga and almost completely out of the transition forest, away from the highly acidic layer of decaying needles and twigs (the so-called mor humus) of conifers, deep into the central hardwood region where the humus layer (the mull humus) is dark and rich and deep and full of nutrients. And it is shallow—shockingly shallow. That is the biggest difference of all. Superior is 1,300 feet deep, Michigan and Ontario around 900, Huron 750. Erie at its deepest is 210, and that is a local anomaly. The Lakewide average depth is only fifty-eight feet, and much of the western end is barely half of that. Of all the Great Lakes, Erie is the only one whose bed does not reach below sea level.

	ONTARIO	ERIE	HURON	MICHIGAN	SUPERIOR
length (mi)	193	241	206	307	350
width (mi)	53	57	183	118	160
surface (sq mi)	7550	9910	23010	22400	31800
volume (cu mi)	405	109	850	1171	2933
depth average (ft) greatest (ft)	283 802	58 210	195 750	276 923	487 1330
coastline US (mi) Canada (mi) total (mi)	328 384 712	474 397 871	837 2990 3827	1638 0 1638	1245 1481 2726

Given parameters like that, it is not too surprising to find that, while the other Great Lakes are clearly oligotrophic, Erie is firmly mesotrophic or even borderline eutrophic—always has been, always will be. To say that, though, is both to oversimplify and to ignore human activities. Erie's basin is morphometrically complex, with some characteristics that make mesotrophic nutrient levels act, at certain times and places, like eutrophication. And the nutrient levels themselves are no longer mesotrophic. What we have seen on Lake Erie is a process called "cultural eutrophication"—a huge artificial influx of certain nutrients, primarily phosphorus, which impose the worst form of eutrophic excess, the algal bloom, on top of a basically mesotrophic system. The Lake becomes a monster that stinks and exudes thick mats of green, decomposing slime. It is no wonder that 1960's journalists latched so gleefully onto the term "dead" for this vast morass of so-called water.

The primary component of an algal bloom is, of course, algae. To say that, however, is not to pin things down very far: There are roughly 30,000 different species of algae, half of an entire biological phylum, the Thallophyta (which also includes the fungi). Algae are water-dwellers, the most primitive of the "green" plants—those that contain chlorophyll. Although there are many-celled forms (the familiar giant kelp of the Pacific coast, which may grow to a length of 200 feet, is one), most algae are single-celled organisms; the individual plants normally cannot be seen without a microscope. Multi-plant masses are another matter; given the right conditions of temperature and nutrition, they may grow in such great numbers that they dye the water green. This is the phenomenon known as the algal bloom.

In some algae, the cells grow long, thin filaments which become entangled with each other, forming colonies in the shape of streamers several inches or even several feet long. It was one of these so-called filamentous algae—a cyanophytic (blue-green) species known as *cladophora*—which bloomed so profusely in Lake Erie during the 1950's and 1960's. Hundreds of square miles of it formed great mats up to two feet thick on the Lake's surface; pieces of the mats thousands of acres in size broke free and washed up on the beaches. Water intakes were fouled; drinking-water supplies took on the distinctive, disgusting taste of rotting vegetation. In the Lake's western end the Bass Islands looked as though they had drifted off course and ended up in the Sargasso Sea, with cladophora literally everywhere. "It looks as if it had dropped off the Ancient Mariner and smells terrible," complained science writer Gladwin Hill in the *Saturday Review*.

All this was merely unpleasant. The blooms of cladophora also had another effect, however—one that made them not just disgusting but downright lethal. It was they, it turned out, that were responsible for the mayfly deaths and for the anoxic conditions in the Lake's central basin. And that was something to be really concerned about.

It was, in a sense, not the algae but the shape of the Lake's bed that was the culprit. Lake Erie, as has already been pointed out, is morphometrically unusual. At the southern limits of the continental glacier's reach, in a region largely underlaid by hard dolomitic bedrock, it was not carved out as deeply as the other four Lakes to begin with—and it has silted in more since (the sediments in its bed have been measured at depths of at least 100 feet). Its basin is crossed by two prominent underwater north-south ridges, the upturned edges of two of the nesting bowls of the Michigan Structural Basin. The western ridge begins at Point Pelee and heads south, broadening as it goes; the Bass Islands, Pelee Island, and Kelleys Island are all above-water exposures of it. The eastern ridge begins at Long Point and runs south to the short Pennsylvania shore; the great bar of Presque Isle at Erie is part of a glacial moraine piled up on its southern end. The ships of Perry's 1813 squadron were built behind that morainal bar, in the protection of the eastern ridge; they were sheltered by a hole in the western ridge, Put-in-Bay on South Bass Island, the night before engaging the English at the turning point of the War of 1812. This is a small point but important. Thus does geology influence history.

The presence of the ridges divides the Lakebed into three separate basins, named by geographers for their positions along the Lake's axis: the western basin, the central basin, and the eastern basin.

The western basin is the shallowest of the three; it is this part of the Lake that rarely exceeds thirty feet in depth. It never develops a thermocline—a summer temperature stratification—and its natural character is clearly eutrophic.

The eastern basin is the deepest, exceeding 100 feet for much of its area and reaching the Lake's maximum depth of 210 feet at a spot a few miles off the tip of Long Point; it stratifies thoroughly, with a clearly defined thermocline between June and September, and most limnologists classify it as oligotrophic, although it has some meso-trophic characteristics.

The central basin is a bit of an enigma. With an average depth of sixty feet over much of its area, it is deep enough to develop a thermocline for most of each summer—but just barely. The warm, well-mixed water above the thermocline (the epilimnion) contains most of the central basin's water; the cold, still water below it (the hypolimnion) is only a few feet thick. Since the thermocline prevents the circulation of water from the epilimnion to the hypolimnion—trapping the hypolimnion waters and not letting them reach the surface of the Lake where they can be exposed to the air—the amount of oxygen dissolved in that tiny hypolimnion at the time of spring overturn (when the thermocline forms and the Lake stratifies) is all the oxygen that will be available to life in the depths until fall over-turn (when the thermocline breaks up again).

Under natural conditions, that was not normally a problem: The BOD was moderate, and the mayfly nymphs and other bottom-dwelling animals—and the whitefish and similar cold-water species that seek shelter in the cold hypolimnion during the summer months —had enough oxygen to make it through from overturn to overturn. Under the conditions imposed by cultural eutrophication, however—the conditions of algal bloom—there was a dramatic change. Individual cladophora cells are not long-lived, and a two-foot-thick mat of the stuff contains an astronomical number of plants, most of them in various stages of dying. The dead ones fall out of the mat, cascading to the bottom as a deluge of microscopic bits of plant matter that has been likened to an underwater rainstorm. On the bottom, decay sets in. The bacteria that bring about decay are high oxygen users; BOD shoots up. The hypolimnion—that thin, almost nonexistent central-basin hypo-limnion—rapidly loses its oxygen. The fish migrate, if they are lucky. The mayfly nymphs, which cannot migrate, die.

To get a handle on the anoxia in the central basin, therefore, it was clearly necessary to get a handle on the algal blooms. What was causing them, and why had they not shown up earlier? The single answer to these two questions was very simple indeed. Years earlier, Commodore Perry had dispatched a succinct, immediately famous

message from Lake Erie: "We have met the enemy and he is ours."
Now, in the 1960's, cartoonist Walt Kelly's laconic possum Pogo
rephrased Perry's sentence into a Lake Erie message for modern
times: "We have met the enemy and he is us."

All those years of using Lake Erie as a garbage dump were beginning to catch up with us.

The facts—once they started coming into view—were both as-
tonishing and disgusting. For decades, it turned out, residents of the
Lake Erie region had been blithely living beside, and drawing their
drinking water from, what amounted to an open sewer. At opposite
ends of the Lake, the cities of Buffalo and Detroit were pouring tens
of thousands of tons of sewage into the water every day in a virtually
untreated form: Neither city used more than the simplest variety of
primary sewage treatment, the settling basin. The Detroit River was
carrying more than 500 million gallons of domestic wastewater, and
roughly twice that amount of industrial effluent, into Erie each and
every day—a total waste stream of nearly 1.6 billion gallons, with a
pollution content of more than 20 million pounds. The river's waters,
said the Public Health Service, were "polluted bacteriologically,
chemically, physically, and biologically, and contain excessive coliform densities as well as excessive quantities of phenols, iron, ammonia, suspended solids, settleable solids, chlorides, nitrogen compounds and phosphates." That was why the beaches of Point Pelee,
just down current from the mouth of the Detroit in the hydrologically constricted western basin, were so badly fouled. The Buffalo
River was in even worse condition: Studies of it showed no life at
all—not even anaerobic, pollution-tolerant life such as sludgeworms
—in its bottom sediments, and far too much life—up to 500,000
coliform bacteria per 100 milliliters—in its water. ("Unbelievable!
Disgusting!" exclaimed Buffalo Mayor Chester Kowal after an eye-
opening, eye-watering boat trip up the filthy sewer-river he normally
never saw.)

The problems were literally all around. "All major tributaries of
Lake Erie are grossly polluted," announced Charles Northington of
the Public Health Service. At Cleveland, the Cuyahoga River was so
laden with floating logs, oil, old tires, paints, and flammable chemicals that the city had been forced to declare it a fire hazard. It also
carried Cleveland's sewage—from three plants, only two of which

had secondary treatment capability. At Toledo, the Maumee was providing 3 percent of the Lake's water and nearly half its sediment load; most of these sediments came from agricultural lands and were heavily laden with fertilizer and biological wastes. Down the Thames and the Grand and the other rivers draining the rich soils of Ontario's Arrowhead came more than 2,000 metric tons of phosphorus each year. The percentage of Erie Basin residents served by sewage systems delivering only primary treatment ranged from 20 percent in the Ohio section of the basin to an alarming 78 percent in the New York section—and even when the sewage plants were set up for secondary treatment, there was a catch-22 that meant the Lake was unprotected much of the time. Most sewers around the Lake were so-called combined systems in which storm runoff and sewage were carried by the same set of inadequate pipes: During storms of any size, the runoff rapidly overwhelmed the treatment facilities, and the overflow—containing a large amount of totally raw sewage—was simply passed around the treatment plant entirely and dumped into the Lake without any treatment whatsoever.

In the Lake itself these problems were compounded, during the spring and early summer, by that peculiar Great Lakes phenomenon, the thermal bar. Like a vertical thermocline, the thermal bar prevents mixing of the warm shore waters with the cold waters of the open Lake. Pouring out of the sewers, the pollutants were trapped on the shoreward side, multiplying their effects on beaches and shore wetlands by immense amounts. It didn't help any that the season of the thermal bar was also the breeding season for virtually every fish in the Lake—and that most of them used those shallow, superpolluted shore waters to breed in.

Of particular concern to the rapidly awakening scientific community were the new, exceedingly popular man-made soaps—the detergents. Algae, like all living things, need certain elements in their diets, among them relatively large amounts of nitrogen, calcium, sodium, potassium, and phosphorus: If any one of these is in short supply, the algae will stop growing whether or not they have a sufficient supply of the others. Whichever of the primary nutritive elements is used up first is the "limiting nutrient," the one that controls the algae's population; as long as sufficient supplies remain of the other elements, addition of the limiting nutrient alone is enough to spur new growth. Lake Erie's limiting nutrient, it turned out, was phosphorus. Detergents contained a great deal of phosphorus, in the form of phosphate additives included in the detergent mix to "soften" the water and make the cleansing power of the detergent-compound itself more effective. Primary sewage treatment had no effect on phosphates whatsoever, and secondary treatment didn't have much; they were mostly passing through the treatment plants and into the Lake. The phosphorus-starved algae were latching onto them like gluttons in a candy store. The "primary productivity" of a body of water is a measure of how much extra carbon—the primary element of life—is bound up in living things in the water each day. Two hundred milligrams of carbon per square meter of water surface is considered high. In phosphate-enriched Lake Erie the astounded scientists found primary productivity running an incredible 7,340 milligrams per square meter.

To be fair, we must emphasize here that detergents were not the only culprits. Human and animal wastes also contain large amounts of phosphorus; so does agricultural runoff from farm fields treated with phosphate fertilizers. Various industrial processes, including sugar refining and silk production, depend at least partially on phosphorus; match heads contain large amounts of it (there were sugar refineries and silk and match factories in the Lake Erie basin). Nevertheless, it was detergent phosphates that bore the brunt of public indignation once the contribution of phosphorus to Lake Erie's problems was exposed in the press. The reason was simple: None of those other things were apparent in the water. Detergents were.

This visibility was a quirk—it had nothing directly to do with phosphates. Detergent molecules are long, asymmetric structures: One end of the molecule is attracted to dirt, the other to water, a peculiarity that gives the detergent its ability to remove dirt from soiled objects. The molecules come in two forms, straight and branched, which have nothing to do with their cleansing ability but a great deal, indeed, to do with their sudsing. The suds of the straight molecules break down rapidly; those of the branched molecules decompose slowly or not at all. Detergent manufacturers were locked in an absurd advertising battle over who had the "longest-lasting" suds. For this reason—and only this reason—they were using branched molecules, the branchier the better. The resultant suds were piling up everywhere. Great mounds of them drifted down the rivers and washed up like snow on the Lake Erie shore, mixed in with decomposing algae and dead and dying fish from the Lake's anoxic bottom. For sheer repulsiveness these scenes have seldom been equaled anywhere on the planet.

Belatedly realizing their mistake, the detergent manufacturers switched over, in the early 1960's, to straight molecules, and "long-lasting suds" was replaced as an advertising slogan by "biodegradable." It was too late. The mountains of suds on the Lakeshore, together with scientists' testimony about detergent phosphates, had fingered detergents as the principal villain in Lakewide cultural eutrophication. And the problem with the phosphates was not that they were not biodegradable. The problem was that they were.

By the mid-1960's, public indignation at Lake Erie's condition had reached the ignition point. A Cleveland auto dealer named David Blaushild instituted a petition campaign to "Save Lake Erie" and was overwhelmed by the result: More than 1,000,000 signatures poured into his office in a few short months, many accompanied by letters calling the Lake things like "cesspool" and "industrial wastebasket." In April 1965 Blaushild turned the whole pile over to Ohio Governor James A. Rhodes, who accepted them with glee, shipping them off en masse to Lyndon Johnson's Secretary of Health, Education, and Welfare—former five-term mayor of Cleveland Anthony J. Celebrezze. "We are past the talking stage," Rhodes wrote in a cover letter, "and past the deploring, the study, and the study-the-study stages . . . we want action, and we want it now!"

The Governor's table-thumping was mostly for public effect: Celebrezze—as Rhodes well knew—was already on his side. Two years before, shortly after taking office, the Secretary had requested a Public Health Service study of the Lake; this study was nearly complete, and hearings on it were being prepared for the coming summer. The previous October, the State Department—responding to Celebrezze's not-so-gentle prodding—had quietly requested a similar study of Lake Erie, Lake Ontario, and the upper St. Lawrence

River from the International Joint Commission on Boundary Waters (IJC), a quasi-judicial body set up under the auspices of the Boundary Waters Treaty of 1909 to coordinate U.S. and Canadian policies regarding water resources shared by both nations. The killing of the Great Lakes was primed to become not just a local but a national— even an international—cause célèbre.

The State Department's request to the IJC was particularly interesting because it specifically asked for a study of more than one Lake. Cultural-eutrophication problems and industrial pollution were suddenly turning up all over the Fifth Coast. Lake Erie was leading the way, but the other Lakes did not seem to be far behind. The others were all deep, nutrient-poor, and aggressively oligotrophic, so there would be no Lakewide algal blooms as had been seen on Erie, but parts of them—in some cases, very large parts—were proving to be susceptible just the same.

There was, for instance, Saginaw Bay—an immense arm of Lake Huron, fifty miles long, twenty-five miles wide, and for the most part well under thirty feet deep. Flowing into it, the Saginaw River drained a large, rich basin of mixed industry and agriculture similar to that surrounding Erie's Maumee. Much of the Saginaw Basin grew sugar beets; the refining of the sugar, a phosphorus-using process, was done at the town of Sebewaing, "Michigan's Sweetest City," on the eastern bayshore. Large manufacturing facilities—paper mills, automotive plants, chemical plants—were located at Saginaw and Midland and Flint and Bay City. Saginaw Bay was shallow and warm and receiving nutrients by the ton. It was exceedingly eutrophic, more so even than Lake Erie.

So was Green Bay. Cut off from the body of Lake Michigan by the Door and Garden peninsulas and the island chain that links them —the western limb of the Niagaran Cuesta—Green Bay has little cross-circulation with the main Lake and is ecologically almost a separate body of water. Like Lake Erie and Saginaw Bay, it is shallow, mostly under seventy feet deep and never more than 120; over its entire southern third the depth never exceeds thirty feet. The Fox River, running into the southern end, drains the agricultural heart of Wisconsin—a basin of rich soils and productive farms similar to those of the Maumee and the Saginaw drainages. Green Bay has a large *natural* eutrophication problem. The Indian tribe that Nicolet encountered on its banks called themselves Winnebago, which means "stinking water"; the French themselves called the place Baye des Puants, which translates as "Bay of the Stinkers." The English name "Green Bay"—in use at least since 1815—refers to the appearance of the water following an algal bloom. Given these bits of colorful local history, it is not too surprising to find that cultural eutrophication ran rampant here even earlier than it did on Lake Erie. As far back as the 1940's, the city of Green Bay was forced to close its water intakes in the bay and build a 25-mile-long pipeline across the Door to the cleaner waters of Lake Michigan. Beaches all around the bay had been closed on and off by the health authorities for years.

A particularly nagging problem at Green Bay was the effluent of the pulp and paper industry. The Green Bay drainage basin contains one of the highest concentrations of paper mills in North America; there are twenty-one of them along the lower Fox River, between Lake Winnebago and the city of Green Bay, alone. The effluents from these plants are heavy with ammonia. Some of this ammonia comes from ammonia-based coating processes within the plants; some comes from the use of ammonium bisulfate as a solvent to free cellulose fibers from wood pulp—an essential step in paper making; and some comes, ironically enough, from waste-treatment facilities at the mills, where it is used both to neutralize acids in the effluent and to provide nutrients for bacteria in biological waste digesters. All of it, whatever its source, ends up eventually in the bay.

In high-enough amounts—and these are not very high—ammonia can be directly toxic. The principal problem with it in Green Bay, however, is not its toxicity but its contribution to the eutrophication process. There is a nice little positive-feedback loop involved here. Ammonia is a nitrogen compound, and it can be used by many plants —including algae—as a nutrient. In this role, of course, it fuels growth rates. The resulting overgrowth of algae raises the surrounding water's pH level, making it less acidic: The higher pH levels slow down the decomposition of the ammonia, making more of it available for use as plant food. The circle goes on and on, the snake eating its own tail forever and ever, each new increment of ammonia added to the water causing more eutrophication than the last. BOD, of course, escalates rapidly. In fact, total oxygen demand in the water goes up astronomically, because ammonia not only feeds BOD, it also has a high chemical oxygen demand (COD) of its own. Even slowed down by the algae/ammonia feedback loop, it decomposes readily. In the process, it uses up slightly under 4.5 units of dissolved oxygen for every original unit of undecomposed ammonia.

There were other problems in Lake Michigan besides those of Green Bay. Most of them were grouped around the south end of the Lake, a region known to hydrologists as the south basin. There is a prominent underwater ridge in Lake Michigan that runs roughly from Milwaukee on the Lake's west shore to Holland on the east, cutting off deep-water circulation and separating the south basin hydrologically from the rest of the Lake. The basin is relatively small and shallow—less than one-fourth of the Lake's surface area and only a little over 300 feet deep (as opposed to the nearly 1,000-foot depths north of the Milwaukee-to-Holland abyssal ridge). It also happens to be precisely that part of Lake Michigan that extends south of The Line, into the broad Working Tier stretching from Chicago to Toronto; about its shores are grouped Lake Michigan's greatest cities and heaviest concentrations of industry. It was receiving huge loads of pollutants and not passing them on very well to the rest of the Lake, and it was a mess. There were 252 sewer outfalls, most of them carrying untreated sewage, on the lower few miles of the three little rivers falling into Milwaukee Harbor. The industrial agglutination to the south of Chicago, around Gary and Hammond, Indiana, had long since overwhelmed the poor little Calumet River; now known as the Calumet Sag Channel, it had been dredged, straightened, bermed, and dumped brimful of wastes to the point where it was essentially lifeless. Even the hardy, pollution-tolerant oligochaetes had abandoned it. Debris and filth from factory outfalls in Michigan City washed up in mile-long windrows on the Chicago beaches. (Chicago itself dumped its sewage down the Chicago Sanitary and Ship Canal into the Mississippi River. That was a stroke of luck. If it hadn't been for that canal, the south basin would likely have been a much deader sea even than Erie.)

Lake Ontario's problem was a little different from the others. Ontario's bed is remarkably regular and uniform, with much deep water and no large area of shallows; though it has the smallest surface area of any of the Great Lakes, its average depth is greater than that of any other except Superior. Its hypolimnion is up to 750 feet thick. Even with the huge excess of nutrients pouring out of Lake Erie over Niagara—plus the substantial amounts added by its own watershed —there was no way on God's green earth that Ontario could ever have any significant region of anoxic bottom waters. It could and did, however, have something nearly as bad: a virtually complete ring of shoreline eutrophication. Because of its remarkable uniformity and great average depth, Ontario's thermal bar is particularly well developed. In season, its nearshore waters—especially areas of relatively broad shallows such as Toronto Harbor and the Bay of Quinte— were as putrid and cladophora-filled as its neighbor's to the southwest.

Of the five Lakes, only Superior escaped major problems. There was no eutrophication in Superior; and given its depth, its position at the top of the great chain of freshwater oceans, and the rockbound, nearly sterile quality of its watershed, the limnologists who had studied it didn't think there ever could be. Thus was born the myth of Superior's invulnerability. It was not quite time for that myth to be rudely shattered.

The U.S. Public Health Service's hearings on the problems of Lake Erie took place in Cleveland and Buffalo over the first two weeks of August, 1965. They were extremely heated. There was Senator Gaylord Nelson of Wisconsin, for example, accusing industries around the Lake of turning it "from a body of water into a chemical tank"; there was Congressman Charlie Vanik of Ohio, chiding the steel industry for failing to use "any visible devices" for pollution abatement—and noting pointedly that "the steel industries almost universally use these processes for water pollution control except where the steel industry is located on the Great Lakes." There was Congressman Weston Vivian of Michigan, lambasting the paper mills in his congressional district for pouring "volumes of what can best be labeled as 'goop' " into streams leading directly into the west end of the Lake. "The paper mills do have facilities for cleaning the effluent from the mills," Vivian added accusingly. "Now, when the officials of the mills know I'm about to visit, these facilities are always operating. But when I visit unannounced, they're shut off."

Much of the testimony centered around the maladroit and technologically terrifying Detroit sewers. Expert after expert testified that Detroit's museum-piece sewage-treatment system was rudimentary at best, that its antiquated combination design, its overworked storm bypass, and its lack of any treatment beyond settling basins were all criminally inadequate to take care of the massive 600-million-gallon waste stream that poured forth from the city each day. Attacked from all sides, Detroit grew testy. It would cost at least $100 million to upgrade the collectors and convert the sewage plant from primary to secondary treatment, the city asserted sniffily. That was too much to spend to clean up someone else's water. It was a waste of money; they weren't going to do it. A couple of Michigan congressmen exploded. "Neither the city of Detroit nor any other municipalities or industries concerned have any God-given right to befoul the waters of the Detroit River or Lake Erie!" snapped liberal Democrat John Dingell. Conservative Republican Gerald Ford was nearly as angry. Pointing out the absurdity of serving the city that gave us the automobile with what he called a "horse and buggy" sewage plant, the future President remarked that it was "a strange anomaly to have water officials from the city of Detroit attempt to minimize the problem of Detroit River pollution and suggest that secondary sewage treatment would be a waste of money."

That was at the Cleveland phase of the hearings. The Buffalo phase was similar, except that there the adamant government polluter was not a city but the host state of New York, and the excuse given for inaction was not money but states' rights. Lake Erie's pollution, New York insisted, was best taken care of by the various state governments. The Feds—represented in this case by the Public Health Service—should keep their cotton-pickin' hands off. When pressed, however, New York admitted that its state health agencies had not been policing, or even *monitoring*, waste discharges into the Lake by Buffalo's industrial plants. Lake Erie was an international waterway; New York was just a state government. It wasn't New York's responsibility. Caught in this contradiction, New York at first displayed the wide-eyed innocence of a child with his hand in the cookie jar who parries a scolding by insisting that it was really the cookie that did it. New York was at the downstream end of the Lake, state officials insisted, so the state couldn't possibly be contributing significantly to its problems: It was all Detroit's fault, and Cleveland's, and

Toledo's. By the end of the Buffalo hearings, however, New York
—unlike Detroit—had repented of its sins: Maybe it was a little bit
their fault after all. When the other states of the Lake Erie Basin
prepared a document condemning the Lake's polluters and request-
ing federal assistance in cleanup activities, the Empire State quietly
added its signature at the bottom.

The Public Health Service's hearings were the first of their kind,
but they were not to be the last: Suddenly, Lake Erie was everyone's
issue. Congressional hearings followed, and state hearings, and provincial hearings, and scientific congresses, and interstate conferences.
The International Joint Commission completed its study of Erie and
Ontario and requested permission to do another—on the upper
Lakes, this time. The national press took the theme of a "dying"
Great Lake and ran with it; soon a bewildering variety of articles
were appearing in publications ranging from *The New York Times*
and *Newsweek* to *Scientific American* and the *Saturday Evening Post.*
Time called the Lake "critically ill . . . a North American Dead Sea."
Barbara Tufty of *Science News* described it as "a wasteland, a lifeless
body of water that has lost its sparkle and vitality, and is being
hastened to its wretched fetid death by man's affluent [sic] wastes and
increasing activities." In the *Saturday Review,* writer Gladwin Hill
took dead aim at "state and local water and health officials parrying
implicit criticism of their activities and defending their areas against
stigma":

> Life would be simpler for everybody if their position were substan-
> tial. But it is negative. . . . Their argument against corrective steps
> is that "we have no assurance of what they'll accomplish." This is
> rather like arguing against transferring from a sinking ship to a
> lifeboat on the ground that one doesn't know where the lifeboat is
> going.

The industrial and municipal organizations fought back—after a
fashion. In December, 1965—four months after the Lake Erie hearings—they held their own water pollution conference in Washington, D.C., under the sponsorship of the U.S. Chamber of Commerce,
where—in the admirable phrase of environmental writer Gene Ma-

rine—they "made a noise like a baby guinea pig with his foot caught in his cage." They weren't doing anything, and it was the right thing to do anyway. Governor Henry Bellmon of Oklahoma took the podium to assure them that one of the principal purposes of a waterway was to be "a repository of waste." The delegates applauded. Water was made to be polluted; that was its highest and best use. What was all the fuss about?

The general public, however, wasn't buying that line anymore. The general public's feelings were summed up nicely by limnologist Ralph O. Brinkhurst in an offhand remark at another meeting, a conference on changes in the biota of Lakes Erie and Ontario sponsored by the Buffalo Society of Natural Sciences in 1969: "In this day and age," sputtered Brinkhurst, "in a society which is so affluent— to have to paddle in its own sewage is just disgusting." That was the key: disgust, spreading and rampant. If Lake Erie could die, were the other Lakes safe? Was anything? Demands for action spread swiftly beyond the boundaries of the Great Lakes Basin. Environmental groups saw a dramatic upturn in membership: Earth Day was proclaimed. In a very real sense, the death of Lake Erie marked the birth of the modern environmental movement.

On June 22, 1969, the Cuyahoga River helped things along by living up to its billing as a fire hazard. Several linear miles of the Cuyahoga in the industrial section of Cleveland—a smoky wasteland of factories and dumps and slag heaps known as "the Flats"—went massively up in flames, and the fireboat *Anthony J. Celebrezze* had to rush upstream from its berth in the city's wharf district and put out the river. It wasn't algae that was burning, it was industrial waste, but the point was driven home: All that talk about a "dying Lake" wasn't just rhetoric. The water the Lake was receiving from its tributaries was grossly polluted. At about the same time that the Cuyahoga caught fire, a couple of newsmen were being shown around the Detroit waterfront by a municipal official who was assuring them loftily that the river was not as bad as it had been made out to be. As he spoke, two ducks swooped in for a landing on the river, drifted sedately for a moment, began choking, keeled over, and died. Governor Rhodes had been right four years before when he said the study stage was past. It was time for action.

It came, ponderously. By the end of 1972—three years after the

Cuyahoga fire, and eight years after David Blaushild's petition drive
—a legal framework for protecting and cleansing the Great Lakes
and other North American waters was at last in place. The principal
components were:

 • The U.S. Clean Water Act of 1972. Passed as a set of massive
amendments to the Federal Water Pollution Control Act of 1956, the
U.S. Clean Water Act set nationwide water-quality guidelines and
industrial- and sewage-effluent standards; provided for penalties
against polluting industries; and committed the federal government
to supply major funding assistance for building and upgrading local
sewage-treatment plants. Detroit, Cleveland, and Buffalo could no
longer legally get away with their antiquated, primary-treatment-only
facilities. That alone would make a significant difference to Lake Erie.

 • The Canada Water Act of the same year. Similar to the U.S.
Clean Water Act, the Canada Water Act went much further in at
least one significant area: It legislated a reduction of detergent phosphates to 5 percent by weight. The U.S. law had set phosphate
standards for sewage-plant effluents, but the lawmakers had caved in
to the pressure of the powerful and determined detergent industry.
The Act hadn't mentioned detergents at all.

 • The International Great Lakes Water Quality Agreement
(GLWQA) between the United States and Canada. Signed the same
year as the two Water Acts were passed, the GLWQA defined the
two nations' joint goals for Great Lakes protection and cleanup and
established a framework for cooperative research and abatement actions. A beefed-up International Joint Commission was put in charge
of carrying out the agreement, with an International Great Lakes
Water Quality Board to assist them. (The GLWQA was updated and
greatly strengthened in 1978.)

 • A set of various cooperative agreements among government
units around the Lakes. These included an interstate pact among the
four Lake Michigan states to reduce phosphate emissions; a similar
pact among the five Lake Erie states; and, to the north, the Canada-
Ontario Great Lakes Water Quality Agreement, a joint federal-
provincial effort to coordinate information and enforcement of
water-quality standards, which was put into place in 1971 and which,
not incidentally, became the model upon which the International
GLWQA would be constructed the next year.

• Various state, provincial, and local laws aimed at sewage-effluent standards and the control of phosphates, ranging from short-term experimental limits (the state of Wisconsin) to outright phosphate-detergent bans (Chicago; Akron, Ohio, on the Cuyahoga above Cleveland; and the state of New York).

• Industry/municipal agreements and industrial self-regulating pacts. These varied broadly in direction and effectiveness, from responsible efforts through miserable excuses to out-and-out hostility to any control at all. The two extremes were both reached on the Cuyahoga River. The three steel companies operating in Cleveland were apparently as horrified as anyone over the state of Lake Erie, once it had been adequately called to their attention: Even before those celebrated Public Health Service hearings in 1965, they had voluntarily entered into an agreement with the Ohio Water Pollution Control Board to clean up their effluents—including a self-imposed standard of zero discharge for cyanide-laced "pickling water"—into the Cuyahoga. But at the same time that the steel companies were acting with at least a minimum of horse sense, the soap companies were persisting in acting like the other end of the horse. They fought Akron's phosphate-detergent ban tooth and nail through the City Council—and then, when it passed the council unanimously anyway, proceeded to throw a tantrum all the way from the council chambers to federal court, where they sued petulantly to have the ban set aside as a matter outside the city's jurisdiction. (The suit was declared "frivolous" and slapped down almost immediately. *Sic semper cum tirades.*)

By 1975 there had been a noticeable improvement in Lake Erie's condition. That summer the algal bloom failed to appear for the first time in over a decade; the usual anoxic desert did not develop on the floor of the central basin, and the beaches were able to remain open. The Cuyahoga's color had moderated from black to a still opaque but much more attractive light brown, and the river was no longer considered flammable; the Lake itself had turned from green back to blue. Fish—and live ducks—had returned to the Detroit River. The

floating scum and debris on the Lake's surface were gone; the stench
had disappeared. Phosphate loadings in the incoming waters were
down by 50 percent or more. The hue and cry of the 1960's and the
strenuous efforts of the early 1970's had apparently paid off. The
agencies, the activist organizations, and the industries shook hands
and walked off, patting each other on the back. The miracle had been
accomplished: The Lake had been saved. The public stopped paying
attention.

They shouldn't have.

The hue and cry and the strenuous efforts were almost exclusively directed toward the abatement of what is loosely called "conventional pollution," the kind that comes out of residential and municipal sewers. In this there had been at least the appearance of
success. But conventional pollution was not the Lakes' only problem;
in fact, it was not even remotely their most serious one. Beneath the
cosmetics of conventional-pollution repair, the real problems—
shoreline erosion, man-made toxins, excessive water consumption
and diversion, wetlands destruction, and a great mass of others—
were still going on. Unfortunately these problems, unlike the algae,
did not generally stink, and there was little to call people's attention
to the uncomfortable fact of their existence. Dealing with the algal
blooms and the other symptoms of cultural eutrophication, it has
now turned out, was a little like performing plastic surgery on a
patient in the last stages of terminal cancer. There has been a vast
improvement in appearance, but underneath it all the Lakes are still
dying.

And even the cosmetic repairs may be illusory, more eye-shadow
than substance. There is strong evidence that the much-vaunted
improvement in Lake Erie's condition has been far less our doing
than we would like to believe. Scientists studying the Lake's phosphorus balance have lately turned up a distressing fact: Though the
phosphate content of the inflowing waters has been greatly reduced,
there has not been a corresponding decrease in the amount of phosphates available to algae in the receiving waters—the Lake itself. In
the Lake, that amount has held almost completely steady.

"We think there's a lot of recycling of material in the bottom
that's coming back up," says Dr. Charles Herdendorf. A tall, fit man
of middle years who looks as though he has just come from a vol-

leyball game on the beach, Herdendorf is the current head of Ohio State University's Franz Theodore Stone Laboratory on South Bass Island. The Stone Lab, as it is called affectionately, is run partially on moneys obtained from Washington, D.C., through the Federal Sea Grant program. Ohio, that epitome of midwesternness, is a Sea Grant State—a fact that never fails to astound people who have forgotten about the Fifth Coast.

In an open aluminum boat we cruise around Put-in-Bay, circling the small islet known as Gibraltar, where the main buildings of the Stone Lab are located. "We're not seeing much decline in the chlorophyll concentrations yet," Herdendorf remarks from the wheel. "That's a good measure of the amount of algae, the amount of chlorophyll in the water. It hasn't gone down as we had expected it would. We're doing some research on it up here, and we think that a certain percentage of the phosphorus in the particulates on the bottom is bioavailable. And that's a big concern."

Indeed it is. Limnological dogma has always held that once phosphorus has latched onto particulate matter—sediments—and settled to the bottom, it is out of the ecosystem, and that what is known as "total phosphorus content" (the amount of phosphorus of all forms actually present in the water itself) is the key to eutrophication. Now Herdendorf and his students are discovering that it is the *bioavailable* phosphorus—the amount that can be used directly by living organisms—that really counts. This is only indirectly related to the phosphorus loadings of the Lake's tributaries. Reducing tributary loading will reduce the water's total phosphorus content, but with the sediments, and the algae themselves, chock-full of the stuff, that reduction may not mean very much. "Turnover time"—the amount of time necessary for a phorphorus molecule to go from the water into the cellular structure of an individual alga and back into the water again for use by the next plant—has been measured in Lake Erie at the somewhat incredible rate of one minute, and when things are cycling through the ecosystem that fast the amount in the water at any one time may be largely irrelevant. Cutting the phosphorus loading to the Lake was necessary to keep things from getting any worse, but getting better, unfortunately, seems to be another matter entirely.

"All the models that have been developed for telling when Lake

Erie's going to be well again are based on total phosphorus concentration," states Herdendorf. "And that's probably wrong."

So why the appearance of improvement? Why the change back from green to blue water, the shrinking of the anoxic area in the central basin, the healthier and more attractive beaches? Herdendorf smiles. "Something has happened that bears on that," he says. "We are running right now about two feet above the all-time mean water level for Lake Erie. Now, these peaks have happened in the past, but they've definitely been cyclical, at intervals of ten to twenty years. The thing different about what's happened now is that it's never gone down. We've had a hydrologic jump. And the people at the National Oceanic and Atmospheric Administration, at the Great Lakes Regional Office up there in Detroit, are saying privately, 'Well, gee, maybe it's not *ever* going to go down.' Well, the thing that concerns me is, I still think it's got to go down *some* day. And I'm afraid these high levels may be much of the reason for the return of the fisheries and the revitalization of the Lake."

He gestures at the blue water beneath us. "Looks great now, doesn't it?" he says. "But if it dropped two feet I think you'd see a pea-soup Lake again."

XIII Change

The Men who manage the boats, their wages is commonly from one hundred to two hundred dollars for the year. They are obliged to perform all that is required of them, to row the boats, to carry the baggage on their backs, across the portages. When at the trading post, they perform all the menial services, such as fishing, chopping wood, and cooking etc. at present they are seldom allowed perquisites, formerly it was an indespensible rule; but it is gradually losing ground. Some now get a few trifling articles of clothing; tobacco, soap, salt etc. their labour is very hard, for in a few years they are compleatly broken down in constitution, they have to work more like beasts of burden than men, and when they can procure the means they will go into all kinds of excesses; exposed constantly to change of heat and cold; which soon brings them to an untimely grave.

William Johnston, *Letters on the Fur Trade* (1833)

Just my luck. The only voyageur I'll ever see in my life, and he's wearing a Timex watch and driving a Japanese pickup.

Rod Badger, remark made upon seeing one of the costumed interpretive staff at Grand Portage

T he Great Lakes of today bear only a superficial resemblance to the Great Lakes Champlain and his companions found. There is the same wide blue water, the same dance of wind across the surface, the same wavelash against the shore, but the context is different. The great brooding forest is gone now, in most places, replaced by farms and homes and factories and acre upon acre of concrete; the shore the wavelash falls against is likely to be armored by riprap, or hiding behind a man-made breakwater, or extended by fill far into what used to be Lake, or all three. The wetlands are mostly filled in or dredged out. Shoreline trails have been replaced by freeways; forty-foot canoes have given way to 1,000-foot diesel freighters. Basic geography has changed: Man-made watercourses have turned the Door and Keweenaw Peninsulas into islands, reversed the Chicago River, bypassed and dried up—in certain seasons—the falls at Sault Ste. Marie. Inflowing streams are broader, warmer, heavier with sediment. Even the Lakes' agelong regimen of annual rise and fall, as basic to them as breathing, has been altered. Outlet works on Superior and Ontario now "control" Lake levels, subjecting the greatest bodies of fresh water on earth to the whims of politicians and engineers (though that control is probably not as great as the politicians and engineers claim; like the proverbial pet tiger in New York City, when you take a Great Lake for a walk, the place you are going to take it is anywhere it wants to go).

Beneath the surface, the changes have been even more profound. It has not just been a matter of species change—drastic as that has been. It has also been a loss of innocence. What mysterious deeps there were in those wild transparent waters, what dark profundal passages, what manner of unknown fishes! Today we know most of the fishes intimately. We should—we put them there ourselves. None of the species that currently dominate the Lakes—the alewives, the lampreys, the smelt, the carp, the Coho and Chinook salmon— were there when the explorers came. The salmon still wouldn't be if we didn't help them. For reasons that remain undiscoverable by fisheries experts, these Pacific Coast species thrive in the Great Lakes but do not breed there. The fishery on them is strictly put-and-take, with hatchery-raised fish planted by the tens of thousands for the benefit of wide-eyed Great Lakes sportsmen who do not care about the big beasts' antecedents as long as they put up a good fight before they can be drawn into the boat.

(There is, curiously enough, one Pacific salmon—the Pink—that is breeding in the Lakes, but it is not one that the sportsmen seek and it was not brought here on purpose. Several decades ago a large cargo of fertilized Pink salmon eggs on its way to an experimental plant in Hudson Bay was held temporarily in a hatchery on Ontario's Nipigon River, at the north end of Lake Superior; and when the holding was over and the cargo had been moved on, it was discovered that some 10,000 eggs had been left behind. They were flushed down the

hatchery's sewer. Two years later several hundred Pinks were observed attempting to spawn in the sewer. They have spread out since,
and have colonized most Lake Superior tributaries and a few on Lake
Michigan; they have not overbred, and have apparently fit into the
Lakes' altered ecology quite well. They are a principal predator on
alewives, which is much to their credit. There is only one problem.
They are humpbacked and stunted and ugly as sin, and no fishermen
want anything whatsoever to do with them.)

It would, of course, be foolish to argue that all these changes were
necessarily evil. Change is just change, a null-valued fact of existence;
it is only human observers who decide whether that change is en-
hancement or deterioration, good or bad. Change has always taken
place, whether or not we cause it and whether or not we like it. There
were no whales in Champlain's *Mer douce,* but there had been a few
of them there a couple of thousand years before he arrived. Human
engineers reversed the flow of the Chicago in 1900, but in a sense they
were merely putting it back where it belonged; it was once a legiti-
mate natural outlet to Lake Michigan, and remained one probably as
recently as the time of Christ. Human waste-disposal practices have
pushed Erie over the brink from mesotrophic to eutrophic, but the
shallow, sediment-rich Lake was probably pretty close to the brink
to begin with, and would undoubtedly have made it on its own
sooner or later. As Charles Herdendorf once put it, "Whether man
showed up or not, Lake Erie would be dramatically different from
the other Great Lakes. It's just the wrong depth. Sorry."

Having granted that point, however, one must also state that
many of the changes—by nearly any measure we can put to them—
are deteriorations. This applies particularly to those changes that are
byproducts of desired and consciously created change: the arrival of
the lampreys and the alewives, for instance, when all we wanted was
ships. "Much artificial work has been necessary to obtain from the
Great Lakes their maximum service," wrote one commentator
proudly at the turn of the century. "The lakes have attained their
present commercial power and prestige only by herculean human
effort." God didn't make it right, so we had to fix it. Well, maybe
so: but at least God knew what He was doing and what the effects
would be. We don't. We call what we do "management," but it is
really tinkering. We change things without paying any attention to

what they are connected to; we pull the table leg out to scratch our backs and then complain loudly that the table and everything on it is falling down on top of us.

Today, North America's Fifth Coast and the waters off it are under what can only be described as a state of siege. The besiegers are good, well-meaning people: our neighbors, our friends, our relatives. Ourselves. They/we seek only to make life better (richer, easier, more affluent). We cannot be blamed for seeking means to those ends. The problem is that the means we have found are slowly but surely killing the Lakes. The killing is going on quietly; we cannot see it unless we look. But it is there. It is there as surely as the sedimentation of the streams was there when we cut off the timber, as surely as the lampreys were waiting off the coast when we built the canals, as surely as the algae had the capacity to bloom if someone would only give them enough phosphates. We are about to go on a tour of several hells—hells present and hells to come. They are man-made hells, but they were not made on purpose. They were made because we projected a bright future, built toward it, and only belatedly discovered that it was so bright because we were burning our birthrights to power it.

This is, of course, a common human failing, and has been going on a long time.

Back in 1679, Father Louis Hennepin saw the Lakes from the deck of La Salle's *Griffon* and was moved to ecstasies about the future that awaited them. "It were easy to build on the sides of these great Lakes, an infinite number of considerable Towns which might have Communication one with another for Five Hundred Leagues together, and by an inconceivable Commerce which would establish itself among them," he wrote some time after the voyage. Well. There is no need to quarrel with Father Hennepin; obviously his vision was accurate. But there was a darker side he didn't see. One evening on the Lakes he penned the following passage:

> The country on both sides of this beautiful Strait is adorned with fine open Plains, and you can see Numbers of Stags, Does, Deer, Bears, by no means Fierce and very good to eat, Poules d'Inde and all kinds of Game, Swans in abundance. . . . The rest of the Strait is covered with Forests, fruit Trees like Walnuts, Chestnuts, Plum and Apple

Trees, wild Vines loaded with Grapes, of which we made some small wine. There is Timber fit for Building. It is the place in which Deer most delight.

A perfect spot, surely, for one of Hennepin's "considerable Towns," and one was soon built there—but not, to our everlasting shame, as Hennepin must have pictured it. The "considerable Town" has totally spoiled the "beautiful Strait." Who today would recognize that paradise-on-earth as the location of downtown Detroit?

XIV Dumps

Dioxin, PCB's, Mirex, DDT's, phosphorus; they've told me, you
name it, we've got it. I believe them.
                    Mayor William Cahill of Oswego, N.Y., speaking
                        before a congressional subcommittee hearing
                              on water pollution, July 9, 1982

The city of Oswego, New York (population: 20,000), lies at
the mouth of the Oswego River, halfway between Mexico
Bay and Little Sodus Bay on the low southeast shore of Lake
Ontario. It is a peaceful little place, the home of a branch of the State
University of New York and the Lake Ontario terminus of the New
York State Barge Canal. A modest port facility handles grain, textiles,
chemicals, and oil-well supplies. The streets are tree-lined, narrow,
and quiet; the place has an almost somnambulant air about it, belying
what has been at times a very stormy past. This is the site of the first
British settlement on the American north coast, and it did not come
easily. In 1720, the government of New York Colony—proclaiming
loudly that the French should not be allowed to monopolize the
Indian trade on the Great Lakes—sent a party to the mouth of the
Oswego to establish a trading post. The post was closed down,
forcibly, by the French. The British reinvested it and built a fort to
protect it; the French burned the fort down. This Anglo-French
give-and-take continued until the French and Indian War in the
mid-eighteenth century, at which point it became a tussle between
the British and their own colonists. Several more forts were built and
burned during the Revolutionary War and the War of 1812. The last
was built at Oswego at the time of the Civil War, and it was not

burned. It was not even attacked. It stands today at the foot of
Seventh Street—a huge stone structure, star-shaped and bermed with
turf, its defenses menacing and untried. Beneath the gaping cannon
mouths, picnickers frolic; below them, on the Lakeshore, swimmers
sun themselves on glacier-polished outcrops of Pre-Cambrian granite, isolated southern exposures of the ancient Canadian Shield.

A few miles east of the fort along the Ontario shore lies the mouth
of a small stream called Wine Creek, and it was there, on an idyllic
little patch of rural land along Seneca Road a half mile or so upstream
from the Lake, that a country-western radio station called WSGO
built itself a brand-new broadcasting studio and transmission tower
in the early 1960's. A short distance to the north of the new studio
lay the edge of a large piece of vacant property owned by three
Oswego businessmen in the name of Pollution Abatement Services,
Inc. (PAS); beyond the PAS land sprawled the broad, sparkling
waters of the Great Lake. Rural homesteads, small farms, and a utility
parts and service yard or two lay scattered about among fallow fields
and copses of hardwoods. The breeze blew up the creek at night,
bringing with it the scent of the Lake. The air was sweet.

Although the WSGO management had been told at the time they
purchased their building site that there were no immediate plans for
development of the PAS property, they were not too surprised when
a truck arrived one day shortly after the station went into operation
and began unloading rolls of cyclone fence. Land under corporate
ownership that close to town was sure to get something on it sooner
or later. What was disturbing was not the fence itself but what
appeared inside it: first an incinerator, then barrels—fifty-five-gallon
drums, thousands upon thousands of them, multicolored, corroding
about the seams, and full of God-knows-what. Some were stacked
neatly in rows; some were tossed into heaps; some were emptied into
a huge pit, flattened, and flung aside like beer cans on the shoulder
of a monstrous freeway. The pit was called, somewhat loosely, a
"lagoon." It was open to the air, it was full of foul liquid, and it
smelled to high heaven.

"The stench was overpowering," says Bill Schlemir, wincing at
the memory. "Everybody was getting headaches." Schlemir—a big,
beefy man with an intricate, Texas-sized belt buckle and a wild

red-brown beard—is WSGO's chief engineer. It is a lovely July day in 1983, and we are standing beside the cyclone fence behind the station, gazing into what was, until very recently, PAS domain. The barrels are gone now, and the lagoon has been filled in, but there is still a faint reek of chemicals in the air. The ground between the fence and the station is somewhat soggy: Chemical-laden water—"leach-ate"—seeping through the ground from the improperly lined lagoon had briefly turned the area into a toxic marsh, and squishy places remain here and there. We have been stepping gingerly.

Schlemir gestures at the station's transmission tower, rising in a low-lying area a few feet from the fence. "We've only got half a ground plane," he says. "Just what's out in front of the station. Back here it's just garbage. The leachate ate it. We had a guy, used to come back here to check the antenna—he was the only one who would go. He wore hip boots, and even then he hated to do it. And then the cleanup crews came along, and they wore oxygen masks." Schlemir chuckles. "Sorta made him wonder what he'd been doing to him-self. . . ." The cleanup crews, it must be emphasized, were not from Pollution Abatement Services, Inc. They were from another waste-disposal firm, SCA Chemical Services, Inc. of Model City, New York. SCA was under contract from the U.S. Environmental Protec-tion Agency to take care of PAS's mess. Cries for help from the radio station and its neighbors—first through normal channels and then, when that didn't work, broadcast rather pointedly over the air—had finally brought results. By that time, though, what had started out as a minor annoyance had escalated into a major disaster. There were between 8,000 and 15,000 barrels behind WSGO's studio and several thousand others scattered around at various nearby sites, including barns, sheds, road rights-of-way, an abandoned milk-processing plant, and a number of open fields. Four hundred barrels of unknown content had been buried beneath a parking lot at a Lakefront develop-ment called "Glimmerglass Lagoon," a little over a mile from the Oswego campus of the State University of New York; 1,500 more had been tossed into the wetland along Ox Creek, near Bowens Corners in the southwest corner of Oswego County; another 8,000 or so had been surreptitiously dumped in the county-operated Volney Landfill, across the road from the county airport near Fulton. Back at the original site, chemical-laden leachate from the improperly sealed lagoon had seeped into Wine Creek, passed downstream to its mouth, and spread a slick a half-mile wide over the surface of Lake Ontario. Hundreds of fish had turned belly-up. So had Pollution Abatement Services: In 1977, declaring themselves "hopelessly insolvent," the members of the consortium had—as one observer put it a few years later—dropped everything and simply "walked off the site."

They had not taken their mess with them. It was still there.

Six hundred miles to the west of Oswego, where the state of Indiana elbows its way up between Michigan and Illinois to grab a forty-five-mile stretch of shoreline on the southern tip of the Lakes, lies the greatest expanse of fresh-water dunes on this planet. Acre after acre, mile after mile, the great wind-sculptured piles of sand stretch along the Lake Michigan shore, crowned by sawgrass and the circling flight of gulls, the surf pounding at their feet, the vast blue mirror of the water stretching northward beyond sight. Coasting along this shore in his big canoe, Henry Schoolcraft found it "barren and uninviting," a "dreary prospect of sand banks" broken only occasionally by the mouth of a sluggish river or the gaunt, haunted spars of a wrecked ship. Today's visitor is likely to come away with a much more favorable impression. In the midst of the densely populated megalopolis that surrounds southern Lake Michigan, the skyscrapers and the factories and the industrial harbors and the canals and the ubiquitous layer of urban grime Southside Chicagoans know simply as The Dirt, the Indiana Dunes are quite literally a breath of fresh air. The soul's horizons expand; the heart retunes. Time itself seems altered, smoothed, and mellowed like fine wine, made to be sipped slowly and savored to the last drop. It is these attributes that caused Congress in 1972 to set aside 12,000 acres in the heart of the Dunes as the Indiana Dunes National Lakeshore.

Merely setting aside an area, however, does not save it. The Dunes are an anomaly, an open-space island in the midst of one of the most heavily industrialized shorelines on earth, and they are quite literally set upon from all sides. On the eastern park boundary is a huge coal-fired power plant run by the Northern Indiana Public Service Company (NIPSCO); on the western boundary is U.S. Steel's plant complex at Gary. Smack dab in the center of the park, dividing it into two segments, is the Port of Indiana's Burns Harbor complex —a second NIPSCO power plant, a Midwest Steel plant, a Bethlehem Steel plant, and one of the Lakes' most heavily used commercial wharves. These facilities and many others nearby, in Gary, Hammond, and East Chicago, are the headwater springs of a massive stream of industrial wastes. There are strong, well-meaning attempts made to keep this stream from backing up and flooding out of its banks into the park. The attempts are not always successful.

"Exciting would be one way to put it," says Ron Hiebert about the Lakeshore's problems with its industrial neighbors. A stocky, bearded man in his mid-thirties, Hiebert is a Park Service staff biologist, working out of research headquarters in a former private residence on Lake Front Drive. Picture windows in his second-floor office look out on the bathers and breakers of Beverly Shores Beach and the enormous, transcendent sheet of ocean-blue water beyond them. A faint faraway line marks the place where Lake meets sky: Specks of distant sails are silhouetted against it.

"NIPSCO's Burns Harbor facility was getting rid of its fly ash in settling ponds dug in the sand," Hiebert says quietly. "It's seeped through and flooded and contaminated the park wetlands. There's a large slag pond on the edge of Miller Woods, on U.S. Steel's property: We really do not know what's in there. There may be a lot of surprises. Sink a well and smell the groundwater—it smells like diesel. We monitor the water quality on our beaches weekly, and we've had to close them occasionally. During storms the sewage plants in nearby cities overflow and cause us all sorts of problems."

There are dozens upon dozens of abandoned waste dumps and caches of fifty-five-gallon drums, many of them unmapped, most of them unlined, and all of them potentially dangerous, scattered throughout the wasteland that is the Gary/Hammond industrial complex. The East Chicago sewage system, ten miles to the west, receives phenol- and ammonia-laden wastes from several steel mills and other industries; it is an antiquated combined system, with inadequate overflow lagoons, and it regularly discharges these wastes into the waters of Lake Michigan. A three-way suit against the city by the

U.S. Environmental Protection Agency and the states of Illinois and Indiana has so far not brought results. In August, 1977, a fire of spectacular dimensions ravaged the five-acre Mid-Co Corporation waste dump and solvent-recycling facility in Gary, a mile or so from the Park boundary and not far from the shore of the Lake. More than 40,000 barrels of industrial wastes, many of them exceedingly flammable, had been "stored" at Mid-Co out in the middle of an open field. Investigators probing the site after it had cooled found soils and water contaminated by phenols, chromium, cyanide, arsenic, and lead. They also found a 200-square-foot sludge pit of unknown depth and contents, and an in-ground storage tank containing what the official reports termed "an unidentified pink substance." Mid-Co owner and operator Ernest DeHart was subsequently sued by the Environmental Protection Agency; cleanup began, under court order, in 1980. It was expected to last several years and cost more than $5 million.

Gazing out the window at the bathers and the big Lake, Hiebert smiles sadly. "I've heard rumors," he says, "that this place is an experiment with the Park Service to see if a park can function this close to a major population center. I don't know—sometimes I don't think they're gonna succeed."

Three hundred miles northeast of the Indiana Dunes, on the rural Lake Huron shore above Saginaw Bay, the small town of Oscoda, Michigan (population: 7,500), snuggles compactly inside the final curve the Au Sable River makes on its way to lose itself in the enormous waters of this second largest of the Great Lakes. The city was born as a lumber port—a gigantic statue of Paul Bunyan still stands in the city park, and at least one local restaurant features a wall decor of misery whips, circular saws, and double-bladed axes—but today its principal focus is the canoe. Oscoda is World Headquarters for the Sawyer Canoe Company ("North of Highway 20, where the storied Au Sable meets Huron's ice-blue waves, we build canoes for the time of your life") and the eastern terminus of the annual Au Sable River Canoe Marathon, a 15-hour, 240-mile test of endurance that is considered the supreme event of canoe racing. To a canoe enthusiast like Rod Badger, it is almost as important a station-of-the-cross as Grand Portage. Traveling the Fifth Coast, Rod and I stopped in Oscoda for a tour of the Sawyer plant with company president Bob Gramprie. Rod wore his pilgrim's T-shirt—the one with the birch-bark canoe—and trailed Gramprie slowly through the plant, asking various questions about belly bands and Kevlar layups and asymmet-rical vee/arch hulls. Driving away afterward with a brand-new Saw-yer X-17 stowed safely atop the car, he relaxed visibly for the first time all morning. "If I act a bit odd for the rest of the day," he said, "it's because I feel like I've just been to the Vatican and had an audience with the Pope."

Canoes are not the only thing manufactured in Oscoda, however. There is also a small auto-parts plant, employing perhaps 200 people, and during the early 1970's, this plant was using substantial quantities of the industrial solvent trichloroethylene (TCE). The used material was dumped out behind the building. A firm link has never been established, but it is almost certainly not coincidence that caused the appearance of TCE in nine drinking-water wells near the plant over the period 1973–78. TCE is a powerful carcinogen—a cancer-causer—with side effects including headaches, nausea and vomiting, and heart and kidney disease. The wells are closed now, and the resi-dences they served have been connected to the Oscoda city water system. The cost was $140,000. It was borne by the city, with the help of a grant from the Federal Health Administration. There was no provable connection to the auto parts plant. It didn't pay a cent.

Once upon a time, pollution was simple. Pipes put it in streams; the pipes were connected to sewers, or factories, or both. To stop the pollution you plugged the pipes, or ran their contents through a treatment plant of some kind to render them harmless before deposit-ing them in the water. This was the model nearly everyone sub-scribed to back in the 1960's, when Lake Erie was dying. The prob-lem was sewage treatment, or rather, lack of it; the trouble with factories was that their effluent was going into the rivers untreated.

Someone went up the Milwaukee River in a power boat and counted nearly 100 waste outfalls in the first mile above the harbor. Run those outfalls through factory treatment plants, and then pipe them into the sewers where the municipal plant could treat them a second time, and the problem would be solved. It was undoubtedly this preoccupation with sewers that led the early pollution crusaders to concentrate on nutrient pollution—eutrophication—instead of industrial wastes. Eutrophic waters are fed by improperly treated sewage. Improperly treated sewage also carries bacteria, which thrive in the eutrophic receiving waters. To test for bacteria was to test for pollution. The "coliform count"—an enumeration of coliform bacteria, a ubiquitous resident of the mammalian gut whose presence in water indicates the arrival in that water, sometime in the recent past, of untreated feces —became the main index of polluted waters. The coliform count was enshrined into U.S. law by the Safe Drinking Water Act of 1974, and it remains the principal test in use today.

Unfortunately, there are a couple of very serious problems with this reliance on sewage-treatment technology and the coliform count as indicators of pollution.

The first problem is that many industrial wastes destroy coliform bacteria. They also destroy sewage treatment plants, especially those which rely on biological digesters—in essence, bacteria farms—to render human wastes harmless. This presents health officials with the twin dilemmas of increased wastes in the receiving waters and the concurrent failure of their principal test to spot those increased wastes. Water may be literally stinking with all sorts of dangerous substances and still test out as perfectly healthy.

The second problem is that not all pollutants reach the receiving waters—streams, rivers, or Great Lakes—from pipes. Runoff over the ground brings them, too; so does runoff *through* the ground, trickling from spilled wastes down between the soil particles to dark aquifers where it oozes unseen downgrade until sometime, months or years in the future, it seeps out through an underwater spring and destroys a once productive wetland. Pollutants can be recycled when chemical-laden sludge is stirred up by ships in harbors or by dredging operations. They can even come through the air. Years ago, we were taught that rainfall was essentially distilled water. Today we know better. A raindrop falling through polluted air sweeps up pollutants as it falls, and by the time it reaches the ground it can be a veritable chemical factory. That is why the area around Sudbury, Ontario, is barren of vegetation, and why so many lakes in Killarney Provincial Park, on the north shore of Georgian Bay, have become so acidic they will no longer support fish.

Water polluted by sewage effluent—nutrient-enriched water, eutrophic water—*looks* polluted. It is discolored, thick, and opaque; it smells of decay. There are *things* in it. The trouble with the other common forms of pollution is that they often exhibit none of these clues. Water may be grossly polluted and yet so clear and sparkling that it seems not only harmless but beautiful, desirable, and downright healthy. This type of pollution, known as "microcontamination," involves dissolved chemicals that may be present in microscopically small amounts but are so extremely dangerous that even amounts so small they can barely be quantified—a few drops of the chemical mixed into a billion drops of water—may be unsafe. If you can find them at all there is a good chance there is too much of them.

Consider, for example, dodecachloropentacyclodecane (popularly known as Mirex)—a pesticide once scattered widely about the southeastern United States in an attempt to eradicate the fire ant. Mirex is so dangerous that the 1978 Great Lakes Water Quality Agreement between the United States and Canada takes the unprecedented step of declaring the allowable levels of the substance in water as none at all ("less than detection levels as determined by the best scientific methodology available"). It was never used in the Great Lakes Basin, but it was manufactured there, in and around the city of Buffalo, and significant amounts of it have found their way into the Niagara River and Lake Ontario—at least 2,000 pounds from a single source, the Hooker Chemical Company's Hyde Park Landfill on Bloody Run Creek, alone. Ironically, Mirex was chosen for the fire-ant campaign largely on the basis of its relatively low toxicity to mammals; it takes a great deal of the compound to poison a mouse, let alone a human. Unfortunately, however, toxicity is not the only measure of a chemical's hazards. There is also carcinogenity (the ability to cause cancer); mutagenity (the ability to cause birth defects); and bioaccumulation (the tendency to concentrate in greater and greater amounts as a compound moves up the food chain: Small amounts in the water lead to larger amounts in plankton, still larger amounts in small fish that eat the plankton, and potentially dangerous amounts in big fish that eat the small fish). Mirex is a bioaccumulative carcinogen and mutagen. The amount of it in the waters of Lake Ontario is absurdly small, measurable in parts per trillion if it is measurable at all. The amount of it in the flesh of fish swimming in the Lake is something else again. The U.S. EPA and the Canadian Ministry of the Environment have both defined the acceptable level of Mirex in items intended for human consumption at 0.1 part per million. The flesh of fish from Lake Ontario has been measured at several hundred times that amount. It was this evidence of bioaccumulation that led the State of New York, on September 14, 1976, to announce a total ban on the consumption of most of the Lake's species of game fish—a ban that lasted for two years and nearly destroyed the state's infant salmon-stocking program.

Microcontaminants are almost all man-made. Nearly all of them are "organic" chemicals, those whose structure is based on the carbon atom; most of these organic chemicals are members of an even more restrictive group, the phenols and their relatives—chemicals of sometimes extraordinary complexity, which hold in common the basic six-carbon, six-hydrogen ring structure of the benzine molecule. A smaller but still major group are the specialized benzine derivatives known as "halogenated hydrocarbons," compounds in which one or more of the hydrogen molecules in the benzine ring have been replaced by halogens—fluorine, chlorine, bromine, iodine, or astatine. It is this group which poses the greatest danger to living things. A pinch may kill; a microscopic speck may pose a substantial cancer risk. Thousands of pounds of them are released into the Great Lakes and their feeding waters each year.

And make no mistake: Though these chemicals are called microcontaminants, they are not always present in micro amounts. In the water in large-enough quantities, they are quite detectable by human senses. The water develops rainbow slicks on its surface; its bed becomes stained orange or red or blue or brown. Life in the water and along its banks disappears. Many of these substances evaporate easily—the technical term is "volatilize"—and the air above the water soon becomes heavy with the sickly-sweet smell we think of as "chemical." All these clues are apparent even to a casual observer. The incredible thing—the unforgivable thing—is that even given these characteristics, the health crews who come out to test the water often subject it only to a coliform count. Water reeking with chemicals, water in which a bacterium could not survive more than five microseconds, is given a coliform count and pronounced drinkable. That is all the law provides for, that is what the test crews are used to doing, and that, by God, is all that is going to be done.

Unfortunately, there are hundreds of places—perhaps thousands of places—around the Great Lakes Basin where what the law provides for is nowhere near enough.

Today, microcontamination is recognized as a far greater problem for the Great Lakes Basin than eutrophication ever was. The reasons are not hard to grasp. This is the industrial heartland of North America—the center of manufacturing for two nations. Chemicals are both made and used here, in vast quantities. They are also discarded, often with incredible abandon—behind factories, in vacant lots, in gravel pits, in unlined holes dug in the sand. From here they find their way, usually quite rapidly, into the Lakes. More than 400 man-made substances known or suspected to be human health hazards have been found dissolved in Fifth Coast waters, and the list grows annually.

Once in the water, the contamination is likely to be there essentially forever. There is no way to decontaminate a Great Lake; the only solution is to wait for natural processes to work, and that often takes a very long time—if it happens at all. Many of these substances are extremely stable and cannot be broken down by natural processes. There is almost literally nothing that can be done about them.

One hope has been that the pollutants will be taken up by the sediments in the Lakebeds and thus rendered harmless—and this is happening to a certain degree. Particles of soil falling through the water pick up chemicals as they go and carry them to the bottom. A rather odd side effect of this is that Lake Erie—for all its encircling industry—may be the cleanest of the Great Lakes from the standpoint of toxic chemicals. "One of the problems Superior has," points out chemist Kent Fuller of EPA's Great Lakes office in Chicago, "is that it's so clean that it doesn't have the sediment particles, or even the microbiota, for the toxicants to sorb to and then sink out of the system to the bottom of the Lake. Once in the water, a molecule tends to stay there. Whereas Lake Erie, which gets probably the heaviest load per square mile of toxicants, is in many respects better off, say, than Lake Michigan or Lake Huron. Because it has such a tremendous sediment load—such a tremendously high level of productivity —that the toxicants are being carried out of the system, to the bottom."

Unfortunately, though, this sedimental journey—while useful in the short term—may not really be helping us very much over the long run. As Ohio State University researchers are discovering with phosphorus in Lake Erie, pollutants can easily be recycled into the system from sediments, so that what was once looked upon as a long-term ace in the hole—the natural flushing of the Lake water, over hundreds of years, out the St. Lawrence and down to sea—may not clear everything out as we once thought it would. And even if it did, we would only be exchanging pollution of the Lakes for pollution of the oceans. As pollution experts are fond of pointing out, pollutants never go away—they just go someplace else.

We must face facts. Our waste-disposal technology is abysmally bad, and the Great Lakes are suffering severely because of it. Even the best technology available is likely not to be good enough. Consider that ill-fated PAS site in Oswego, with which this chapter began. Granting that it was run in what charity insists we must call an incompetent manner; granting that its "high-temperature" waste incinerator never incinerated anything sufficiently, and was in constant violation of county and state clean-air ordinances while it was running, which wasn't very much of the time; granting that the firm took in more wastes than it could handle, and types of wastes it had no permit to handle, and ended up not handling them at all but merely dumping them off-site; granting all that, one must still ask: What did we gain when the cleanup crews came in? Pollution never goes away, it just goes someplace else. The only way to clean up the PAS site was to move the waste materials. They reside now near Model City, New York—still in a landfill, still in the Lake Ontario watershed. There are indications that this landfill is leaking as well. Chemicals have turned up in nearby creeks and abandoned sewers, and there have been local citizens' ground-swell attempts to shut the place down, so far without success.

Well, what else do we do with the stuff? Burn it? That pollutes

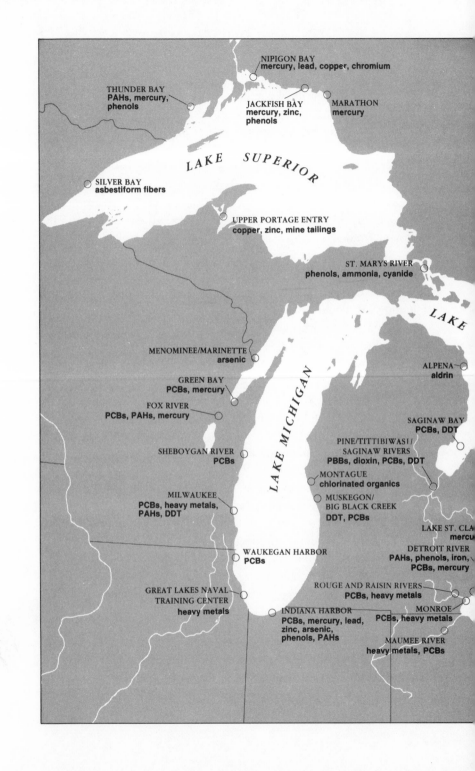

Toxic Substances in the Great Lakes System

SERPENT HARBOUR
heavy metals, DDT

SPANISH RIVER
PCBs, DDT, heavy metals, phenols

HURON

ARNIA
AHs, lorinated ganics

GRASS RIVER
PCBs

CORNWALL/ MASSENA
DDT, PCBs, heavy metals

KINGSTON
arsenic, selenium

COBOURG
PBBs, PCBs, chlorinated organics

TORONTO
PCBs, Mirex, heavy metals

MISSISSAUGA
arsenic, selenium, phenols

CLARKSON
phenols

LAKE ONTARIO

OLCOTT
PCBs, Mirex, DDT

OSWEGO HARBOR
Mirex

HAMILTON HARBOUR
PCBs, zinc, iron, cyanide

ROCHESTER HARBOR
heavy metals, phenols

ST. CATHERINES
PCBs

NIAGARA FALLS
(Love Canal)

ST. CLAIR RIVER
heavy metals, PCBs, chlorinated organics, mercury

NIAGARA RIVER
Mirex, PCBs, phenols, PAHs, heavy metals, mercury, dioxin

GRAND RIVER
PCBs, DDT, mercury, arsenic, lead, phenols

BUFFALO RIVER
Mirex, PAHs, phenols, PCBs, pesticides, heavy metals

THAMES RIVER
PCBs, DDT

LAKE ERIE

ANDOTTE
orinated organics

ASHTABULA RIVER
heavy metals, PCBs, HCB, HCBD, PAHs

PORT COLBOURNE
heavy metals

ROCKY RIVER
hlorinated organics

GRAND RIVER
phenols

CLEVELAND
heavy metals, ammonia, PCBs, phenols

BLACK RIVER
heavy metals, phenols, cyanide

SOURCES: U.S. Environmental Protection Agency, 1980 and Canada-Ontario Agreement Review Board, 1982

the air. Convert it chemically to something else? Even when possible, that is horrendously expensive, and it often only gains us another potentially hazardous substance. Put it in deep injection wells, several thousand feet below the surface, in stable geologic formations? That has been tried, not always with a great deal of success. On April 14, 1968, one such well operated by the Hammerhill Paper Company of Erie, Pennsylvania, literally erupted, pouring four million gallons of concentrated wastes directly into Lake Erie before it could be capped. In the late 1970's, drinking-water wells near a Dow Chemical Company injection wellfield at Hemlock, Michigan—in the Saginaw River watershed twenty miles or so above Lake Huron—turned up significant levels of at least eight industrial chemicals, including tri-chloroethylene, carbon tetrachloride, PCBs, toluene, and "an uni-dentified halogenated hydrocarbon." The levels seemed quite low; but geese were being born in nearby farms with their wings on backward, cows and horses were dying, and humans were complain-ing of a variety of symptoms ranging from headaches to full-body paralysis. Placed in the well water, fresh-water shrimp did not sur-vive. A link was never proved to the injection wells, but where else could the stuff have come from?

One proposed "solution"—one that has been seriously studied, which shows you how desperate we have become—is to take the wastes generated in the Great Lakes region, haul them out to the deepest parts of the Lakes, and deep-six them. Leaving aside such technical questions as to how many toxins, carcinogens, and so on would be released on the way down—and such philosophical ques-tions as to why we should choose to solve pollution in one part of the Lakes by producing it in another—just what sort of society does this "solution" make us out to be, anyway? The deepest parts of the Lake beds are well below sea level; wastes deposited there will be there for geologic time. Eventually the sediments containing them will turn to rock. Will future geologists date our era by the strange, dangerous chemical composition of its shales and limestones and sandstones?

Whatever solution we finally choose, it will have to be found soon. The hazardous-waste elephant is running away with us. There are roughly 60,000 major generators of toxic wastes in the United States, and they are producing nearly ninety billion pounds of the stuff each year. Up to 90 percent of that production—according to EPA estimates—will be disposed of improperly. Approximately one-fourth of that production, and of that improper dumping, will be within the Great Lakes Basin—and that is just on the American side. The Canadian side has similar problems. Canadians produce less waste in total amount, but a greater percentage of it is produced in the Great Lakes Basin and is finding its way into the Lakes. On June 21, 1982, for example, the Ontario Ministry of the Environment served a Control Order on the Algoma Steel Mill in Sault Ste. Marie, Ontario, charging its effluent with exceeding MOE standards for suspended solids, oil, grease, cyanide, zinc, phenols, solvent extractables, dissolved iron, sulfite, and ammonia; phenols remained above safe levels in the river from the Algoma plant all the way downstream to Little Lake George, a distance of approximately ten miles. And for three weeks in 1980 (March 21–April 13) leachate and runoff from two waste dumps owned by Eldorado Nuclear, Ltd., near the Lake Ontario north shore community of Port Hope, overflowed into the Lake at a rate in excess of 40,000 gallons per day—elevating radium levels in that section of the Lake to forty times safe drinking-water standards.

A baker's dozen more hazardous-waste outrages around the Great Lakes, drawn from the better than 1,000 such incidents reported to government authorities over the last ten years:

• Near the mouth of the Cuyahoga River in downtown Cleveland, a routine fire inspection in March, 1979, disclosed 6,000 barrels of toxic wastes stored haphazardly on an 8.4-acre site belonging to a firm called Chemical and Mineral Reclamation, Inc. Four thousand of the barrels were in what the official report described as "a weather-beaten warehouse"; the remainder were out in the open. A substantial number in both places were leaking. Labels on the barrels identified at least thirty-two separate hazardous chemicals, including acetone, chromic acid, heptane, hexane, methylene chloride, ketone, tetrachloroethylene, toluene, 2,4-dimethylpentane, 2-methylpropanol, and a mysterious substance called only "paint and miscellaneous solvents." The site was within the river's flood plain and just half a mile from the city center's populous Public Square. A U.S. District Court ordered the site cleaned up, and all of the drums were removed by November, 1979.

• In April, 1983, a "preliminary finding" published by the EPA found more than forty microcontaminants being released by the Dow Chemical Company's Midland, Michigan, plant into the Tittibiwasi River, a tributary of the Saginaw and of Lake Huron. The toxics cited by the EPA included 2,3,7,8T—the most toxic form of dioxin, a halogenated hydrocarbon some 10,000 times more potent than DDT. "We sent them what we call a Section 308 letter," says Larry Fink of the EPA in Chicago. "They refused to comply with the terms of that, and we had to sue them." Dow swiftly agreed to a settlement. As this is written in late 1985, the company is completing work on a sand filtration system designed to cut their dioxin discharges from the current 50 parts per quadrillion to 10 ppq by 1987. That is a great improvement, certainly—but it is still thirty times as much as the EPA and the state of Michigan would like to see. The original Michigan Wastewater Discharge permit issued under the terms of the settlement, Fink states, called for dioxin discharge limits of 0.3 ppq. The 10 ppq in the current permit is not a health official's safety standard; it is a lawyer's compromise.

• In Montague, Michigan, a tiny hamlet a few miles north of the quiet old lumber port of Muskegon on the east shore of Lake Michigan, the Hooker Chemical Company dumped some 20,000 barrels of hazardous wastes on an 880-acre site near White Lake—a sandbar-isolated embayment of Lake Michigan—prior to October 1979, when operations ceased at the site under the terms of a consent decree worked out between company lawyers and the Michigan Department of Natural Resources. Many of the barrels appeared to have been slashed open with an axe to allow their contents to leak into the ground, perhaps the most simple-minded method of "waste disposal" ever conceived. Over thirty hazardous substances were identified at the site, including C-56—a chemical precursor of Mirex—and "the highest levels of dioxin ever measured in Michigan." Leachate from the site was migrating through the ground and exiting into White Lake at the rate of 1 million gallons per day.

• Also near Muskegon, the Story Chemical Company collected and stored an unconfirmed number of leaking solvent drums, contaminating nearby wells and requiring a state-funded cleanup; and a company called Bofors Lakeway, Inc. discharged wastes into an unlined lagoon near Big Black Creek for several years, contaminating

the creek over a distance of at least seven miles with dichlorobenzi-
dine, benzidine, aromatic amines, benzine, and toluene.

• Possibly the highest concentration of leaking hazardous-waste
dumps on the North American continent is found in the vicinity of
Niagara Falls. A by-no-means complete list would include Love
Canal, where 239 subdivision homes and an elementary school were
built (over company protests) on top of a leaking Hooker Chemical
Company dump containing some 21,800 tons of toxic materials; the
Wheatfield site, fifty acres of land owned by the Niagara County
Refuse Disposal District, which received wastes from Hooker, Du
Pont, Goodyear, and Olin Chemical Company plants; the "S"
Landfill, a four-acre fill in the Niagara River composed of cinders,
stone, slag, dirt, Carborundum abrasives, and 70,400 tons of Hooker
Chemical Company wastes including (but not limited to) endosul-
fan, benzine hexachloride, tetrachloroethylene, and hexachloride;
the Model City site, where radioactive wastes left over from World
War II's Manhattan Project are migrating toward Lake Ontario in
open ditches; and the 102nd Street site, where between 1940 and
1972 Hooker and Olin together deposited some 90,000 tons of hazardous wastes (including Lindane, tetrachlorobenzene, and numerous phenols) on a twenty-one-acre landfill bordering the Niagara
River upstream from the City of Niagara Falls' drinking-water intakes.

• During one 20-minute period on an early morning in July, 1983,
more than 47,000 gallons of wastewater laden with "soap"—a halide-
rich by-product of wood-processing—overflowed into the Spanish
River from storage tanks at the E. B. Eddy Forest Products Ltd. plant
in Espanola, Ontario. Four days later it spilled out of the mouth of
the Spanish and spread over six square miles of Lake Huron, killing
an estimated 100,000 pickerel, perch, muskellunge, and other game
fish. Many of the dead fish were loaded into pickups and trucked to
the plant gates by outraged members of the North Shore Anglers'
and Hunters' Association. "We wanted the staff to take a look and
take a whiff," NSAHA spokesman James Vance told *Maclean's*
magazine, adding angrily, "I don't think anybody will be able to
measure the damage that has been done . . . not even ten years from
now."

• In St. Louis, Michigan, on the Pine River—a Saginaw Bay

tributary—the Veliscol Chemical Corporation dumped between
160,000 and 190,000 pounds of PBBs (polybrominated biphenyls)
into the Gratiot County landfill between 1971 and 1973.

• In Door County, Wisconsin, in 1979, 1,200 gallons of gasoline
leaked from an underground storage tank at a high school, permanently contaminating seven nearby wells; three of the wells, redrilled
at school expense, were contaminated again two years later when the
newly replaced tank was "topped out" too far by an overzealous
supplier, spilling a large quantity of gasoline onto the ground, where
it was washed into the aquifer by county firemen trying to prevent
a fire hazard from developing.

• At Thunder Bay, Ontario, the nearshore waters of Lake Superior around the mouth of the Kaministikwia River—once an alter-
nate route to the Quetico Highlands for the Hudson's Bay Company
and other fur traders shut out of the Grand Portage by the North
West Company fort at its foot—are today so heavily polluted by
heavy metals, toxic organics, and so-called "conventional pollutants"
(sewage and bacteriological wastes) released from the industrial
megacomplex on the river's delta over the last several decades that
fish caught there cannot be eaten and much of the time the water is
not even safe for recreational uses.

• And in Walton Hills, Ohio, BASF Wyandotte and the Dow
Chemical Company have been charged by the Ohio attorney general's office for discharging unknown amounts of mercury into Lake
Erie. Ohio has filed a $45 million suit against the two companies,
including $10 million for cleanup, $25 million for compensatory damages, and $10 million for punitive damages.

We do not know what we are doing. We do not know what we
are doing. The wastes build up, the waters become contaminated, the
residents become ill, the plants die, the fish die, the Lakes die, and
we shrug it off as a necessary byproduct of "progress." One-fifth of
the world's fresh-water supply lies in these immense bodies of water:
one-fifth! That is what is at risk. Do we need all these chemicals? Do
we need to throw them away? Where? Why? Time passes, industries
pollute, governments procrastinate, Champlain's "sweet seas" become an unidentified EPA agent's "world's largest sewer," and nobody but a few cockeyed environmentalists apparently gives a damn.

XV Sludge

Moving water carries sand, silt, and small particles of soil; standing water drops them. From this simple geologic truth comes the wearing down of mountains and the slow infilling of lakes and oceans. It is a natural process that has always gone on and will do so until the end of time. Rivers move; they carry loads of silt with them, eroded from the uplands. Entering still water, they slow down and stop, letting go of their loads, forming great fan-shaped deltas off their mouths. Currents in the deep pick silt and sand from the deltas and transport them further, spreading them in layers throughout the lake or ocean. Some currents, aided by gravity, carry their loads downslope to the profundal depths of the bed; here, because they can go no further, they stop. Other currents move parallel to the shore. The sands and silts move with them. Back eddies swirl in coves and bays and behind peninsulas; the shore currents slow, the sands and silts drop out once more. Bars form. The process is continuous, subtle, and much more rapid than most people realize. More than eleven million metric tons of silt and sediment enter the Great Lakes from their tributaries each year; another forty-nine million tons are moved about by shore drift. That is sixty million tons of sediment deposition and rearrangement annually—nearly 1.2 million tons per week.

Because light objects tend to remain suspended in water longer than heavy ones, the sediments are sorted as they are deposited: big particles on the bottom and close to shore, small particles on top and further out. It is the small particles that are the primary problem. At a certain size—two microns in diameter, roughly the size of fine-grained clay—they become remarkably efficient at picking up and holding chemicals on their surfaces, a process known technically as "adsorption." Falling slowly through the water, these particles act like thousands of tiny vacuum cleaners, sweeping up pollutants as they go. Dioxins, phenols, phosphorus, mercury, halozines, pesticides, and nearly everything else that happens to be dissolved or suspended in the water are all adsorbed molecule by molecule and carried to the bottom. This is good for the water but bad for the bottom. Like an animal accumulating pollutants in its body fat, the lake accumulates them in its sediments—a process that is every bit as dangerous for the lake as it is for the animal.

Animals exposed to high concentrations of pollutants often develop localized malignancies—tumors. Lakes, too, have localized malignancies from high concentrations of pollutants. These are the limnetic equivalent of tumors—the trouble spots, the places where the symptoms of poisoning first begin to show up. And along the Fifth Coast, the worst of them all is at Waukegan, Illinois.

The story actually begins more than 100 years ago, in the summer of 1882. Chester A. Arthur was President of the United States; John Peter Altgeld had just been elected Governor of Illinois. The Chicago Cubs were winning the National League pennant for the third year in a row (there was as of yet no American League). And thirty miles to the north of the pennant celebrations, up by the Wisconsin border, the citizens of the little coastal community of Waukegan—having sought and secured the necessary appropriations from Congress—were beginning the excavation of a commercial harbor in the sand flats bordering Lake Michigan in front of their city.

It was not a simple job. There were no natural openings in the coastline in the Waukegan vicinity—no coves, no bays, no river mouths, hardly even a curved beach. The little stream the city had been built on was inadequate to float anything larger than a small canoe, and an earlier attempt to enclose a harbor by building a breakwater had met with failure when the half-completed structure washed away in one of the big Lake's oceanic storms. Waukegan was a waterfront city with no waterfront; it was a federally designated United States Port of Entry, but it had no port to enter.

It did, however, have the sand flats. They lay at the base of the clay bluff the city was built on and extended as much as a half mile out to the edge of the boundless water, where the ships came up over the horizon from Mackinac and steamed right past to the honest-to-goodness Port of Entry at Chicago. A harbor could be dug in that sand; it could be connected to the Lake by a narrow channel, and the mouth of the channel could be protected by a smaller and more secure breakwater than the one the storm had run away with earlier. Then perhaps some of the ships would slip in past the breakwater and up the channel instead of steaming past, and the docks would fill with commerce, and Waukegan, which had begun to show signs of stagnation, would grow and prosper once again.

That, at any rate, was the scenario the city had managed to sell to Congress in the spring of 1882. Twenty years later the work was done; and during the next half-century Waukegan, which had stabilized at around 7,000 people before the harbor project was completed, grew rapidly—just as had been predicted—to a population of over 50,000. Manufacturers came, drawn by the new port facility; for the most part they built their factories at the base of the bluff, on the flats near the water.

Among these manufacturers was a boatbuilder named Johnson, who diversified into outboard motors in the early years of the twentieth century. The company expanded rapidly. In 1929, Johnson Motors merged with Evinrude and several others to form the Outboard Motors Corporation; and in 1936 a further merger resulted in the formation of a company called Outboard Marine, which by 1970 had grown to dominate the American pleasure-boat business, as well as holding large shares of the market for chain saws, snowmobiles, and similar equipment powered by small gasoline engines. Through all these changes, though, the company continued to build its increasingly popular Johnson outboard motors at the old plant location on the sand flats beside Waukegan's artificial harbor. The Johnson plant was progressively run; it was a major employer of the Waukegan work force; and it was generally looked upon as a boon to the community.

An assessment, as it turns out, that—due in part to a curiously coincident set of occurrences halfway around the world and in a completely unrelated field—was eventually going to be subject to a great deal of change.

In 1881—the year before Waukegan began construction of the harbor that led to all this activity—a group of organic chemical compounds called araclors was synthesized in a laboratory in Germany for the first time. Araclors were a byproduct of the investigation of coal tar, which was transforming the science of chemistry during the latter half of the nineteenth century. Long thought of as merely an ugly nuisance, coal tar—a sticky black residue left over from the manufacture of illuminating gas from coal—had turned out to be a virtual cornucopia of exotic hydrocarbon-based compounds with unusual and often mystifying chemical properties. Most of these compounds were built around the benzine ring—six hydrogen atoms and six carbon atoms, arranged in the shape of a closed hexagon.

Many benzine derivatives were useful as artificial dyes—a characteristic that had been the original impetus for their study. The araclors were not among these. They were thick, colorless, odorless fluids, chemically inert and almost impossible to break down by heat or pressure. There were more than 100 varieties of them, and they all appeared quite useless. The German chemists noted their properties, set the compounds aside, and went on in their search for dyes and other more interesting materials.

In 1929—the year of Johnson's merger with Evinrude—a use was finally discovered for the "useless" araclors. Their high stability and resistance to heat and pressure, it turned out, made them excellent lubricants and hydraulic fluids for industrial applications such as aluminum die-casting, which requires presses capable of exerting pressures of more than 2,000 tons per square inch. Once one application was found, others soon followed: as insulators for electrical transformers and capacitors, as constituents of ink and of "carbonless" carbon papers, as ingredients of paint and plastics, as road-dust suppressors, as hardeners in certain metallurgical processes. The Monsanto Corporation, a chemical firm founded in St. Louis in 1915 by a pharmaceuticals clerk who was tired of seeing everything in the store brought in from Europe at tariff-inflated prices, sought and received permission to manufacture araclors in America. The company sold them under that name, but by that time chemists were calling them something else. The new name was based on the compounds' chemical composition. Since the basic araclor molecules were composed of two modified benzine rings, they were properly called biphenyls; since each benzine ring had two or more chlorine atoms replacing its normal hydrogen atoms, they were called polychlorinated. And since "polychlorinated biphenyls" was too much of a mouthful even for an organic chemist, the araclors (or Araclors, since that was now properly a trade name) became known among scientists by a three-letter abbreviation: PCBs.

In 1954, the Outboard Marine Corporation—which had recently converted to die-cast aluminum construction in its outboard motors —purchased the first small shipment of what would eventually amount to approximately ten million pounds of this "useless" fluid for use in their plant on the flats beside Waukegan's artificial harbor. It was cheap, and the chemists had assured everyone that it was almost completely inert, so it seemed pointless to be particularly careful with it. By the company's own estimates, approximately 20 percent of the material—some 100,000 tons of it—leaked from the machinery, spilled, or was otherwise lost in the plant, where it was washed down drains and discharged into Waukegan's proud artificial harbor. PCBs are slightly heavier than water. Most of those 100,000 tons sank to the bottom of the harbor and stayed there.

Meanwhile, elsewhere in the world, the doubts were beginning. At first they were just hunches. DDT, the widely used "miracle" pesticide of World War II, had turned out to be perilously dangerous when loose in the environment—building up alarmingly in the body fat of predators, interfering with the reproductive abilities of birds and mammals, killing shellfish and other invertebrates, disrupting food chains, and generally wreaking havoc. DDT and PCBs were closely related to each other; both were chlorinated hydrocarbons originally derived from coal tar. Would PCBs, too, turn out to be dangerous? Laboratory work in Sweden in 1966 suggested that they would; and two years later that suggestion was tragically confirmed by an incident in Japan. In Kitakyushu City, on the northern tip of the island of Kyushu, more than 1,000 people came down with moderate to severe symptoms of a mysterious poisoning: acne-like skin lesions, jaundice, nausea and vomiting, abdominal cramps, swollen limbs and joints, and severe lassitude. Mothers gave birth to gray-skinned, weakened, undersized infants with running discharges from their eyes. Analysis of the victims' body fat pointed to the villain: PCB concentrations averaging in the neighborhood of seventy-five parts per million (ppm). The PCBs, it eventually turned out, had come from a leaking transformer in a local rice-milling plant. A batch of rice oil had become contaminated by the leaked compound; the two fluids are strikingly similar in texture and color, and the PCBs had no taste or odor to give them away, and the contamination had gone undetected until it was too late. Five people died.

Since PCBs, like DDT, are bioaccumulative—meaning that they tend to remain in the body, building up to higher and higher levels as each successive dose adds to the amount already in storage—long-term consumption of food containing even very tiny amounts of the material could be predicted to have the same eventual effects on the consumer as the unfortunate citizens of Kitakyushu City had suffered from short-term consumption of high amounts. Clearly, PCBs were not the benign material they had been made out to be. Monsanto voluntarily limited production of the compound in 1970, selling it after that only to manufacturers of high-load electrical equipment; and two years later the federal government banned the stuff altogether and initiated a survey of possible sites of serious PCB contamination around the country.

Four years later, in the fall of 1976, they came to Waukegan Harbor.

What they found there was classified information for a number of years, subject to a protective court order issued at the request of the Outboard Marine Corporation, but the protective order was lifted in 1981, and a year later the Water Quality Board of the International Joint Commission on Boundary Waters, in its 1982 *Report on Great Lakes Water Quality*, was able to spell out for the first time the singularly complete extent of the contamination of Waukegan Harbor. The harbor, the board noted with careful understatement, was "grossly contaminated with PCB." The bottom sludge was a nightmarish concoction of chemicals with a PCB content of as much as 500,000 milligrams per kilogram (mg/kg); the water itself was carrying as much as three micrograms of the supposedly insoluble stuff per liter. Fish from the harbor showed whole-body accumulations of as

much as seventy-seven ppm—more than the victims of the Kitakyushu City incident had shown in their fatty tissues alone (PCBs, like
many other chlorinated hydrocarbons, are strongly lipophilic—
meaning that they tend to concentrate in their victims' body fat—so
whole-body concentrations of the compound are normally considerably lower than fat concentrations). Fishing was banned from the
harbor; dredging also had to stop, because dredging activities would
stir up the sludge and resuspend it in the water. The Environmental
Protection Agency and the State of Illinois sued Outboard Marine
and were in turn sued by the company. Attempts began to find ways
to remove the sediments and dispose of them safely; but no really
satisfactory method turned up.

Today, four years later, it still hasn't.

"Nobody knows what to do about it," says Jane Elder, midwest
representative for the Sierra Club, with a territory covering Wisconsin, Michigan, Minnesota, Indiana, Illinois, and Iowa. She works out
of a windowless basement office near the University of Wisconsin in
downtown Madison. "There are some fancy high-tech things they
may be trying," she explains, "where they sort of set up a vacuum
system so that when you're dredging, the water doesn't leave the
exact dredge area. But even if you dredge it successfully, the thing
you've got is a bunch of toxic sludge that nobody wants to landfill.
And the question of what you do with toxic sludge once you get it
is one that's never been satisfactorily answered."

That is the crux of the matter. What do you do with the stuff?
Do you place it in a diked-disposal area on the edge of the harbor?
Do you transfer it to railroad cars or tank trucks—with all the hazards
the transfer entails—and take it off somewhere and bury it? Do you
take it out to the middle of the Lake, close your eyes, and let go? Not
one of these "solutions" seems satisfactory. The argument goes on;
the dredges sit idle. The silt, which up until the PCBs were discovered was dredged out regularly, builds up. The water is at pleasure-
boat depth now, and soon it will not be even that. The artificial
harbor Waukegan developed so proudly out of its sand flat a century
ago is well on its way back to being a sand flat again.

There are many ways for pollutants to enter the bottom sediments of a lake. There are industrial waste pipes and sewage outfalls;

there are shipping discharges, ranging from massive accidents to bilge cleaning and even deck hosing. There is "nonpoint runoff" from streets and parking lots, and upland sediment derived from sprayed and fertilized fields and forests and carried into the coastal waters by rivers like the Maumee and the Fox and the Saginaw. There are mine tailings. All these things end up on the Lakebeds, where they are covered by "normal" sediments and mixed into the bottom mud by the turbulence from storm currents and passing ships. The result is "in-place pollutants"—toxic sludge. Waukegan Harbor has the worst known case of it, but it is not alone: There are plenty of others just a notch or two down the scale.

There is, for example, the lower end of Green Bay, Wisconsin, near the outfall (this sewer-engineering term seems particularly appropriate here) of the Fox River. The bottom sediments in this area, says the IJC's Great Lakes Water Quality Board, are "grossly polluted, with high concentrations of volatile solids, chemical oxygen demand, total Kjeldahl nitrogen, oil and grease, mercury, phosphorus, lead, zinc, and ammonia . . . [and] with PCB in excess of 10 mg/kg [milligrams per kilogram]." The main sources of these contaminants are the sixteen paper plants and seven municipal sewage outfalls along the lower Fox River. Several of these sources—Appleton Paper, Consolidated Paper, Fort Howard Paper, Nicolet Paper, the Green Bay Metro sewage plant, and three or four others—were still discharging ammonia and/or phosphorus in excess of permit standards at least as late as 1982; three (Fort Howard, Wisconsin Tissue, and the Bergstrom Paper Company) were recycling printed papers containing, in the printers' ink, significant quantities of PCBs (Wisconsin law specifically exempts paper recyclers from most restrictions on working with PCBs). The PCBs were supposed to be contained within the plants, but they often were not. Measurements of the effluent from the Fort Howard mill in 1981 found it running a PCB concentration of 4 micrograms per liter, well above clean-water standards.

In Milwaukee Harbor the situation is much the same. There are phosphates, oil and grease, Kjeldahl nitrogen, PCBs. There is not as much ammonia as in Green Bay, but there are significant quantities of lead, zinc, cadmium, and copper. There is chlordane and DDT. The principal current source of contamination seems to be the Milwaukee sewer system, an antiquated combined design that overflows regularly in wet weather. Milwaukee is working on its sewers, but if the current plan is followed, it will be 1996 before it comes into full compliance with federal and state effluent standards. Meanwhile the toxic sludge continues to build.

At Collingwood, Ontario, on the south shore of Georgian Bay— a major winter-sports center and one of Canada's loveliest small cities —harbor dredging is under severe restrictions owing to sediment contamination by heavy metals and organochlorides, including PCBs. At Jackfish Bay and at Nipigon, on the wild north shore of Superior, harbor sediments are so thickly coated by wastes from pulp and paper manufacturing that dredge spoil cannot be disposed of in open water but must be confined, for reasons of health, behind dikes and levees. And at Port Hope, on the north shore of Lake Ontario, "contingency spills" from the Eldorado Nuclear Plant on the edge of the Port Hope Turning Basin have added to the severe sediment contamination already in place from industrial and shipping discharges prior to 1945 to create a deadly mix of heavy metals, uranium, radium, and PCBs that cannot, with current technology, be safely dredged at all.

Canada's worst in-place pollutants problem—and one of the worst anywhere—is in Hamilton Harbour, at the west end of Lake Ontario. Tucked in behind a three-mile-long sand and gravel bar (deposited by the glaciers but shaped by the Lake), the five-square-mile harbor serves its nation's greatest concentration of heavy industry, a place known to its neighbors, somewhat derisively, as Steeltown. In that confined space the results have been devastating. Hamilton Harbour's sediments, the Great Lakes Water Quality Board reports,

> . . . exceed the provincial guidelines for open-water disposal with respect to iron, lead, arsenic, zinc, copper, nickel, mercury, chromium, total phosphorus, total Kjeldahl nitrogen, ammonia, ether extractables, and oil and grease. . . . PCB levels in sediment exceed provincial guidelines for open-water disposal along the south shore and in the deep water areas. . . . Organochlorine pesticides and their metabolites have been detected in sediments at average levels close to 10 µg/kg [micrograms per kilogram].

In 1982, the principal continuing sources of pollutants were two steel firms, Stelco and Dofasco, which exceeded Ontario Ministry of the Environment effluent standards for a variety of microcontaminants, including cyanide (Stelco); suspended solids, ammonia, and ammonium thiocyanate (Dofasco); and phenols (both plants); before the inauguration of a new sewage treatment plant at the beginning of that year, the Hamilton sewers had been a third major contributor. All effluents are expected to be in compliance with government standards by 1987, but the problem will remain. Trapped behind that confining bar, the sludge is going nowhere. "The sediment contamination problem," notes the Water Quality Board with typical understatement, "will persist over the long term." For Hamiltonians, cyanide, ammonia, and phenols—like diamonds—apparently are forever.

Next to Waukegan Harbor, the worst problem spot on the Lakes is probably the Indiana Harbor and Ship Canal at Gary, sixty-odd miles to the south. Here the sediments are, in the International Joint Commission's words, "heavily polluted for all conventional pollutants and heavy metals." Bottom samplings by the Indiana Stream Pollution Control Board and the U.S. Environmental Protection Agency have turned up oil and grease levels as high as 175,000 mg/kg; phosphorus and lead levels of 15,000 mg/kg each; iron concentrations of 325,000 mg/kg; and volatile solids concentrations of a whopping 609,000 mg/kg, or more than 60 percent of that particular sample. The source of these contaminants is the Hammond/Gary industrial ganglion of steel plants, chemical factories, plastic plants, coal-fired generators, and others—probably the world's largest single concentration of heavy industry. Most of these plants currently meet all state and federal effluent standards, but this is misleading, for two reasons. Since the Grand Calumet River here has almost no natural flow— the whole river is currently composed of effluent—the standards are significantly lower than they are elsewhere. And many of the industrial plants meet these reduced standards by simply not releasing any effluent of their own at all, at least directly. Instead, they have connected themselves to the overloaded municipal sewage facilities at East Chicago, Hammond, and Gary. None of these plants is currently in compliance with either state or federal standards at the best of times—and all of them are combined systems with little storm runoff capacity, which release massive amounts of heavily contaminated effluent in the worst of times. The "floatables" from the effluent drift up on nearby beaches, closing them (the beach at Hammond's Lake Front Park has had to be posted so often for "temporary" hazardous conditions by the health authorities that they have finally closed it permanently); the rest of the effluent—cyanides, phenols, ammonia, halogens, old Uncle Tom Cobbley and all—becomes part of the sludge.

In-place pollutants are a sticky problem—in more ways than one. Bottom muck is, after all, a part of the ecosystem—a natural phenomenon that water-borne life has adapted to over the billions of years of geologic time. It is the home of mayfly nymphs, oligochaetes, and other invertebrates. Close to shore, plants root in it. Fish eat the invertebrates and the plants, and are in turn eaten—by larger fish, by birds, by animals, by humans. Pollutants in the muck are thus transferred up the food chain right to the top, bioaccumulating as they go. In this way do PCBs, picked up by sediments and carried "harmlessly" out of the water, still end up on our plates.

They may also end up once again in our water. It is known that sediments readily adsorb many organic chemicals and some heavy metals; it is not known how readily they give them up again. Sludge may be a sink for pollutants, but how full can the sink get before it overflows and the pollutants return to the water? This is a problem that is just beginning to receive serious study. The bottom sediments of Lake Erie are apparently contributing to the Lake's continuing phosphorus problem: There are still elevated levels of PCBs in the water of Waukegan Harbor, where no releases have taken place for over ten years. Some recycling of pollutants is clearly going on. How much is it? How dangerous? The answers are not yet available, but the hints we have seen have not been very comforting.

The most difficult thing about in-place pollutants, however, is not what they do *down there*; it is what they do when they are brought back *up here*. This is not a problem that is likely to be solved soon. Toxic dredge spoil is like any other toxic waste: a thing virtually impossible to get rid of with current technology. About all that can be done with it is to stockpile it, and that doesn't solve the problem, it merely transfers it. What does one do, eventually, with the stock-piles?

"In some cases the best thing to do may be to just leave it down there," states Jane Elder somewhat wearily. "Landfills are certainly an inadequate solution. The idea that just by burying it you take care of the whole problem is so primitive—and yet, that's what we do with most of our toxic materials." And in Windsor, Ontario, Pat Bonner of the IJC agrees. "What do you do with the sludge?" she asks rhetorically. "Do you stir it up and remove it? Do you cover it up? If you're going to remove this stuff, where is it safe? What makes it safe? What are the conditions? We just don't know. So is it safer to leave it where it is? I still don't know that, either."

And there is this little problem with much toxic sludge: It *has* to be moved. It often cannot be merely secured in place, although this is probably—as Elder suggests—the preferable method. Harbors are usually built at the mouths of rivers, so that eleven-million-metric-ton wallop of silt that enters the Lakes each year down their tributaries does so through the harbors. They must be dredged to keep them usable. If they are too dirty to dredge—as the citizens of Waukegan are finding to their sorrow—they soon fill in. Ships cannot enter; docks stand idle. And in a waterfront town, idle docks spell economic disaster.

So in most places along the Fifth Coast, the dredging goes on. The toxic spoil comes up; the barges fill and are towed away. Most are currently towed outward. In the center of the Lake, in deep water, the tows stop and the contents of the barges are released. This is the time-honored way of doing things. It makes more sense, certainly, with toxic sludge—a thing of lake bottoms, anyway—than with other forms of toxic wastes for which the same sort of fate has been suggested. But what is it doing down there?

No one knows.

And as if to emphasize our ignorance—nature has a way of high-lighting these things—certain disturbing reports have lately come from the Delaware Basin. There, in the salt-water estuary where the Delaware River meets the Atlantic, chlorinated hydrocarbons for which there are no apparent landward sources are beginning to show up in the bottom sediments. According to Dr. Gerald Hansler, the former EPA engineer who is currently chairman of the Delaware

River Basin Commission, the most likely source of these chlorinated
hydrocarbons is the sediments themselves. Chlorinated effluent from
city sewage systems—a result of the almost universal practice of
adding a little chlorine to city water as a biocide—has combined with
chemicals in the sediments to actually create the toxins right there in
the bottom muck. The estuary has become a vast chemical factory,
and it is slowly poisoning itself.

Now, consider this: Twenty-four million people drink the Great
Lakes. Virtually every drop of that drinking water is chlorinated first
—and then returned to the Lakes. What is happening on the Delaware is surely happening here as well. What are we doing? What sort
of Frankenstein's Monster are we building down there, deep in the
once-beneficial sediments beneath the beds of the greatest reservoirs
of fresh water on the face of the earth?

XVI Shores

What is the highest and best use for the Great Lakes? What should we do with them, and which of us should do it? Assuming for the moment that we can solve the eutrophication problem, and the toxic-wastes problem, and the in-place pollutants problem, and all the other problems that continue to plague us—it is just barely possible, given global cooperation for the sake of this global resource, that these things might one day be done —to what use should the rejuvenated waters and the lands that adjoin them be put? Or, assuming that we cannot solve all these things, and the Lakes are doomed to die, how should they best be conserved, used, and maintained through their declining years? These enormous sweetwater seas must serve variously as drinking-water reservoirs, as shipping lanes, as swimming and fishing holes, as industrial process and cooling water, as trash dumps, and as scenic backdrops. To what extent do these uses conflict? When they do, which ones should take precedence? Or will another use altogether—energy production of agricultural irrigation or something as yet totally unthought-of— prove more important, eventually, than all current uses put together?

Nowhere are these problems more clearly apparent than when addressing the question of shoreline use. How much of the shore should be public, and how much should be private? How much of the Fifth Coast should be devoted to parklands, how much to homesites, and how much to industrial frontage or recreational development? How much infilling should be allowed? What sort of erosion controls are needed? Should NO TRESPASSING signs be allowed on the beaches? Why? Where? These questions are being addressed right now. We cannot postpone them; they *will be* answered. Our choice is not whether or not to answer the questions; it is whether to answer them intelligently and aggressively, or to sit back and just allow the answers to happen.

In all too many cases, we appear to be doing the latter.

The shore is the interface between the earth and the water. It is a dynamic place, a place of movement and interaction and change. The water beats on the land, in waves; the land washes away. Currents eddy, slowing, depositing sand; the land builds up. Bays are enclosed by bars and become separate lakes. Islands and headlands are worn down. Erosion goes on constantly, much faster than most people realize. Not long ago there was an island off the American north coast called Little Steamboat, at the western end of the Lake Superior archipelago known as the Apostle Islands. Little Steamboat was owned by an absentee landlord, an out-of-stater who rarely visited the area. One fine day this out-of-stater took it into his head to come take a look at his property. Arriving at the nearest town— Bayfield, Wisconsin—he chartered a boat and headed out to the spot the maps showed as his own little corner of the Apostles. There was nothing there but water. A storm had come and gone three years previously and taken his island with it, and he had been paying taxes on a featureless section of Lake Superior ever since.

Erosion takes place all over the Great Lakes, but the damage— in human terms—tends to be concentrated in three places: the eastern shore of Lake Michigan, the southern shore of Lake Erie, and the red-clay region of Lake Superior, along the northern Wisconsin coast. At roughly $100 million per year, this damage is not small. It is a problem that clearly needs a solution. Unfortunately, we have yet to come up with one. Partly this is due to the magnitude of the problem—the strength of the forces involved, the length of the coastline subject to those forces, the dollar costs of the proposed remedies. Mostly, though, it is due to none of these things. It is not the problem's size that stops us; it is our woeful underestimation of it—an underestimation caused by our blissful ignorance, in general, of the workings and implications of the whole erosion process.

For this reason, we had better begin right now by examining this process in some detail.

Erosion is essentially a mechanical phenomenon; though limestone can dissolve and sandstone can come unglued, breaking down the matrix in which the grains of ancient sand are held, the vast majority of erosion is a matter of simple physical wearing-down, of water literally plucking out pieces of the land and carrying them away. The water has to be moving to do this, of course; so the main agent of erosion in a standing body of water such as a lake or an ocean is wave action, and the main theater where the action takes place is a narrow band extending from a few feet above still-water level to a few feet below—an area known to geologists as the "zone of breakers."

Waves are caused by the wind; their crests are perpendicular to the wind's direction, and they drive onto the shore with the wind behind them. They are a so-called harmonic phenomenon, which means they tend to be of equal size and spaced equal distances apart; this size and distance is dependent largely on two things, the force of the wind and the *fetch*, which is a geologists' (and sailors') term for the length of the water surface over which the wind is blowing. The stronger the wind and the longer the fetch, the higher the waves will grow and the further apart their crests and troughs will lie. Since waves, once started, carry their own energy, they can spread well beyond their source: If the fetch is long enough, the waves will continue far beyond the dying-out of the wind that started them. The enormous fetch of the ocean is the main reason why its breakers are never still. (The Great Lakes are very nearly in the same category.)

Only the wave energy passes from crest to crest; the water molecules themselves stay in place, describing small vertical circles as the waves pass over them. These circles tend to be larger near the surface and smaller as depth increases, until at a certain point—roughly half as far below the water's surface as the distance from the crest of one wave to the crest of the next, a distance known as the *half-wave depth* —they disappear altogether and the water remains still. A wave approaching the shore begins to "feel bottom," as geologists put it— begins to expend energy on the Lakebed—at about the half-wave depth, and the zone of breakers extends from this point to the *run-out height*—the point where the energy of the wave finally dissipates as it runs up a beach or a bluff.

The energy expended by waves of a given size is constant, but their effect on the shore varies considerably from place to place along a coastline. This is due to variations in the coast itself. Steep bluffs erode more rapidly than long flat beaches, because the zone of breakers is much narrower on a steep shoreline, and the wave's energy— since it must be concentrated into a smaller space—is greater per square inch. Shores made of small-grained materials like clay or fine sand erode faster than shores made of coarser stuff, simply because small things are easier for the water to carry away. Soils erode faster than rock; soft rock (like sandstone) erodes faster than hard rock (like granite). Waves that have picked up sand and are carrying it around with them erode rock much faster than waves of clear water with the same fetch and height, because the sand acts as an abrasive, literally sanding away the rock as though it were a carpenter with a piece of wood and a piece of sandpaper; for this reason, rocky coasts downcurrent from sand beaches are worn down more rapidly than coasts made of the same rock but located elsewhere.

Once it is eroded away into the water, of course, a particle of shoreline is not going to stay there very long; it is going to be set down somewhere. This is the often-ignored other half of erosion— a process called *deposition*. By this means, bars and spits are built up, beaches are extended, bays are filled in. Often—too often—the designers of erosion-control devices pay little or no attention to deposition. This is a mistake. The two processes are tied inseparably together, and to interfere with one is also to interfere with the other —and while the interference with erosion can often be planned, the concurrent interference with deposition usually cannot. Thus does trying to solve one problem, as usual, beget another.

Deposition does not depend, as erosion does, on wave action; instead, it depends on current patterns. There are two main types of these.

One type, the *offshore current*, flows down the side of the Lake toward the bed, away from the shore; it is generally caused by the pull of gravity on waves falling back from the shore into the water, though convection or the presence of underwater springs may also enter into the picture. Offshore currents carry their loads out toward the center of the Lake, and are responsible for the flattening of beaches and the slow filling-in of the Lakebed.

The other type, the *longshore current*, flows parallel to the shoreline. It is largely wind-driven, a result of waves hitting the beach obliquely instead of straight on; but in a large-enough body of water —and the Great Lakes definitely qualify—there is also a measurable "Coriolis effect," a clockwise swirl (in the northern hemisphere) caused by a combination of gravity and centrifugal force as the earth tries to turn out from under the water resting upon it. Sand carried by longshore currents, known as *shore drift*, can move from point to point along the coastline with amazing rapidity. Sand eroded from one beach builds up other beaches further down the line, a process called *beach nourishment*. Longshore currents running suddenly off a point and into deep water slow down and deposit their drift, forming spits; deflected into bays, the currents may eddy aimlessly, slowly dropping their loads, filling in the bay and starving the beaches beyond it. Longshore currents are a major shaping force for shoreline features, probably much more major than most of us realize. If you look at a map of Lake Michigan, you will see, scattered along its eastern shore, numerous smaller lakes—Crystal, Glen, Elk, Torch, Charlevoix, and perhaps two dozen others—separated from the main Lake by what appear to be extremely narrow necks of land. Those necks are harbor spits that have been extended across the mouths of bays to form bars. The lakes behind them were once embayments of Lake Michigan. Shore drift has cut them loose and turned them into separate bodies of water.

Because it is a geologic anomaly—an exception to the general rule that earth-shaping processes move with exceeding slowness—shoreline erosion has always been a perplexing problem for humans, who have yet to find a rational means of dealing with it. We approach the subject with an almost complete dichotomy of purpose. On the one hand, we seek to deny its existence, building roads, homes, and other structures on pieces of land the Lake is about to claim; and on the other, having inevitably failed in this course, we seek to deny its *right* to exist, sorting through our modern bag of technological tricks for ways and means of stopping geological processes in their tracks.

Traditional means of tackling the problem of erosion are all mechanical; the building of some protective structure that will keep the

Lake from eating away any more of its shoreline. This is in keeping with the standard human desire to "conquer" nature, to tame it and put it in its place so that we can do what we want where we want to do it. It is an approach that seldom works. We cannot deny erosion; it exists. Geology is real. The forces involved are massive, the rules they play by are fixed and immutable. We cannot alter these rules or abrogate them. The only thing we can do is to change the milieu in which they work—and like so many other changes, like canals and pesticides and long-lasting suds and the tall smokestacks that solved immediate-vicinity air pollution problems only to give us acid rain, the changes we make in our attempts to control erosion often lead to other changes, unforeseen but major, which follow immediately from the desired change and have a way of coming around and haunting us for years afterward.

One of the most common forms of structural erosion-protection is the *groin* (or groyne)—a low wall running perpendicular from the shore out into the surf. The theory behind the groin is simple: If the longshore currents are blocked, they will stop, dropping their loads of sand and silt and building up the shore in the vicinity of the groin instead of eroding it away. The theory is sound and—when looked at from the standpoint of the groin's immediate upcurrent vicinity— works quite well. It is only when you cast around for a broader look that you run into the flaws.

Near Michigan City, Indiana, on the eastern end of the Indiana Dunes National Lakeshore, there is a massive, mountainous pile of moving sand known as Mt. Baldy, whose 123-foot height above Lake Michigan makes it one of the tallest active dunes in the world. From the summit the views are schizophrenic. To the north, looking out over the Lake, you can see nothing but sand and sky and water and white gulls flying—a primitive place, a place out of time, lifted straight out of Schoolcraft's *Journal* or Father Hennepin's *Travels*. But to the west, far away across the Lake, the towers of Chicago rise, dim and distant like a waterborne mirage; and to the east, much closer —so close it seems almost in your lap—looms the giant Northern Indiana Public Service Company (NIPSCO) coal-fired power plant at Michigan City. To build that power plant and its enormous mush-room-shaped cooling tower as close as possible to the water, NIPSCO took down a dune called the Big Slide, a dune even larger than Baldy. To keep it there, they built a groin.

You can see the groin from the top of Baldy as well. Five feet above wave level, several hundred feet long, it sticks out into the blue Michigan waters like a causeway to nowhere. It works, too. Behind it, on the eastern side, the sand builds up. The shoreline is extending; erosion has been turned around. The power plant is safe.

The National Lakeshore is not.

At the Lakeward foot of Baldy, Park Service naturalist Robert Fudge showed me the evidence: a steep three-foot scarp in the sand running the full length of the beach, straight and clean as if it had been made by a bulldozer. It is an erosion line, and it was not there before the groin was built. The sand collecting on the far side of NIPSCO's structure is the sand that should have nourished this beach. Now it has been cut off, and the beach is suffering from malnutrition. Eventually the scarp will eat its way back into Baldy itself. Baldy is moving away from the Lake, but the scarp is moving faster; over the long run—perhaps fifty years, perhaps one hundred, perhaps five hundred—the dune is doomed.

And not just Baldy. The whole Lakeshore is going. "Much of the Dunes area is now being stripped away," writes the Indiana Geological Survey in its booklet *Legacy of Sand.* "In many areas of the state and federal parks . . . the rate [is] more than 15 feet per year. Portions of the old Lakeshore Drive have been undercut and washed away by longshore current and wave action. . . ." Some of that would be going on anyway—it is the nature of coasts to change—but it has gotten much worse since the power plant went in. NIPSCO has solved its own erosion problem, but it has significantly increased erosion problems for its neighbors. That is what groins always do.

Just behind the scarp there is a strange area of sand, alien in texture and color and full of impurities. When I questioned him about it, Fudge flashed a quick grin. "Artificial shore drift," he explained. The alien sand was the work of the Army Corps of Engineers; somebody told them Mt. Baldy was disappearing, and they happened to be dredging reasonably pure sand out of a nearby harbor, so they dumped it on Baldy to replace the sand the currents no longer bring.

"Doesn't seem too intelligent," I observed.

Fudge nodded. "I thought so at the time," he said, "but I didn't say anything. At least they were trying, and anyway, you'll notice it's disappearing as fast as the regular sand. It looks a little funny, but it's not going to be a problem for very long."

There are several structural methods besides groins that have been tried in an attempt to solve the problem of erosion.

One approach is to construct *dolos,* concrete or steel barriers placed just offshore so that the waves will strike them instead of the shoreline, dissipating their energy harmlessly and leaving the shore alone. Dolos work splendidly: They stop erosion cold, and they have a minimal effect on shore drift. Unfortunately, they are extremely expensive—in the neighborhood of $70 per protected meter of shore —and unless they are placed far out in the Lake, well beyond the half-wave depth of even the most severe storms, the sand erodes away beneath their feet, causing them to collapse and need replacement every few years. They are also—to put the matter as delicately as possible—ugly as hell. Thus they are useful only in areas where price and aesthetics are no object.

A variation on the dolo approach is the artificial sandbar—the "artificial shore drift" that Fudge laughed about on Baldy, but placed out in the Lake instead of just being dumped on the beach. Natural-appearing and extremely effective, the artificial sandbar—like the dolo—stops waves from hitting the shore by absorbing them against its own Lakeward side. Shore drift is deflected further out into the Lake, but is otherwise unaffected. Artificial sandbars are much cheaper, and far less visually obnoxious, than dolos—but they are even more subject to erosion. Unable to carry the shore away, the waves and currents take the man-made sandbar instead. Replacement must normally be done annually.

Functionally speaking, the best mechanical erosion control of all is probably shoreline armor—concrete seawalls, riprap, or armor stone placed directly on an eroding shore so that the waves find nothing small enough to carry away. Armor works splendidly, and it has even less effect on current patterns than dolos and artificial sandbars do. But there are drawbacks to armor as well. It cannot be used for beaches, only bluffs—an armored beach being essentially a useless one. Unless it extends down below the half-wave depth, the armor—like the dolo—is doomed, sooner or later, to be undercut and to fall into the Lake, requiring replacement. And—also like the dolo —it is ugly. Riprapped shorelines, in particular, look more like the aftermath of a horrible accident than a rational means of erosion control. Raw hunks of shattered stone lie over the bank at crazy angles like petrified vomit; the Lake laps disconsolately at them. Effective, yes: The shore stays put, the water remains clear. But who would choose on purpose to go there and see these things?

And people *do* go there—lots of people. Because of their dynamism—there is always something happening there—shorelines are favored spots for human use. This is a valid role for the Lakes, certainly, but it is hardly a role without problems. These problems are of two kinds. Some—as we have just seen—are problems the recreationists have with the Lakes. The rest are problems they have with each other.

Two hundred miles or so north of the Michigan/Indiana border, well up the eastern shore of Lake Michigan where the water is cold and clear and almost as clean as Superior's, a vast, hulking bluff called Sleeping Bear Dune looms out of the Lake like a wall, many miles in length and 400 feet or more in height. It is sometimes called the tallest sand dune in the world, but this is not strictly true; though a true dune forty feet high or so perches up there on top, most of the bluff is composed of small gravels and coarse sand grains too large for wind-moving. Sleeping Bear is a glacial moraine—one of the lateral moraines left behind by the huge Lake Michigan lobe of the continental glacier when it packed up and left for the weekend some 12,000 years ago last Friday. The dune on top was deposited a few thousand years later, sort of as an afterthought, by the Nipissing stage of Lake Michigan; it has been raised up there high above the Lake by a combination of water-level retreat and the slow isostatic rebound of an earth rid, after thousands of years, of the billion-ton dead weight of the engulfing ice.

These rather prosaic facts can be stored up ahead of time and read about in books. The visual impact of the place cannot. This is one of the most dramatic coastlines in North America, perhaps in the world. Rising almost directly from the surf behind a tiny striplet of beach, the face of Sleeping Bear heaves skyward like the flank of some enormous buff-colored animal, hulking and severe. To the north and south are more bluffs, more perched dunes on more morainal deposits, part of a great chain of which Sleeping Bear is merely the tallest; offshore lie two large islands, North and South Manitou, morainal likewise, bluff-ringed and dune-capped like the nearby shore. Viewed from the heights of any of these bluffs, the sunset is spectacular; viewed from water level, from South Bar lake or the little beach at the mouth of the Platte River, it is even more so. The sky flames; the black water and the light-colored bluffs reflect it. The sun sinks slowly, a round orange ball, quenching itself in the deep waters far out beyond the horizon. There is a breeze from the Lake and a smell of great distances. Talk falters and disappears because there is nothing to say that would not sound irreverent. The sun sinks in silence; the dark descends, and the sky is full of stars.

Because of its obvious attributes, the Sleeping Bear region has long been known as prime vacation country. Tourism is the major industry here, and has been at least since 1920, when a small part of the Dunes became D. H. Day State Park—the first state park in Michigan. Despite this unity of purpose, however, serious shore-use conflicts have boiled about Sleeping Bear for a long time, and they continue to simmer along today. These questions are ones of proportion. How much of the shoreline should be left in its natural state, and how much should be developed with motels and marinas and docks? How much beach should be public, and how much should be private? What developmental rights do private landowners have? When do these conflict with the rights of the public to have access to the dunes, to see unspoiled beachlines and bluff faces, to watch a river run unfettered over a natural bar and lose itself in the broad cold waters of a great fresh-water sea? How important are these conflicts? Who should resolve them, and how should they be resolved?

At the center of the storm over these questions lies a 60,000-acre federal preserve called Sleeping Bear Dunes National Lakeshore. It is a peaceful place, but it has had a remarkably contentious history. Though it was designated by an Act of Congress fifteen years ago —in 1970—it still exists mostly on paper. Two-thirds of the land within the Lakeshore boundaries remains in private hands. Development on those lands has been frozen by law pending their acquisition by the government, but that acquisition has been proceeding with agonizing slowness. Congress has authorized the purchase of the lands, but so far has failed to give anybody the money to follow through.

"It's a cloud over the land," says Sleeping Bear Resource Manager Max Holden. "We've got people who want to sell to the government, but we can't do a thing without money. But they can't do anything either, because there's been a restriction placed on their deeds that says that land use cannot change. So they can't develop it, and they can't sell it to us. It's a real catch-22 situation. What are they supposed to do?"

Needless to say, those deed restrictions have been challenged in court, on the grounds that they are what is legally referred to as a "taking without compensation": that the government has taken something away and given nothing in return, a clear violation of the search-and-seizure clause of the U.S. Constitution. The courts, however, have ruled the restrictions valid. Compensation, they have said, has been given—in the form of freedom for the landowners within the Lakeshore to remain on their lands as long as they want. A clause known as "category three" in the Lakeshore's enabling legislation forbids the condemnation of lands purchased before 1964, and Congress has since extended that right to all private lands within the preserve whatever their date of purchase. No one within the Lakeshore can be forced to give up his land if he doesn't want to. This "right to remain" is rather intangible, of course, but so is the right to develop. A right for a right seems fair enough. But if the land can be neither developed nor condemned, just what is supposed to be done with it?

"You know," muses Holden, "the basic idea of making a park out of private lands is a real problem. It was hard enough in Alaska, where the land was all public anyway. And on top of that, to make a park not just out of private land, but out of land with historic use patterns going way back—" He sighs. "I don't know. I think we're finding out that it's damn near impossible."

Sleeping Bear's problems are large, but they are unfortunately not unique. Everywhere preservation has been attempted along the Fifth Coast there has been the same pattern—the same private development, the same belated recognition of a public need, the same battle over the cause of preservation as a public good, the same agonizingly slow process of incomplete land acquisition within inadequately large boundaries. The root of the difficulty is the Lakes' ancient enemy: complacency. They still seem too big to damage. Why bother preserving anything when it is impossible to develop it all anyway? A comfortable attitude, but wrong: It is *not* impossible. Of the Great Lakes shoreline, 83 percent is in private ownership and subject to development at any time; 50 percent has already been developed. In some areas—Michigan's South Basin, the Ohio coastline, the east end of Ontario—nearly 90 percent has been developed. How much is too much?

At Indiana Dunes National Lakeshore, preservation was delayed long enough by infighting among politicians on various levels that the area was sundered by the Burns Harbor facility, with its steel mills and power plants and industrial docks. The fragmented National Lakeshore that remains is beleaguered and overcrowded; thousands of visitors every day jockey for a place in the sun, overrunning the surf, squeezing into the few square feet of natural shoreline left, and in the process damaging it seriously, perhaps irrevocably. "We have a 600-car parking lot at West Beach," laments Ron Hiebert. "Normally in the summer that will tend to be full. Surrounding that beach area we have some of our finest examples of ecosystem, and they're among all those people. They're just getting trampled."

At Grand Portage National Monument at the mouth of the Pigeon River on the Canada/Minnesota border, inadequate funding means that Park Headquarters must be located in rental quarters forty miles away. "In the winter," says Historic Specialist Don Carney, "you walk to work, and that's fine. In the summer you walk to work and then get in the car and drive forty miles. It gets old quick." There is no visitor center and, with an operations budget of barely $300,000 per year, little hope of one soon. "We've got a $1.2 million item for preliminary work in the budget," says Carney resignedly, "but with the deficit and all, it'll probably be knocked out."

At Apostle Islands National Lakeshore near Ashland, Wisconsin, the Interior Department itself—with James Watt then at its head— nearly perpetrated the greatest outrage of all: the resale back to private individuals of already purchased federal land within the boundaries of an admittedly inadequate park. The place was Sand Island;

the prospective buyers, a prominent midwestern family which had contributed heavily to Republican political campaigns. The family had once owned part of the island, had sold it to the government for use as part of the Lakeshore, and now wanted to buy it back. Mr. Watt was more than willing to sell; it took the combined pressure of an outraged public and an outraged Park Service to dissuade him.

"We got wind of it," recalls the Sierra Club's Jane Elder, "and we said, 'This man's out of his *mind.*' We've been trying for years to acquire these parklands, and now he's trying to sell them back to the very people we tried to acquire them from. Now, I have nothing against [the prospect purchasers]—but they have no more right to special privileges from the Interior Department than I do. And even if they did, where do you stop? If you were another landowner up there who had been bought off your property, or pushed off, or whatever else you want to call it—why wouldn't *you* have the right to come back? And pretty soon the parks aren't public parks any- more."

Apostle Islands Ranger Don Brown makes much the same point. "It would open a whole can of worms," he says. "Once land here was sold back, people in Yellowstone or Yosemite or Alaska could say, 'Hey, why not us, too?' Besides, what we need here in the Apostles is *more* land, not less. Look at Bear Island. We own most of the island, but we can't open it to the public. All the spits are privately owned and covered with NO TRESPASSING signs. There's no place to land. We don't even go near the place ourselves."

And even what is actually in Park Service hands—and has little problem remaining there—may be inadequately protected. It is not just things like James Watt's attempt to sell off the Apostle Islands; it is development within the Lakeshore themselves, under Lakeshore ownership. Much of this development is not desired by the Park Service, but it is likely to go ahead anyway.

At Sleeping Bear, the main reason the Lakeshore legislation was finally pushed through in 1970 was that the looming specter of mas- sive shoreline development seemed to be gathering itself to pounce; indeed, had—in too many places—suddenly done so. Within a few months of each other in late 1968, marinas, blacktopped parking lots, bulldozed roads, motels, and housing developments appeared in the three critical Lakeshore areas of South Bar Lake, Otter Creek, and the mouth of the Platte River. Local citizens were outraged; many of them, cool to the Park idea before, became strong and active supporters almost literally overnight. A Save Sleeping Bear committee was formed, with the Democratic and Republican party chairmen from Leelanau County acting as co-presidents. Lobbying shifted into high gear. Within eighteen months the Lakeshore bill was signed into law and the worst of the developments came tumbling down.

Now—though not in precisely the same places—they may have to go back up again.

The Lakeshore management has strived for a natural shoreline. That is their mandate from Congress; that is the way a national park, in general, should be run. But in doing so, they have run afoul of Michigan state law. The state requires developed Harbors of Refuge —safe, well-protected areas for storm moorage of small boats—every fifteen miles along the coastline. Since the Lakeshore is forty miles long, the law mandates that it have be not just one but two developed harbors—with all the submeanings the word "developed" entails.

"We wouldn't mind just building a dock," says Max Holden ruefully, "but that's not what they want. No one is hearing us. We're talking about a dock and people are hearing 'harbor.' It may happen like a juggernaut. We're saying we don't want the responsibility to provide overnight slips—we don't want to sell bait. But nobody's listening."

And so it goes. In the Pictured Rocks National Lakeshore in northern Michigan, inadequate roads and road signs—the fruit of a dubious relationship between the Park and surrounding Alger County—make travel almost impossibly difficult; in the Apostle Islands National Lakeshore the road and sign situation is similar. Coastal state parks—with the exception of those on Wisconsin's Door Peninsula, Minnesota's North Shore, and lower Michigan's Thumb—are widely spaced and poorly funded. That is the U.S. situation; in parts of Ontario the situation is somewhat better, but in other parts, it is much worse. From Bruce Mines to Walford—a distance of eighty-five miles—the Trans-Canada Highway remains within a few miles, and often within less than a mile, of Lake Huron. There are no Lakeside parks in this entire distance—not even a scenic turnout. The Lake is entirely bordered by private property through here; there is no public access. The highway might as well be a hundred miles from the shore. At no place along that splendidly scenic stretch of inland sea is the water even glimpsed.

In her basement office in Madison, Jane Elder props her elbows on her desk, laces her fingers, and rests her chin on them. "The trouble with the National Lakeshores," she says reflectively, "is that they aren't officially National Parks, and they aren't Seashores. They're Lakeshores, which is sort of an odd category. So they often get the short shrift of things. In terms of the National Park System they're really low on the totem pole. We're extremely close, with these areas, to many of the major population centers of the Midwest, and they are heavily used, and they ought to be given the same kind of consideration that the other units of the National Park System get. But in many cases their seasonal employees have all but been eliminated. We've had to fight all the way for acquisition. In Sleeping Bear Dunes, we have court orders that are almost five years old, and we're just now starting to pay them off. The people didn't know what to do with their land, because they didn't really own it, but they hadn't been paid for it either. And so local relations fester, and there's a lot of local bitterness in all these areas."

She sighs deeply. "We've missed so many opportunities. There's a really depressing book written in the late 1950's, a National Park Service document called *National Lakeshore Opportunities in the Great Lakes.* It lists all the places where there are open shorelines, and natural places of beauty. And one of them on Lake Erie was Cedar Point, near Sandusky. Cedar Point is now one of the biggest amusement parks in the Midwest. The things we've lost just in the last twenty years are nothing short of tragic. We're trying in Michigan to get a wilderness bill passed through Congress this session. And out of the public lands that are adjacent to the Great Lakes shoreline, there's only two areas that we can nominate for wilderness. That says something really sad about what's left."

XVII Superships

In the late morning of Friday, June 26, in the still-innocent year of 1959, a bald, elderly man and an attractive, dark-haired young woman stepped aboard the young woman's boat in the little Montreal suburb of St.-Lambert, on the southeast bank of the great St. Lawrence River. Five hours and twenty-six miles later, at the small upstream town of Beauharnois, they disembarked amid the popping of flashbulbs and the whirr of newsreel cameras. Dwight David "Ike" Eisenhower, President of the United States, and Her Most Royal Majesty Elizabeth II, Queen of Great Britain and Sovereign of the British Commonwealth, had just ridden the royal yacht *Britannia* through the lowest lock-and-canal section of the St. Lawrence Seaway; and the Seaway—more than 100 years in the planning, five years and nearly $500 million in the building (and with at least another $150 million planned for but not yet spent)—was now officially open for business.

There was a ceremony. Speaking partly in English and partly in excellent French, the Queen said that the Seaway was "bound to exercise a profound influence on the maritime trading nations of the world." Speaking mostly in English, with one sentence sort of in French, the President called it a "technical and commercial triumph" and a "magnificent monument to the enduring friendship of our two nations and to their partnership in the development of North America." From England, 81-year-old Poet Laureate John Masefield contributed a bit of doggerel for the occasion:

> . . . Today, this Nation offers to mankind
> This moment, when the passion in old foes
> Is blest and sublimated and combined
> To give Man's utmost for the best man knows. . . .

Great Lakes boosters, needless to say, were ecstatic. The Lakes, crowed historian Harlan Hatcher, were now "truly the 'Mediterranean of North America,' " connected to the sea by "a new wonder of the world . . . the fourth greatest engineering project ever completed." (He didn't identify the other three.) Canadian novelist Hugh MacLennan envisioned a "Laurentian empire along the former agricultural reaches of the upper river"; *The New York Times* spoke fulsomely of "a boundless prospect of trade and expansion" for the Lakes cities and central North America. These rhetorical flourishes were expected, inspiring, and inaccurate. Away from the ceremony, out there in the real world, the Seaway was already in deep, deep trouble.

Much of the trouble, there at the beginning, was little things: delays, minor accidents, unexpected side effects (one is tempted, after the Lakes' experience with lamprey invasions, spawning-stream warming, and so forth, to ignore the contradiction and speak of "the usual unexpected side effects," but let that pass). The Seaway had actually been in operation for more than eight weeks before the two heads of state dedicated it, and the inevitable shakedown was going on. The *Britannia* was not the first, but the 1,875th, ship to use the St.-Lambert locks; she passed through unscathed, but some of the others hadn't been so lucky. The very first vessel through, back at the Seaway's real opening on April 25—the Dutch freighter *Prins Wilhelm George Frederick*—had left a fair amount of her paint on the lock walls. Others had done more than just scrape paint. The day before the dedication, the new lock had been closed for several hours for emergency repairs, and there had been some question as to whether it would be operational for the *Britannia*'s passage. Up at the Welland earlier in the week, an accident in one of the locks had tied up Seaway traffic for most of a day. The salt-water skippers, unfamiliar with Lake and canal sailing conditions, were having their troubles. A ship loaded to the twenty-six-foot draft mark in a salt-water port will sink nearly a foot deeper in fresh water, untuning the fine maneuverability which the salties—used to being pushed around in harbors by tugs—weren't very good at anyway. Even as the Queen and the President spoke so glowingly near Montreal, the Liberian freighter *Monrovia* was foundering in Lake Huron off Alpena, Michigan; she had collided with the Canadian ore carrier *Royalton* the day before, and was well on her way to the fresh-water version of Davy Jones's locker.

More disturbing than these nautical mishaps, however—which had as yet caused no loss of life—was the economic impact of the Seaway system. This was very large, but it was not quite so large as its backers had hoped it would be, and it went off in some odd and unexpected directions. Foreign water-borne trade did indeed increase hugely, up from a pre-Seaway level of 750,000 tons per year (brought in by shallow-draft freighters through the original fourteen-foot-deep St. Lawrence lock and canal system) to 20 million tons during the Seaway's first year of operation. But the boomers had expected 25 million that first season, and the system had been designed for 80 million, a figure it has never come close to reaching then or since (the highest annual cargo figure so far recorded is 1977's 57.5 million tons, off the design maximum by nearly 30 percent). Great Lakes port cities did benefit—as expected—from the increase in trade, which offered greatly increased revenues as well as lending a dashing, cosmopolitan, seaboard flavor to certain bland Midwestern cities as the crews of foreign vessels went on leave (it was at this time that Duluth, Minnesota, became the United States' second leading seaport). But there were tradeoffs. To get their share of the new trade, Fifth Coast cities had to build millions of dollars' worth of new harbors and offloading facilities; though the Seaway had been constructed to a channel depth of twenty-seven feet, there were in 1959 only four ports that deep on the entire Great Lakes system.

To the consternation of shipowners, the American and Canadian shipping industries gained nearly nothing; almost all of the new trade came in foreign bottoms. Their operating costs were lower, so their rates could be cheaper. In his 1966 book *The Great Lakes Reader*, Ohio writer Walter Havighurst lamented this "hard new reality":

> Foreign shipbuilding costs are less than half the cost in this country, and there is a still greater difference in costs of vessel operation. On

a British ship under the Liberian flag Chinese seamen are paid fifty cents a day. At four hundred dollars a month a deckhand on an American freighter draws more than a captain on many foreign vessels. . . .

The trade itself was not all as welcome to the Lakes region as it might have been; it included foreign steel, foreign rubber, and—most insulting of all—foreign automobiles, which steamed right past Detroit and Windsor on their way to docks in Chicago and Milwaukee and Thunder Bay. And as a kind of crowning derisive blow to these millponds that dared to think of themselves as oceans, the vast majority of incoming "salties"—foreign and American alike—had no on-board facilities for handling human wastes. "Nineteen naval vessels that visited Milwaukee for the Seaway celebration had no sewage collection or storage system built in," pointedly complained Arve H. Dahl of the U.S. Public Health Service a short time after that celebration had departed for other ports. "Wastes discharged from these ships which carried 8,000 marines and sailors went directly into the Lake"—into already fouled Milwaukee Harbor.

The worst problem with the Seaway, however, was neither a matter of economics nor of minor physical mishaps—though it had a bearing on both. The worst problem was a matter of engineering. The Seaway, it rapidly became apparent, was underdesigned; it was based around a maximum ship length of only 730 feet and a maximum draft of just 25.5. By the time of the dedication ceremony these figures were already too small, and they have since become ludicrous. In 1959, more than 20 percent of the world's maritime fleet was barred from the Seaway and the Lakes beyond because of size. Today that figure has climbed to somewhere between 40 and 60 percent, and the Seaway is suffering from malnutrition. Tonnage figures have fallen off to 42 million tons per year, barely over half of design capacity. Seaway tolls—originally expected to retire construction costs quickly—do not even meet the system's current operating budget, despite several recent hikes. A few years ago the governments of Canada and the United States were forced to step in and "forgive" the Seaway's debt to them, absorbing the unpaid construction costs in order to keep the system in operation. This was a necessary but controversial move. "They call it a forgiving," fumed one opponent to me a few months later, "but we're stuck with it. The public gets stuck with that debt, nobody else does."

The answer to this problem strikes some people as ridiculously simple. If the Seaway is too small, why don't we just make it bigger? Replace those inadequate 800-foot locks with 1,200-footers; dredge the channels out to 32 feet instead of 27. Turn the Lakes into a nautical superhighway. That was the original design intent of the Seaway, after all. We fell unaccountably short of it the first time around. Let's do it over—and do it right this time.

Unfortunately, this approach is not so much simple as it is simple-minded. It ignores a whole host of complicating factors—beginning with the fact that we are dealing with Lakes, not shipping channels. They are not there just to move cargo across; they are sources of domestic water, too, and homes for fish and waterfowl, and public swimming holes, and the backdrop to some of the most stunningly scenic landscapes in North America. Can we afford to damage or even destroy these uses, just to get a few more salties to Duluth?

Take just the question of channel deepening. Leaving aside the several billion dollars it would cost—what would we do with the material from the channel bottoms? We're having enough trouble with the dredge spoil from merely maintaining the channels and harbors at twenty-seven feet. What happens if we go to thirty-two? It will be the same in-place pollutants problem that we already have, but magnified thousands of times. What, if one is sane, can one possibly do with the top five feet of the bed of the Detroit River?

The thought terrifies environmentalists. "Oh, God, if they ever dredge the Detroit River—!" shudders the Sierra Club's Jane Elder. "That's part of the problem with some of these things. It's awful that it's down there, but it might be worse to bring it back up." The Detroit has the distinction, along with Waukegan Harbor and Hamilton Harbour and Indiana Harbor, of having one of the four worst in-place–pollutants problems in the Great Lakes system. Generations of municipal sewage deposits, of factory wastes coming down the Rouge River, and of shipping spills—small, mostly, but cumulative—have turned what was once among the most beautiful of American rivers into a thing little better than a refuse pit. Nearly every contaminant known to science has been found in the Detroit's sediments at one time or another, often in large amounts. A comprehensive 1981 study by the Ontario Ministry of the Environment, for example, found PCBs in excess of water-quality standards at 78 percent of all bottom sites sampled—and mercury excesses in 34 percent of them. "You go in and dredge," points out Elder, "and what happens is a couple of things. You dredge up the bottom sediments, you resuspend all that stuff—it gets up into the water systems, in the water that the fish are essentially breathing—plus, it goes downstream. But the Detroit River's one of the most critical links in the navigation system. So you've *got* to dredge it out, which suspends it in the water, and sends it down to our poor friends in Lake Erie, as well as the whole river downstream. And the other thing you've got —again—is a bunch of toxic sludge that nobody wants to landfill." It recently took the Michigan Department of Transportation nine years and $30 million to find a home for the dredge spoil from 250 acres of Saginaw Bay. What is going to be done with several hundred thousand times that amount? Who is going to do it? So far, no one has come up with any answers.

There are other problems. "You deepen the channels, you increase the flow," Elder points out. "It flows faster. So you end up with more shoreline erosion. And the faster the flow goes, the more the bottom gets scoured, which keeps the sediments suspended longer. Which may or may not be good—it cleans up the local area faster, but it just moves the problem downstream again. And you have increased destruction of wetland habitat, and the whole thing gets more and more like a gigantic shipping channel." She flashes a dazzling smile. "We're not *opposed* to shipping on the Great Lakes. I mean, it would be sort of silly to be opposed to shipping. But it's a question of how appropriate *big* shipping is, and there's a limit to how much we should spend, as a society, in money and also in the Great Lakes environment, to ship on the Great Lakes."

Others besides environmentalists oppose the development of larger shipping channels. Small shipping firms dislike the idea because, by encouraging the use of 1,000-foot ships, it would make the industry too top-heavy for their firms to survive. A 700-foot ship, they point out, can hold roughly 30,000 tons of cargo; a 1,000-footer can hold more than twice that amount, so the 1,000-footer is therefore considerably more efficient, and is likely to nose out its 700-foot competition. And unfortunately, the bigger vessels are so costly to build and operate that only a few firms—usually conglomerates for which shipping is only a sideline—can afford them. The smaller firms would be driven out of business, idling workers and equipment and destabilizing the industry.

Railroads and trucking firms are also opposed to the superships, for reasons similar to those of the small shipping firms. Government construction of 1,200-foot locks and thirty-five-foot-deep channels, they point out, amounts to a multi-billion-dollar subsidy to the shipping industry, giving it a competitive advantage it does not deserve over rail and highway transit. The shipowners admit freely that they can't afford to enlarge the channels and locks themselves. Should any industry be allowed to operate—at public expense—at a level above its own ability to capitalize? Railroad executives and their employees, as they are fond of pointing out, pay taxes, too. Is it fair for the government to use those taxes to subsidize their competition?

Waterfront property owners along the Seaway and the Lakes fear the increased erosion that would result from the passage of the bigger ships. Fishermen fear the potential destruction of spawning grounds and disruption of breeding cycles on reefs subjected to significantly deeper wakewash. And the smaller Lakes ports look aghast at the money involved. It would cost so much to upgrade port facilities to handle 1,000-foot-long ships, they argue, that only those cities that already have extensive harbors would be able to do so. The 1,000-footers, owned by only a few firms, would call at only a few ports. Those fortunate few would make a killing; the rest of the Fifth Coast would plunge even further into depression than it is now.

Still another issue has been raised by Great Lakes shipping historian Frederick Stonehouse: safety. "The new 1000-foot class lake freighter is an example of technology and the bulk carrier concept gone wild," he wrote in 1977.

It is my personal belief that the 1000-foot (and many of the smaller 800 plus footers) pose an entirely new set of safety problems. For one thing, they are so large that they can't get into many ports or protected areas, forcing them to remain "outside" in heavy weather instead of seeking shelter. The new carriers are far too large to use the Keweenaw Waterway (The Portage Lake Ship Canal) and must make the long exposed run around the Keweenaw Peninsula. . . .

Supership promoters counter these arguments with some of their own. They do not argue that there will not be some social costs involved, but they insist that the benefits of increased efficiency will be worth it. "We have thirteen one-thousand-footers now," says Glen Nekvasil of the Lake Carriers' Association in Cleveland. "It's true that they're built basically for the head-of-the-Lakes trade, and they're not as versatile as the smaller ships. But I've been unaware of a lot of problems. Of course, since they have diesel they require a lot more maintenance. You have as many people on a thousand-footer in the winter as you do when you're sailing, just doing maintenance. But they'll carry a tremendous amount, up to sixty-six thousand tons or more in one load. So for the trade they were built for they're extremely efficient." And Margaret Downs of the Northeast-Midwest Institute, in a 1983 position paper prepared for the Center for the Great Lakes in Chicago, argues that duplication of existing locks by 1,000-footers—the so-called "second lock" concept—would "increase the efficiency of the . . . [Seaway] system, and would provide a contingency in the event of mechanical failure or sabotage. . . . This year, vessel traffic waited nine hours while a valve failure prevented the Poe [lock at Sault Ste. Marie] from opening at the beginning of the navigation season."

All of which is undoubtedly valid, but I remain unconvinced. Partly this is because I sense, with the environmentalists, that the costs will be greater than the benefits; partly it is because I fear, as Frederick Stonehouse does, that the safety issues have been inadequately addressed. Mostly, though, it is because I wonder about those economic arguments. It is not just those called into question by the railroads and the smaller shipping firms that bother me; it is the even more fundamental issue of need. Why are we talking about increasing the system capability when we aren't using it to full capability as it is? How in the world can we justify *that*?

I know the arguments: The system is not being used to capacity because its substandard design prevents modern ships from using it fully, and anyway, the current downturn is not the shippers' fault but the fault of the economy in general. "We're not depressed right now because we have antiquated facilities, or antiquated vessels, or old docks," insists Glen Nekvasil. "We're down because of the recession. When domestic steel production comes back up—power production

—Canada gets going again—you're going to see the Lakes rebound. So what we're saying is—don't mess this up. We're only in a temporary situation."

One hopes that Nekvasil is correct, but the arguments—*as arguments in favor of larger ships and larger channels*—miss the point. Even at its peak, in 1977, Lakes traffic never approached the design capabilities of the current system. It has the ability to handle roughly half again as much cargo as it has ever handled historically, and to do so without any alterations whatsoever. Under those circumstances, talk of alterations seems at best premature. What is needed is not a commitment to build more or larger locks. What is needed is a commitment to build more ships that fit the current ones.

And even if the supership proponents are right and the benefits of 1,000-foot ships outweigh the damages that would be caused by accommodating the Lakes to them, there is still one thing that bothers me. Suppose we go ahead and absorb the costs, do the work, and construct the enlarged system. Suppose we "rebuild the Lakes," as the Detroit *Times* once aptly put it. *What is to guarantee us that once this is done it, too, won't prove obsolete?* Shippers are now saying that the St. Lawrence Seaway was antiquated before it opened. Are we to spend between $10 and $20 billion—the rough cost parameters agreed upon by both supporters and critics—to come up with another obsolete system? If so, what is the point? Already naval architects speak longingly of 1,300-foot Lakes vessels with fifty-foot drafts. Longer and deeper ones—1,400-footers drawing more than ninety feet—have been built for the ocean trade. If we build locks and channels for 1,000-footers with thirty-foot drafts, what is to stop the shippers from demanding them for the 1,400-footers and whatever else lies beyond? When does greater size stop being an asset and start being a liability? Who is to judge?

If you build a boat long enough, it becomes a bridge.

And there is another issue, too, concerning the big ships—one that is not usually brought up in conjunction with them but that belongs there, anyway. The issue is winter navigation—the extension of the navigation season from its current eight-month April-to-December length to eleven months, or even year-round.

Shippers try to divorce the two issues: In fact, the Lake Carriers' Association's official position is in support of the superships but in opposition to winter navigation. While the Carriers, according to LCA President George J. Ryan, "firmly oppose arbitrarily closing the locks each December 15 without first considering the technical, economic and environmental needs of the world we live in today," year-round navigation "was not sought by [the] Lake Carriers' Association and does not have our support. . . . compelling questions must be answered regarding the environmental and economic feasibility of year-round navigation." The season extensions are desirable in some seasons, Ryan maintains, but they should not be blindly instituted as a general rule.

Very well. The position is admirably stated and well considered. One is left, however, contemplating the question of how long it will last. The fact is that ships, harbor facilities, and so forth represent a huge capital investment—and the bigger the ship, the bigger the investment. When the ship is not operating, that investment is sitting idle. Idle capital is an anathema to any business. How long will the owners of 1,000-foot ships hold to that admirable position on winter navigation? How will they defend it to their stockholders?

It is a fact, which must be noted here, that virtually every 1,000-footer constructed so far has been built with icebreaking capabilities. It requires quite a stretch of the imagination to presume that the extra money spent on those capabilities was done merely so the shipowners would be prepared should winter navigation be eventually forced upon them against their will.

Winter navigation is a complex, difficult subject. More than just icebreaking is involved; there are also air-bubbler systems to keep harbors open, and booms to deflect broken pack ice from sensitive shorelines, and (in some incarnations) gates on the St. Clair and Detroit rivers to prevent stray ice floes from coming down from Lake Huron in droves and interfering with the busiest shipping channel in America. There is also the safety issue: Winter is a time of intense storms on the Lakes, storms capable of throwing up thirty- to forty-foot waves, big enough to swamp even a supership. It was a storm of this nature in 1975 that sank the 26,000-ton, 726-foot *Edmund Fitzgerald* in the deep Lake Superior waters off Whitefish Bay, with the loss of all twenty-nine men aboard. How many companions will the *Fitz* and her crew have if winter navigation becomes a regular thing? Under the experimental season-extension programs of the 1970's, the principal winter cargoes—in addition to iron-ore pellets—were chemicals and fuels. These are the most dangerous cargoes of all, from an environmental standpoint. The shippers seemed to be selectively raising the proportion of hazardous cargoes they were carrying during the most hazardous sailing system—a process that hardly reflects favorably on the intelligence of the human race.

"I have a lot of problems with winter navigation," says DuWayne Gebken of the Wisconsin Department of Natural Resources. "And the problems I have are interrelated to a number of other things. You see, when you look at winter navigation, that justifies something else, and that justifies something else, and that justifies something else—and our problem is that we look at these things as though they were isolated, not interconnected. We look for catastrophes. We don't look at the subtle little things that happen in combination with other things that add up to something.

"Let me give you an example. Let's assume that we're looking at the worst possible catastrophe—an oil spill over the Gull Island Shoals in the Apostle Islands. That's a spawning area for Lake trout, whitefish, and Lake herring. It's a very strong genetic stock, it's been around for a long, long time, it hasn't been tampered with—it's withstood the depredations of lampreys, and fishing, and all kinds of things, and it's still there. So an oil spill over it would be disastrous. OK—it very well could happen, I'm not trying to discount the possibilities of that. But rather than spending all that time looking at it, we should be taking what I call a 'sideways' approach—one where we would ask the question, 'What kind of subtle things am I missing that I haven't even thought of?'

"For instance, one of the things that's necessary for winter navigation is bubbler systems to keep the harbors open. Let's say we put one of those in Duluth-Superior Harbor. That's an area that's used for spawning by the burbot—the freshwater codfish. And it spawns in the wintertime, as it happens, in the early winter. Well, suppose the bubbler system interferes with the burbot's desire to go up there and spawn, so it starts failing in its population, and there's fewer burbots. So what does that mean? Well, it so happens that the burbot is a predator on the sculpin. The sculpin lives in rockpiles out in the Lake, in the crevices, and preys on Lake trout eggs; the Lake trout comes along and lays its eggs, and the eggs fall down there into the rocks and crevices, and there's a sculpin down there eating them up. OK. Do you see the connection? Fewer burbot—more sculpin— fewer Lake trout. And it may not be due to an oil spill, it may be due to something else. It's simply that you haven't thought out the problem of what all the relationships are."

The winter ecosystem of the Lakes is a different thing from the summer ecosystem—and no one knows precisely where those differences lie or how they relate with one another. ("It's a virtual black hole," complains Gebken. "We don't know what's going on down there. I don't know that we ever could.") The winter shoreline conditions vary greatly from the summer ones, with fewer plants to hold down the soils, and greater waves to wash them away; ice thrown against the shore from the wakes of winter ships may be a far greater erosion hazard than the waves themselves. Shelf ice out from the shore may protect it from erosion—or it may simply funnel the waves underneath it, causing greater erosion just below the ice line. No one knows. No one knows what effects ship movement will have on winter-spawning fish, or what effects keeping a channel open through the St. Marys River will have on wildlife accustomed to using the iced-over river as a bridge. Most of these things have been studied, but only from the straight-line, catastrophic point of view; no one has, in Gebken's terms, looked "sideways" at the situation.

And the situation—looked at sideways—goes far beyond the direct engineering and environmental impacts. There are a whole set of subimpacts growing from it like flowers opening after a spring rain. "With the year-round thing," muses Gebken, "you're talking about a lot more ice, and a lot more engineering measures. Well, OK. But it doesn't stop there. There will obviously be, as a result of that, increased economic development—and as a result of that there will be more demands upon the waterfront area, and the wetlands, and things of that sort that people will want for development—and concomitantly with that there will be discharges and poor-quality complications. And then you add the possibilities of mining in the bed for mineral deposits, and add to that the Connecting Channels Project [the official name for the 32-foot channel-deepening scheme], and add to that increased fishing pressure—the boats transport commercial fishermen—and add to that the possibility of radioactive waste disposal somewhere in the north—and eventually you have to begin to wonder how many things you can add without having problems."

Nobody wants to eliminate shipping on the Great Lakes. No-body wants to go back to the days of clipper schooners. As Jane Elder points out, it would be ludicrous even to try. But somewhere along the line, we are going to have to draw the line at more. Sometime —*now*—we must decide how many other uses of the Lakes get subordinated to shipping. Are 1,300-foot ships sailing stoically through winter waves compatible with our concept of what the Fifth Coast means to us?

Go out the long, narrow road to Whitefish Point, at the mouth of Whitefish Bay in upper Michigan, some day soon. Sit on the low dune above the beach, as Rod Badger and I did, among the winds and the sawgrass and the soft gray mists, listening to the sound of surf and gulls and the big muted diapason of the Whitefish Point foghorn, gazing out to sea across the Superior Ocean to the point out there, somewhere off beyond the horizon, where the *Edmund Fitzgerald* fought a Great Lakes winter storm—fought, lost, broke apart, and died—not so many years ago. Listen. Watch the breakers, smell the breeze, feel the sawgrass move about you. Listen. Think.

XVIII Pipes

Everything is connected; nothing is separated. All things that happen affect other things. There are no islands. The measurements of dredged channels and harbors along the Great Lakes coast line are determined partly by the shape of ships sailing out of England and Greece and Liberia; the amount of pesticide residue dissolved in Lake Ontario is determined partly by the need for mosquito control in Central America and Indonesia and the Philippines. The demand for automobiles in Los Angeles affects the amount of steel produced in Hammond, Indiana, and that in turn affects the level of cyanide in the waters of Lake Michigan. An event —any event—is like a stone dropped into a quiet pond. The localized splash is immediate; the ripples continue to spread outward long after the stone has sunk from sight.

On June 10, 1982, an extraordinary conference was convened at the genteel old Grand Hotel on the former fur-trading outpost of Mackinac Island in northern Lake Huron. The principal conferees were the chief executives of five of the ten Great Lakes states and provinces—Governor William G. Milliken of Michigan, Governor Albert H. Quie of Minnesota, Governor Lee S. Dreyfus of Wisconsin, Governor Robert D. Orr of Indiana, and Premier William G. Davis of Ontario. Official representatives of Governor Hugh L. Carey of New York and Premier René Lévesque of Quebec were also present. The seven officials had gathered to consider seriously for the first time a problem that would probably have seemed totally unthinkable to an outsider: the very real possibility that someone might soon actually try to drain the Great Lakes.

Drain the Great Lakes? It sounds like a fantasy—a science-fiction scheme, an engineer's wet dream, an environmentalist's nightmare after a midnight snack of pickles and spumoni. It is not; it is real. It is quite literally a pipe dream in that it is a dream of pipes, but it is no fantasy. It is, in a sense, not even new. As long ago as 1927, the State of Illinois and the City of Chicago were sued by the State of New York on the grounds that the diversion of Lake Michigan water into the Mississippi through the Chicago Sanitary and Ship Canal was lowering water levels throughout the Great Lakes system; settled in 1930, this suit was resurrected in 1959 by Minnesota, Wisconsin, Michigan, Ohio, and Pennsylvania, with the argument that completion of the St. Lawrence Seaway had substantially negated the previous settlement. (This resurrected suit has yet to be fully dealt with; at least one party—Wisconsin—continues quixotically to pursue it, "I guess to prove our tenacity," as one state official puts it.) In the 1960's, construction of a "Grand Canal" from Duluth to Minneapolis was proposed in order to use Lake Superior water to augment the declining flow of the Mississippi; and since at least the early 1970's there have been mutterings from the arid states of the southwestern Sun Belt (which Great Lakes residents usually insist on referring to as the "Parch Belt" or the "Thirst Belt") that water from the Great Lakes should be used to ease their rapidly developing water shortages. Except for the Chicago diversions, though—which are relatively minor, and which are more than balanced by diversions *into* the system down Lake Superior's Nipigon and Aguasabon rivers of waters that Nature had designed to flow into Hudson Bay—these schemes have always been sheer speculation, idle fantasies with which sane men could while away their time as they contemplated more realistic solutions to their various water problems. What gave the conference on Mackinac its peculiar urgency was that for the first time something more than speculation had surfaced. On August 28, 1981, at a coal-export conference in Duluth, Vice-President William J. Westhoff of the Powder River Pipeline Company of Billings, Montana, had announced that his company would seek permits to build a 1,925-mile, $2.2-billion coal-slurry pipeline to transport low-sulfur coal from mines in eastern Montana to transshipping facilities on Lake Superior. A coal-slurry pipeline moves coal by crushing it to a fine powder, mixing it with large amounts of water, and pumping the water with its suspended coal particles through large-diameter pipes. Montana law forbids the use of its scarce state waters for slurry transport, so the 10,000 or so cubic feet per second needed for the project would have to come from someplace else. Westhoff's somewhat surprising announcement was that he expected it to come from the Great Lakes.

At Mackinac, the conferees listened soberly to testimony by civil engineer Jonathan Bulkeley of the University of Michigan, who said that the diversions sought by Powder River Pipeline would cost the Great Lakes states at least $115 million per year in lost revenues from navigation and energy production. They heard attorney Robert H. Abrams of Detroit remind them of the old adage that "opportunity flows with water like water." Sitting on the old frame hotel's huge Victorian veranda—the "longest porch in the world"—they posed for informal group pictures. At the end of the conference they released—as expected—a joint statement, condemning in no uncertain terms any and all schemes for out-of-Basin transport of Great Lakes water. That water, they said, should be used for economic development within the Basin, not sold to assist rival developments elsewhere. As Wisconsin's Dreyfus remarked, somewhat pointedly, "The only water we should send out of here ought to go out in cans with malt and barley and hops."

That was the official line. Unofficially, however—and also as expected—there was another, somewhat more troubling line. It showed up unmistakably at the joint press conference held on the day of the governors' departure, where it was expressed best by Michigan's Milliken: Water, he said, "will become for the Midwest what oil was for OPEC." Nearby, Ontario's Davis nodded his head in agreement. "Have you ever considered," he asked rhetorically, "what the Great Lakes would be worth at $25 a barrel?"

Officially, the governors' position on Great Lakes water was firm; as Lee Dreyfus's successor in Wisconsin, Anthony S. Earl, has since put it, "Keep it clear and keep it here." Unofficially, though, it was even firmer: Keep it clear and keep it here *until and unless someone bids high enough for us to turn a good profit on the deal.*

Would that someone turn out to be the Powder River Pipeline Company? Probably not. It was apparent, however, that the governors and the premier were not really looking at the Powder River Pipeline Company. They were looking south and west, beyond the Mississippi, out to the High Plains region of Nebraska and Kansas and Texas and Colorado and Oklahoma—the continental breadbasket, that huge slice of middle America transected by the 100th meridian and irrigated from the Ogallala Aquifer. The Ogallala was about to go belly-up, and the governors and the premier sensed a bonanza in the making.

The Ogallala Aquifer is a U.S. national treasure—a genuine liquid asset, an immense underground reservoir of fresh water lying a few feet below the parched earth of the High Plains from South Dakota south to New Mexico and the Texas panhandle. It is 700 miles long, 300 miles wide, and up to a quarter of a mile deep, and once upon a not-so-long-ago time it contained roughly three billion acre-feet of water. It was the presence of the Ogallala that led High Plains residents, in the decades following World War II, to a virtually complete commitment to irrigated agriculture. In 1950, less than seven million acre-feet per year were being pumped out of the ground in that seven-state region; by 1980, the figure had risen to well over 21 million. That is the water used, among other things, to grow your hamburger. Forty percent of American beef cattle are feedlot-raised on corn irrigated by Ogallala water. Without it, food prices would rise dramatically—and food availability would be nowhere near what it is today.

And we may have to do without it soon. Originally, the Ogallala was thought to be part of a vast "underground river" running from the Rocky Mountains to the Gulf of Mexico, perpetually renewing itself in the manner of all rivers everywhere. This is false. The Ogallala, it has now been demonstrated conclusively, is an underground storage tank rather than an underground river; it is—to use hydrologist's terms—a "non-recharge system." Enough water is being drawn from it to lower the static level in High Plains wells by ten feet each year. Only half an inch is trickling back in. The bulk of the water in the Ogallala is three million years old; it is a lode of fossil water,

left over from before the Ice Age, and it is being mined. In fact, it
is being mined out. By the year 2020, according to current predic-
tions, it will be all gone.

What then will become of all that investment in irrigated agriculture?

The answer is brutally obvious. Either irrigated agriculture will
cease, or another means will be found to provide water to the High
Plains. High Plains residents—for understandable reasons—would
prefer the latter course. Pumps and pipelines, many of them feel, will
do the job. The source to be tapped by the pumps and pipelines?
That's a relatively easy question to answer, too. Once upon a time,
the Ogallala contained almost exactly as much water as Lake Huron.
The obvious thing to replace it with is—Lake Huron.

Can this be done? Technologically, the answer is yes. The knowledge exists; the hardware can be built. It would be perfectly possible
today to construct the necessary pipes and the necessary pumps and
start the water flowing. *Will* it be done? Here the answer is much
less certain. There would be immense costs involved—economic and
otherwise. Would the benefits of having all that water on the High
Plains outweigh the costs of getting it there? Who is to judge—High
Plains residents or Fifth Coast residents? What grounds are they to
use? Whose authority will oversee the transfer, and under what legal
framework? Whose water is it, anyway?

To some, these procedural stumbling blocks in the way of large-
scale diversion of Great Lakes water seem overwhelming. Jane Elder,
for example, finds the likelihood of out-of-basin transfer remote. "It's
a good rallying point," she says, "because it's easy for everyone to be
against, at least here in the Great Lakes Basin. From just about
everybody's viewpoint the Great Lakes are fully committed to being
the Great Lakes. And the Great Lakes Governors have come together and said they're not going to let it go west, and Canada would
just throw fits if we diverted it west, and upstate New York would
have problems—so I think that there's such a natural political alliance
against major diversions that it's not likely to happen, certainly not
in the next decade." And in Chicago, the Environmental Protection
Agency's Kent Fuller makes essentially the same points. "I must
admit I personally think it's a great issue to organize governors
around," he sighs, "but it's just hard for me to imagine that it can

happen. There are two nations involved. And looking at the long history of litigation over diversions from the Chicago River, which is *minute* compared to what they're talking about to recharge the Ogallala, or transport coal, or whatever it is—I just can't imagine that there won't be a hundred years of litigation before you can divert any significant amount away."

Others, however, are much less confident. "It scares the hell out of me," admits Ohio State University's Charles Herdendorf. "It's happening today in the Soviet Union," points out limnologist and large-lakes specialist Wayland Swain—the former head of the EPA's Grosse Ile lab near Detroit—"so it's technically feasible. If we can move six billion gallons of oil a day across Alaska, we can certainly pipe Lake Superior water one hundred sixty miles to the Mississippi or four hundred miles to the Missouri. It will simply be a function of the amount of pressure brought—and if the Ogallala dries up, the pressure may be extreme. If you've ever been thirsty, you know how much you'll pay for a glass of water."

Northern Michigan University biologist Bill Robinson says much the same thing as Swain and Herdendorf. "Diversion may not be a threat now," he told me one late July Sunday in 1983 as we watched the Lake Superior surf pound onto the stony beach at Little Presque Isle Point near the university's Marquette campus, "but after a crop failure or two I think it will be a real threat. You know, it's going to be a tough argument—to see people starving and say you still have to keep the water in Lake Superior. People say it's 'just eight inches off the top,' but then it will be another eight inches, and another eight inches, and another—once you get started, it's so much more difficult to stop. And how much is eight inches of Lake Superior worth, anyway? Some people have proposed that several billion dollars be deposited in a bank somewhere by the states that want our water, so that Michigan can get the interest. But what would the money be used for? If it's used to mitigate the loss of the water, fine; but what if it's used for things that cause more environmental degradation? These things can get to feed on each other."

Or, as Swain once put it in an article on diversions for the *Detroit Free Press:* "Never underestimate the power of environmental stupidity."

Another student of Great Lakes issues who is afraid for the future is DuWayne Gebken of the Wisconsin Department of Natural Resources—and that is particularly significant, because it is the Wisconsin DNR that is likely to bear the brunt of the work of handling permits for long-distance transport of Great Lakes water. "I think there's a substantial possibility that it will happen," he told me gloomily one fine summer day in his Madison office. "Particularly when you look at the development in the southwestern part of the United States—and I don't mean commercial development, but just pure migration of people. The political power is shifting to the southwest. They're the ones that will need the water—and as a consequence, I think the day may come when they'll try to take it."

There will be legal barriers thrown in their way, of course. The State of Indiana has already passed a law forbidding the transfer of Lake Michigan water beyond state boundaries, and other states are considering similar legislation. There have been attempts made by nearly every congressman and senator from the Great Lakes region to gain passage of a federal law covering the same thing. U.S. courts have recently ruled—in a Nebraska case followed with almost obscene interest by every water activist in the Great Lakes region—that coal-slurry pipelines are not utilities and thus have no power to condemn land, which should slow down *that* particular aspect of water-robbing for a while. And there is—not incidentally—the international factor. Canada owns roughly half the Lakes, and that half is not likely to go anywhere without a fight. "You can't have our water," says the IJC's Pat Bonner in Windsor. "It's that simple. As far as Canadians are concerned, the treaty protects them. The Boundary Waters Treaty protects their access to that water. Political will may dumbfound and bind up that possibility, but not for at least fifty years, in my mind."

One extremely basic controversy that remains almost unaddressed is the question of the actual legal ownership of Great Lakes water. Surface navigation rights, Jane Elder points out, are "owned by the federal government. The bottom lands under the Lakes—I'm speaking here of the United States portion—are owned by the states. But the question of who actually owns what you could call the volume of water has in many cases not really been settled. It's hard to decide whether it's state water, or federal water, or whether it belongs to the local municipalities." On that point alone several hundred lawyers could probably easily make a living for the next fifty years.

Gebken admits all this, but he still remains skeptical. "I think we've got several factors working against us here," he says when legal barriers such as these are brought up. "One is the movement of political power to the Southwest, and the increasing economic power the Southwest has versus the diminished economic power that the upper Midwest has. Another thing is the commerce clause of the Constitution, and the right of Congress to regulate economic development between the states. I think there's a reasonable chance that the federal government may side with moving that water out of there. And the third thing is—we have no apparent use for that water. We don't, quote, 'put it to a productive use,' end quote. The fact that it's *there* isn't recognized as a productive use. And as a consequence of that, we may be paying a penalty in the long run for having foregone some short-term economic gains to simply save this for the future, and have it stolen away."

Or, as Tim Weston of the Pennsylvania Department of Environmental Protection put it to me in Pittsburgh, "If we have no reason to want the water, we have no excuse for building the fence."

The results of what Gebken has termed "stealing"—if it should indeed take place—would be frightening. Wetlands would dry up; nearshore water tables would draw down. Shoreline currents would be affected, altering erosion and deposition patterns. "There's a definite correlation between wetlands and lake levels," says the Indiana Dunes' Ron Hiebert. "A ten-foot drop would pretty well start a whole new series. Sandbars would become exposed, and a whole new set of sandbars would have to develop before the area would stabilize. The impact would be drastic. I don't think we understand how much." Agrees Jane Elder: "You'd just incredibly alter the shorelines, and what could live in the Lakes, and probably in many ways their capabilities to sustain and cleanse themselves. I don't think we can afford to do it."

The flow of water over Niagara Falls would diminish by an amount roughly equivalent to that withdrawn by the out-of-basin pipes, seriously affecting the Falls' ability to produce electrical power. (Only half of Niagara's natural flow of roughly 210,000 cubic feet per second currently goes over the Falls; the rest goes down penstocks and through turbines to make electricity with. The reductions due to diversion would have to come, at least at first, entirely from this "hidden Niagara" of penstocks and turbines. In order to keep the Falls falling and the tourists happy, international treaty forbids reduction of the river's flow beneath 105,000 cfs.) In Lake Superior, much of the layer of asbestos fibers deposited by the Western Reserve Mining Company over the entire west end of the Lakebed between 1968 and 1980—currently in the process of being covered over safely by sediments—would be exposed to wave action and come uncovered again. There would be less red-clay erosion on Wisconsin's north coast—a plus—but that would mean less materials in the water for chemicals to sorb to, and thus more chemicals in the water, and that would be a substantial minus. "My guess is the effects on Superior will be both positive and negative," says Wayland Swain, "and what the net balance will be I'm not sure, and I don't think anybody else is, either."

Hardest hit of all would probably be the navigation industry. Lowered water levels mean shallower shipping channels, and this in turn means that ships cannot be loaded as deeply—which means that they cannot be run as profitably. Recent studies by the U.S. Army Corps of Engineers have concluded that for every inch the water level in the Lakes is lowered beneath the current twenty-seven-foot shipping-channel depth, Lakes shippers will lose more than $200 million in shipping fees. For a time these losses could probably be staved off by increased dredging, but this dredging would be horrendously expensive—both economically and environmentally. It must be remembered that we are speaking here of the floors of industrial harbors and shipping channels—the most heavily polluted sediments in the Great Lakes system. We have already discussed what impacts deepening those channels and harbors would have on the water quality of the Lakes. If the level of the Lakes were permanently lowered, just keeping the channels at their current depth would do the same thing.

"We can't allow it to happen," emphasizes the Lake Carriers' Association's Glen Nekvasil. "I feel sorry for the people out in Arizona—but we claim that the best way to utilize Great Lakes water is to keep it here, rather than selling it someplace else. Of course, it's regionalism. But this is important to our part of the country. We don't want to see ourselves run dry, so that another section of the country can prosper." And Nekvasil's boss, Lake Carriers' Association President George J. Ryan, has said much the same thing. In a statement prepared for IJC hearings on diversions and consumptive use held—not coincidentally—at the same time as the governors' conference on Mackinac, Ryan wrote:

> . . . while willing to share the wealth, we will not allow the health of our region and industries to be weakened by indiscriminate siphoning of our life's blood. We need to develop strict but fair guidelines for future consumption levels *now*, before we have a water crisis which rivals the oils crisis of the 1970's. Time and again, elected officials from our region have put aside party labels and united behind the stance that the long-term economic interests of this region will be best served by *selling the availability* of Great Lakes water *rather than selling the water itself* for agriculture and industry elsewhere.

"It would be wild to move Great Lakes water, and Great Lakes jobs, and Great Lakes agriculture, over and down in the country," sums up Jane Elder. "But we ought to, in this country, be taking a serious look at what the natural resource base is—what we can do with it, and what the most appropriate use for that land is—instead of trying to figure out how to make the desert bloom when maybe it shouldn't be blooming."

But there is another problem, too—one that, in the Great Lakes Basin's jingoistic rush to protect its water from the grasping hands of its neighbors to the west, is often ignored. We don't have to "move the Great Lakes over and down," as Elder puts it, to get the unfortunate results pictured by Elder and Hiebert and Swain and Ryan and Nekvasil. It is entirely possible that the Great Lakes Basin will be able to do it quite adequately all by itself.

There are two ways to use water. You can withdraw it, use it for a while, and then return it—or you can withdraw it and use it up. This "consumptive use," as it is called, will remove water from the Lakes and lower their levels every bit as surely as will shipping it off to Montana or Arizona or the Ogallala Aquifer. Currently, consumptive use of Great Lakes water is roughly the equivalent of an out-of-basin diversion of 4,900 cubic feet per second; recent studies by a special committee appointed by the International Joint Commission suggest that the next two decades will see that equivalence rise more than sevenfold, to 36,500 cubic feet per second. Add in diversions of Lakes water out of the Great Lakes *Basin* but still within the Great Lakes *states*—which no state has yet come out in opposition to—and real trouble begins to develop. The IJC committee's 1982 report indicated that this trouble may show up in Lake Ontario as a water-level drop of as much as thirteen feet within the next fifty years.

Where would the water go? The report suggests several possibilities. Municipal and rural/domestic water consumption—water that is drunk or otherwise taken out of the system by households and businesses—is expected to more than double, from 1,200 cubic feet per second today to more than 3,000 cfs by 2035. Water consumption by livestock and by the mining industry is also expected to approximately double. Irrigation and manufacturing water use will roughly quadruple—the former from 350 cfs to 1,200, the latter from its current 2,500 cfs to a whopping 14,200. That is process water, and cooling water lost to evaporation, and water incorporated into manufactured items such as Governor Dreyfus's aphoristic beer and shipped to consumers out of the Great Lakes Basin.

The biggest threat, though, is expected to come from the process of power generation. Currently, power plants within the Great Lakes Basin consume roughly 480 cubic feet of water per second. By 2035 that is expected to rise by as much as *thirty-five times*—to 17,100 cfs. The villain: new means of cooling electrical generation equipment. Explains the IJC report:

> Water for thermal plant cooling currently represents the most significant demand on the Great Lakes in terms of withdrawal and, by the end of the projection period, will become the dominant type of consumption. The majority of older thermal-electric power generating plants utilize once-through condenser cooling systems having high water withdrawals and only minimal measured consumptive losses. . . . In more recent years there has been increased use of "wet" cooling towers in the United States to dissipate waste heat via the evaporation of a portion of the water flowing through the tower.

This process reduces withdrawals, but it is significantly more consumptive. Thus, as old plants are phased out and new plants are constructed, projected total water withdrawal rates for power generation will substantially increase. Although new technology has provided the alternative of "dry" (air cooled–radiant heat transfer) cooling towers, the process is currently not economically viable since the cooling technology is considerably less efficient and consumes considerable energy resources.

"We've got to stop spending so much time looking at out-of-state diversions," says Pennsylvania's Tim Weston, one of the authors of the IJC report. "That's not where the major problem is. We're going after a mouse with a cannon when there's a horde of termites nibbling away at the foundations."

The Great Lakes have always had an economy based on resource extraction. First the furs went, made into ninety-pound bundles and sent forth in the canoes and the brawny arms of the voyageurs; then the trees followed them. Hard on the heels of the trees came the minerals, dug from the ground and piled onto ships to be made into consumer goods and shipped to the far corners of the earth. Through all this, though, it has always been assumed that the most basic resource of all—the water—would remain in place.

Until now.

XIX Rain

S een on a map, Lake Superior bears a striking resemblance to the
head of an immense wolf. The nose lies at Duluth; the neck is
truncated by the long curved shoreline stretching east 180 miles
from Marquette, Michigan, to the U.S.–Canadian border at Sault Ste.
Marie. The great ruff of fur around the neck is separated from the
lower jaw by the bulk of the Keweenaw Peninsula; the lower lip ends
at Ashland, Wisconsin; and the ears are up around Nipigon, Ontario.

Isle Royale is the eye.

Isle Royale is the largest island in Lake Superior—the largest
island in the largest lake in the world. The island is forty miles long
and just under nine miles wide at its widest point, and it is all
wilderness. For all that it is a part of Michigan and therefore of the
Midwest, there is a feel of the Far North to it. It is but recently out
from under the continental glacier, and it has been polished to bedrock. Sawtooth ridges rise nearly a thousand feet above Lake Superior, cupping numerous small lakes and ponds; the climate is cool and
damp, supporting vigorous colonies of mosses and lichens. The coastline is rugged, with rocky, fogswept heads and deep fjord-like harbors. Travel is by boat, float plane, or foot. From the high points
along Greenstone Ridge, on the island's backbone, you can look off
to the northern horizon and see the rugged blue shape of the Sleeping
Giant in Sibley Provincial Park, on the south coast of Canada. You
can also, if you know where to look, see a tiny part of Minnesota. You
cannot see Michigan at all. Michigan lies to the south, and all you can

see when you look toward Michigan is water. Isle Royale is technically a part of Michigan, but it is far removed from the rest of the state. Standing on Greenstone Ridge, you are closer to Fargo, North Dakota, than you are to Michigan's capital at Lansing. You are closer to Hudson Bay than to Detroit. You are on a jagged, tilted backbone of billion-year-old basalt, surrounded by the taiga—the forest of the North, the same type of forest found in Alaska or Siberia or Lapland —and if you listen, you are likely to hear the bellow of a moose or the high, quavering song of a wolf floating past you on the cool, spruce-scented air.

Rod Badger and I came to Isle Royale one day in early August of 1983. We came the usual way, by boat out of Copper Harbor at the end of the Keweenaw Peninsula. The boat, the *Isle Royale Queen*, leaves each morning at 8 for the four-hour crossing over depths of water that approach 1,000 feet. It holds fifty-seven people, and that day it was full. It was cold out on the Lake, and most of the passengers remained indoors, huddled over magazines in the heated cabin. Rod and I did not; we stayed on deck instead, watching the water the boat rode upon. That was why we were going to Isle Royale. It was not scenery we were primarily interested in, though we had brought a canoe along and planned to use it. It was water—water, and what was dissolved in it. Rod is an organic chemist. We were going to look at PCBs.

At first consideration—or even second or third—there would not seem to be more than one or two places in the world that could be less likely to be having problems with PCBs than Isle Royale. PCBs are a human phenomenon; they do not occur in nature. Isle Royale is all nature. Though the island has a history of human occupancy going back to shortly after it emerged from the great Wisconsin Glacier some 10,000 years ago, that occupancy has never been very dense, and by World War II—when the industrial use of PCBs first became widespread—it had dwindled to almost nothing. The entire island and its surrounding waters were made into a National Park in 1940, and since then they have been managed strictly as wilderness. The permanent structures on the island, what there are of them— Park Headquarters and a couple of boat-in, fly-in lodges—are concentrated in three small, widely scattered areas. The surrounding waters of Lake Superior are primeval waters, deep and cold and clear.

Their purity approaches that of distilled water. All of the Great Lakes are more or less oligotrophic, but Superior is oligotrophic to a fault. It is so clean it is almost sterile. Dipping a canoe paddle into the water, you often cannot tell by sight exactly when it leaves air and enters Lake; looking over the edge of the canoe, you can see twenty or thirty feet down into the transparent green water and count the pebbles on the bottom. It is almost like floating in midair.

It was once thought that water this clean and clear could not possibly be polluted. That was before much was understood about microcontaminants—the man-made poisons that dissolve in water without showing a trace and that, even in tiny amounts, can cause serious problems. Microcontaminants can show up anywhere, and Lake Superior, as it happens, is full of them. In these limpidly clear waters there are dissolved pesticides ranging from DDT and Lindane to Toxaphene, Eldrin, and Dieldrin. There are benzine, toluene, and naphthalene. There are metals—zinc, cadmium, copper, phosphorus, lead. Even around Isle Royale—even *on* Isle Royale—there are all these things. More than 800 separate exotic chemicals have been discovered in the waters of the Great Lakes, which water-quality officials have been heard to refer to as the World's Biggest Sewer, and though the concentrations are less here in the northern wilderness, the numbers remain relatively constant. Most of them are as likely to be found here as anywhere. The large question for a long time was, How in the world did they get here? The mundane, horrifying answer has only recently been found.

Just at noon the *Queen* threaded the difficult passage between Raspberry and Smithwick islands in the barrier chain off Isle Royale's southern shore, idled across Rock Harbor, and pulled up to the concrete Park Service dock. Rod and I retrieved the canoe from where it had been lashed on top of the *Queen*, swung our packs aboard, pointed the prow west, and began paddling. The miles and the hours came and went; the shore slipped quietly by. Through gaps in the barrier islands we could see the vast, heart-stopping openness of the world's biggest body of fresh water. The scent of the taiga hung in the air; loons called, heralding a coming storm. Wind-driven swells slapped heavily against the side of the boat. We paddled harder. The wind was from the wrong direction, the overcast was thickening, the loons were calling, and we had nine miles to cover to reach Moskey Basin and a chance to sleep before walking in to Lake Richie—our real destination—in the early morning.

Hazardous-waste contamination of Isle Royale's interior lakes was first documented in the mid-1970's by a U.S. Environmental Protection Agency team led by Wayland Swain—at that time, still head of the agency's Grosse Ile lab. The discovery was largely accidental. Swain and his crew were on the last day of a prolonged cruise on the research vessel *Telson Queen* with the purpose of finding the sources of the troublingly elevated levels of industrial pollutants that were showing up in fish samples from Lake Superior. The levels were low, but they seemed to be Lakewide—and in a Lake that is really an ocean, 350 miles long by 160 miles wide and cupping upwards of ten percent of the world's total supply of fresh surface water, that indicated a highly diffuse group of sources. Conventional wisdom said those sources had to be industrial outfalls or leaking toxic-waste dumps, either on the Lakeshore or on tributary streams. The shore seemed unlikely—Superior's three-thousand-mile shoreline is still largely pristine—so they were sampling the streams. Fish samples were taken at the mouths of all major rivers flowing into the Lake; later these would be compared with each other to find which ones had the most highly elevated levels of pollutants in their tissues. Attention could then focus on the basins of the streams where the highest levels had been found. The trouble was that all previous attempts to zero in on the problem in this manner had failed. The samples from all the stream mouths were uniform, and they were not significantly higher than samples taken from mid-Lake.

It was a mystery.

On this trip, the *Telson Queen*'s crew had decided to take their mid-Lake samples from the waters around Isle Royale; so the final three days of the voyage had been spent in Isle Royale waters. On what was to be the last evening of the cruise they were anchored in Malone Bay, on the south side of the island. The ship was deserted; the crew was ashore, sitting on the dock to escape the mosquitoes, chatting with the resident ranger from the National Park Service's Malone Bay Ranger Station. Talk turned to the island's inland lakes —in particular, to Siskiwit Lake, which lay less than a mile from where they sat. Siskiwit is, by most measures, a very large lake, indeed. Seven miles long, a mile and a half wide, and more than 150 feet deep, it lies cupped in impervious basalt at a level nearly sixty feet higher than the nearby surface of Lake Superior. There is no known connection, surface or underground, between the two bodies of water—and even if there should be an undiscovered one, it would have to be both minute and outflowing, trickling rather than running from Siskiwit outward and down to the surrounding waters of the great fresh-water sea. All these facts, crewman Skip Porter suggested, would make Siskiwit Lake an ideal source for control samples— uncontaminated fish specimens with which to establish the baseline against which chemical levels in the main Lake could be compared. Swain, as mission leader, concurred. It was decided to extend the trip by one extra day to allow fish samples to be taken from Siskiwit Lake.

"We were excited that this wild strain of fish from a remote island site would provide us with data about a pristine wilderness area that might be unique," Swain was to write later, adding—somewhat rue-fully—"We had no idea how unique the data would be."

Whole-body sampling of fish for microcontaminants is a lengthy, cumbersome process, involving numerous steps as the fish is reduced, first to a mash, next to an oily extract—a small amount of Essence of Fish in a test tube on a laboratory rack—and finally a series of ink squiggles known as "peaks" on the paper drum of a gas chromato-graph. The cruise of the *Telson Queen* had taken place in July, but it was December before the results were finally reported to Swain and his colleagues at Grosse Ile. Their immediate reaction, when they saw the figures, was that there had to have been some mistake. Instead of the expected control-sample purity, the flesh of these Siskiwit Lake fish showed chemical concentrations far higher than those found in fish from the surrounding waters of Lake Superior! PCBs, in particu-lar, were present at twice the levels found in the main Lake. That simply couldn't be.

A painstaking search was immediately begun for the goof-up. "We first carefully checked the chromatograms," wrote Swain. "Since all was in order, we assumed that an error had been made in logging the samples. Several hours of methodically checking sample acquisition numbers against records of homogenization, extraction, and analysis demonstrated conclusively that no error had been made. We were confronted with the fact that the values were real."

They checked with the National Park Service. There were—as they had expected—no potential sources of PCBs within the remote wilderness of the Siskiwit Lake watershed: no electrical generators or transformers, no motors, no forgotten barrels of toxic wastes. Nothing. There had been spraying for spruce budworms on the island once, but that was on the other side of Greenstone Ridge, and anyway, the material used was DDT, not PCB. The two compounds are closely related and are sometimes mistaken for each other in chromatograph analysis, but Swain's group knew the difference and had in fact identified both chemicals in those troubling Siskiwit Lake samples. The source was not on the island. Where was it?

There was only one possible answer. The foreign materials had to be traveling to Isle Royale through the atmosphere—the toxic equivalent of acid rain.

As the irony of the situation hit Swain, he burst out laughing. "We had spent two years in, under, around, and on the water of Superior hunting the source of the materials, and all the time we were breathing it!" Accidentally, the crew of the *Telson Queen* had stumbled upon a hitherto unsuspected pollution source of immense and frightening proportions.

The loons, as usual, were right: The rain came down that night in torrents. In our small blue tent by the waters of Moskey Basin, Rod and I did not sleep. To be perfectly fair, however, this was not due to the rain—which was probably toxic rain but was at least polite, and stayed respectfully on its own turf outside the rain fly. It was not rain that kept us awake, but pain. I am a relative duffer at this canoe business, and nine miles of paddling against eighteen-inch Lake Superior swells had taken their toll. My arms were solid pain from shoulder to fingertip; they would not let me get comfortable. I tossed and turned, trying to find a magic position, bumping Rod in the process and keeping him as awake as I. The rain pounded on the fly. From someplace to the west, over the island, came the sound of thunder.

The next morning we walked up the trail to Lake Richie, a little over two miles inland from Moskey Basin toward the southwest. The rain had stopped, but there was a gray mist in the air and clouds hung low over the surrounding ridges. The temperature, this August day,

was somewhere in the low fifties. The trail crossed Richie Creek,
wound through cattails on a series of wooden walkways, then
climbed over open rock outcrops and through deep forest to the
lake's outlet. Off to the left, in view for much of the trail's length, was
a substantial wetland; Rod remarked that he hoped we'd see a moose
before the trip was over. There were occasional piles of fresh moose-
berries beside the trail, and now and then in the wet portions a track,
but we never saw the animal itself.

Lake Richie was cold and clear and dotted with islands. Nothing
moved in the clean water or the surrounding unbroken forest. There
was not a mechanical object within miles; we seemed out of the
twentieth century altogether. It was impossible to think of this lake
as being polluted with sophisticated man-made organic toxins like
PCBs and DDT, but Swain's data were inescapable; the impossible
chemicals were not only there, they were there in potentially dangerous amounts. Back in the car, on the mainland, we had the figures.
The fat of those Siskiwit Lake fish had contained 34.29 parts per
million (ppm) total PCB. It had tested out at 82.57 ppm total DDT
and 11.43 ppm Diethyl Phthalate. At least four other man-made organics—Dieldrin, Heptachlor Epoxide, BHC, and HCB—had been
present in low but quantifiable amounts. The source was toxic precipitation—poisoned rain and snow. Swain's reasoning told him it
had to be that, but just to make sure he asked the National Park
Service to collect some fresh Isle Royale snow. Park rangers oblig-
ingly went in right after a December snowfall and brought him
several garbage-cans full from the surface of Siskiwit Lake. The snow
tested out at 230 parts per trillion PCB, nearly five times the level of
contaminants found in urban snow from the city of Duluth.

Since Swain's work was published in 1978, toxic precipitation—
or, as it is known to scientists, "airborne deposition of toxic chemicals"—has caught the attention of many other Great Lakes researchers. What they have turned up has been sobering, to put it mildly.
According to the most recent figures, approximately 95 percent of all
toxic pollutants in Lake Superior have drifted there through the air.
The figure is 75 percent for Lakes Michigan and Huron, 40 to 50
percent for Lake Ontario, 25 to 40 percent for Lake Erie. The numbers suggest that the problem is very large. It is also very slippery.
How do you find the source of something that may have traveled

over 1,000 miles before you can possibly detect it? How do you control the rain? If you find a pipe spewing pollutants into a lake—even a Great Lake—you can plug the pipe; but how do you plug a cloud? How do you find—let alone plug—several thousand unknown sources of evaporating chemicals scattered over at least a twenty-state area? Where is the legal framework to deal with them? These problems are being worked on, but no one involved in the work expects much in the way of answers.

A few weeks before coming to Isle Royale with Rod, I had stopped off in Madison to discuss the toxics problem with the Sierra Club's Jane Elder. "I think the worst problem the Lakes are facing right now is airborne toxic deposition," she told me soberly. "We're not even quite sure what the scope of the problem is. We don't know exactly where all the stuff is coming from, we just know it's ending up in the Lakes. We don't know how to take care of it—there's no specific regulations that deal with it. There's a lot of interest but very few mechanisms. It's going to probably require federal legislation, and that's going to require money at EPA, and a lot of other things that are very hard to come by these days.

"The problem is, the Clean Air Act is not really designed to deal with a lot of these things we're facing. And the Clean Water Act doesn't recognize airborne sources, and toxic substances law doesn't deal with them either. People like the concept of dealing with airborne toxics, but we haven't figured out yet how to regulate them. You can list some of the most persistent things, and ask that their manufacture be banned—but that's already happened with PCBs. We're in the very frustrating position where a new law might not do it. Do you ban the use of the entire substance, or do you try to set up nonpoint regulations to deal with—you know, fugitive dust, and that sort of thing? We just don't know.

"The toxics are scary. They're the things we have the least amount of capabilities to do anything about, and they're also the ones the Lakes have the least amount of natural defenses against. Phosphates accelerate aging in the Lakes, but in a sense you can stop it, and the Lakes can heal themselves. A lot of the nutrient pollutants you can do that with. And some of the other pollutants, once you stop them, they're biodegradable, and slowly start to go away"—she caught herself and smiled—"I want to say 'away,' but I always say about pollution, it never goes away, it just goes elsewhere. But the toxic stuff, heavens, it's persistent, it lasts for decades, if not forever —we don't know what to do with it, and we don't know what it's doing to us."

Which is not to say we aren't trying to find out.

Since the publication of Swain's work in 1978, hardly a month has passed without the release of at least one new study of airborne microcontaminant pollution in the Great Lakes. These studies carry names like "Accumulation of PCBs in Surficial Lake Superior Sediments: Atmospheric Deposition," or "Net Atmospheric Inputs of PCBs to the Ice Cover on Lake Huron," or "Mass Balance Modeling of DDT Dynamics in Lakes Michigan and Superior," and they are published in obscure places like the *Journal of Great Lakes Research* or the *Journal of the Fisheries Research Board of Canada*. A few have appeared as full-fledged, book-length documents put out by Great Lakes regional organizations. The most complete work to date has been done by the International Joint Commission's Great Lakes Science Advisory Board, which took up the study of atmospheric deposition with a vengeance as soon as Swain pointed out the problem to them, and in 1980 issued a report, *Assessment of Airborne Contaminants in the Great Lakes Basin Ecosystem*, which has become the infant discipline's Bible. The report runs to more than 300 pages, and its text is often thorny with scientific jargon (sample: "PCBs exhibit lipophilic and hydrophobic properties in the aqueous environment, resulting in their ultimate accumulation in the lipid layers of biota," which may be translated roughly as "PCBs in water end up in fish fat"), but its conclusions are models of clarity:

> Atmospheric deposition of airborne trace organics to the Great Lakes Basin represents a serious problem to the health of the aquatic ecosystem. . . . Atmospheric deposition of airborne PCBs is the most serious known toxic organic problem affecting Great Lakes water quality. . . . Where . . . [are] these compounds coming from and what threat do they pose to the ecological and human health of the Great Lakes Basin? Unfortunately, although these questions are finally being addressed, the answers remain in a fog.

That last sentence seems somewhat unscientific, perhaps. But few Great Lakes scientists today are likely to disagree with it.

· · ·

Wayland Swain had left the EPA and the Great Lakes region entirely by the time I got around to looking for him, and no one seemed to know precisely where he had gone. Several months after Rod and I visited the poisoned lakes of Isle Royale, I finally tracked him down in Amsterdam. I say that I tracked him down; actually, he phoned me. "I hear you're trying to reach me," he said. He was, it turned out, teaching limnology at the University of the Netherlands ("They made me an offer I couldn't refuse"). It was 2:00 in the afternoon at my home in Oregon but nearly midnight in Europe. We agreed to talk when he next came to the States.

That was in November. In January he phoned again, this time from Detroit, and we had a long conversation. Yes, he was continuing to follow airborne-toxics research in the Great Lakes; in fact, he was still finishing up a little work of his own in the field. No, Lake Richie hadn't been checked—only Siskiwit and Superior itself—but this was clearly a region-wide phenomenon, and there was no doubt the rest of the island exhibited it too, though the concentrations might well vary from place to place. And yes—emphatically yes—the problem was not limited to PCBs.

Toxaphene, for instance, could conceivably be worse.

"We're just in the process of getting data together to publish a paper on what we found up there," he said. "Again, in the Isle Royale area, and specifically in Siskiwit Lake, we began to see large quantities of parent materials that were similar to PCBs, but weren't. And having separated them out, they fell into a series of convenient peaks, and we analyzed them, and it was clear that it was a Toxaphene compound. And there was a sufficient quantity of the material there to indicate that it wasn't all recent deposition. The closest point of utilization historically of Toxaphene has been the cotton belt in the South—suggesting that the circulation patterns are such that when the jet stream moves north, it drags Gulf of Mexico air with it, and deposits the materials in the colder regions of the Great Lakes.

"We did a fairly complete synoptic survey in 1974 through 1976 of one hundred thirteen sites in Superior, and at that time there was a suggestion on something less than a dozen chromatographs of fish that there was Toxaphene material in the fish samples, the oily Lake trout residues only. And that suggested that the stuff was getting in, but we had no idea where at that point. By 1981, '82, and '83, when we went back to Isle Royale, we were seeing substantial quantities of it—numbers that exceeded the total PCB compound by a considerable margin in some cases. When you would see one part per million of PCB, which was supposedly the problem, you would see four or five parts per million of Toxaphene. Which began to cause us a bit of concern." They had their results checked by several independent laboratories. Everyone's figures agreed. Toxaphene had nosed out PCBs as the number one airborne-deposition problem.

Where was it coming from? Swain didn't know, but he had a hunch. "Since those early days," he told me, "they had begun to use Toxaphene also in the area of the Dakotas. They were using it on a sunflower crop against a root pest, as I remember—a wireworm, or a root borer of some sort, that destroyed the sunflower crops. They used it because it was very cheap to manufacture." They aren't using it anymore. Largely as a result of Swain's discovery of Toxaphene in Siskiwit Lake, and confirmation by others that it is found throughout the Great Lakes Basin in significant amounts, Toxaphene was banned by the EPA in January of 1983.

But it was neither PCBs nor Toxaphene that was weighing on Swain's mind the most. It was a substance we all thought had been dealt with adequately years ago—dichloro,diphenyl,trichloroethane, known to just about everybody in the world as DDT. DDT, it was turning out, was far more resilient than anyone had figured it could be. It had been knocked down and stomped on, but it was coming back.

In November, after our first brief conversation, Swain had sent me a paper he had published a few years ago concerning DDT levels in Lake Michigan and Lake Superior. The levels, the paper said, were declining. The paper, Swain now said, was wrong. "Those figures were perfectly valid up until the time that paper was published, but about a year afterwards we suddenly began to discover that the numbers were going back up again. From what we thought was an irreversible bottom line, there suddenly was in 1981 and 1982 a slight blip upward—and by 1983 it had gone up considerably. Which was difficult to reconcile at first, because the U.S. and Canada have both totally banned the use of DDT in any shape or form. And this is new

DDT material—it's not the degradation product from old leftover stuff getting into the system somehow.

"The only answer, when you begin to think about it for any length of time, I guess—or the only one that seems to be apparent to me—is that now we're beginning to worry about global circulation. And probably what we're seeing is contributions from developing countries, Third World nations, and the communist bloc, all of which are using high quantities of the compound."

Which bodes extremely poorly for the future. Toxic rain, it turns out, is a global phenomenon; once the stuff is spewed into the air, there is almost literally no place on earth that it can't come down again. The poisoning of Isle Royale depends on decisions made in Moscow and London and Belgrade as well as in Thunder Bay and Duluth and Rock Harbor. Global phenomena require global solutions. When was the last time you saw global solutions in action?

The National Park Service officially discourages drinking the Lake Superior waters off Isle Royale without treatment: something about a tapeworm, *Echinococcus granulosus*, that circulates through the island's wolf and moose herds and can be picked up by humans. Privately they will tell you that the water is probably just fine. "I drink it all the time," Resource Manager Stuart Croll told us at Park Headquarters on Mott Island, one of a chain of guardian islets lining the big island to the south. "Not the inner lakes—no. But I think out in the open Lake it's safe enough." The organic chemicals that pervade the water from the rainfall are in amounts too small to worry about for direct consumption; it's the bioaccumulation of those chemicals in fish that one must be concerned about. Wayland Swain's data suggest that you would have to drink Lake Superior water every day for 500 years to equal the dose you would get from eating a single one-pound meal of Lake trout. Armed with this knowledge, I drank several cupfuls of Lake Superior water during that canoe trip with Rod on Moskey Basin. It tasted of the north—cold and sweet and utterly delicious. I suffered no ill effects. I still haven't. I probably never will.

Unfortunately, however, "probably" is the best that can be offered, for when it comes down to specific cases, no one—Swain

included—can offer any certainty. On the phone with him, I made
the mistake of implying from his data that there wasn't much in the
way of human health dangers from drinking the water, and he
quickly corrected me. "I wouldn't put it exactly that way," he said.
"I would say instead that there was a five-hundred-fold increased
chance for problems from eating the fish as opposed to drinking the
water. Is there a problem from drinking the water? Our best guess
is probably no, but related only to that compound [PCB] and similar
ones. The problem is, nobody really knows what the long-term
effects of any of these things are, because there's such a long epidemi-
ological lag time between the time the compound is ingested and the
time any effect can be anticipated. Normally we're talking something
like twenty-five to thirty-five years."

In Windsor some time earlier, I had brought up the same subject
to Pat Bonner of the International Joint Commission. Bonner was
clearly not happy about microcontaminants—and even less happy
about blasé attitudes toward them on the part of Lakes Basin officials.
She made frustrated noises. "We've got twenty-four million people
taking their drinking water out of these Lakes," she said wearily,
"and we don't know enough about it to tell you whether it's a health
hazard or not. We know there's a lot of stuff in there that the treatment facilities are not able to deal with, but we don't know if the trace
amounts that are there are dangerous to anybody. Or may ever be.
The cancer rates in this part of the country are higher than they
should be. Is it the water? We don't know. That's the basic answer."

We *don't* know. That is the frightening thing. We don't know
how much is in there, we don't know what it's doing to us, and we
don't know what to do about it. We don't even know exactly where
it's coming from. All we know is that it falls with the rain and that
it ends up in the Lakes. It is building up there, faster than it can pass
through the system and be removed. The "flush time" for Lake
Superior—the time it would take for all the water in the Lake to flow
out through the St. Marys River and be replaced by water from the
Lake's several hundred tributaries—is on the order of 500 years. Even
if we could stop the poisons right now—which we can't—we would
be long dead before the Lake was clean again.

Back in Madison, Jane Elder had suggested a facetious solution to Lakewide toxics contamination: The fisheries agencies, she said, should concentrate even more than they do today on stocking and rearing Chinook and Coho salmon in the Lakes. As bottom feeders, these Pacific Ocean natives are "good toxics vacuum cleaners," bio-accumulating toxic wastes to beat the band and thus removing them from the water. The only problem would be trying to convince fishermen not to eat them. I conveyed this suggestion to Swain, and he laughed—long. His laugh is warm and deep, hinting at much good humor. "You know," he said, after the laughter had died, "I once suggested much the same thing. I suggested that we solve the whole problem by first stocking salmon, and then selectively breeding Loch Ness Monsters to feed on the salmon. A mated pair of two Beasts and their progeny, and you could control the thing forever. The trouble is that people want to eat the salmon once they're put in there." He laughed again. "Lake Michigan has got to be the only place in the world where you can sit in a small boat under the palls of smoke and so forth belching out of the plants in South Chicago and Gary and catch a beautiful, fighting sport fish and chronic pulmonary lung disease at the same time."

The clouds were beginning to lift by the time Rod and I got back to Moskey Basin, and a weak northern sun was bathing the taiga in pale yellow light. The loons apparently didn't trust it; they were still calling for rain. We struck the tent, loaded our gear, and launched the canoe once more on the limpid, poisoned waters of the great Lake. I dipped my paddle into it, watching the surface cleave cleanly around the Kevlar blade; I trailed my hand in it, letting the water swirl past my fingers, feeling the cold and the wetness and the fluidity. Lake Superior, the North Sweet Sea, Gitchee-Gumee, the Shining Big Sea Water, highway of ore boats and of voyageurs, the wind blowing and the surf slapping and the white gulls flying—a chemical tank. Eventually, inevitably—in a hundred years, or a thousand, whenever the levels have built up far enough—a sterile chemical tank. The fish and other aquatic organisms will be able to take it for just so long. The clouds drift over, borne on the wind from far places, from the Dakotas, or the Gulf, or Asia, or distant Europe; the poisoned drops come down. We test the waters, we see the slow, agonizing changes, and we look, desperately, for ways to stem them. But the clouds come on, the loons are calling for rain, and there is really nothing that anyone who cares enough can ever possibly do.

XX Attitudes

. . . I know I can't go down here and walk on the beach and feel
safe about it. And I know I'm probably overreacting, and I know
a lot of people swim in the water, but I know it's dirty—[laughs]
—and I don't know how they can *do* that.

A Chicago secretary

The problem, perhaps, is one of perception. We always treat
things as we perceive them; and if they are perceived
wrongly, they will be treated wrongly as well.

The way we perceive the Great Lakes is implicit in the way we
have named them: the Great *Lakes.* To name something is to classify
it, and we have classified the Great Lakes with all other lakes on the
continent. They are supposed to be bodies of still water surrounded
by land—minor features, temporary interruptions in the landscape.
But they do not fit the mold.

Once with geologist Larry Chitwood I followed the coastline
road around Wisconsin's Door Peninsula, an eighty-mile-long, eight-
mile-wide sliver of Silurian limestone that juts out into Lake Michigan like the point of a giant neolithic knife, separating the main Lake
from Green Bay. Up the Green Bay side, out to the tip where the
Door itself lies, the *Porte des morts,* Door of the Dead, the rocky strait
that forms the entrance to Green Bay and has killed so many ships
and men, and down—I almost said "down the ocean side." Down the
Lake Michigan side. On the Green Bay side the road stayed mostly
high, with views from the bluffs over the endless water. The bluffs
were white limestone, cradled in green foliage; the water was blue,
from that distance; it was lined with narrow, bright beaches. The
beaches made graceful curves at the feet of the bluffs. At intervals the

road came down to edge the water, and there were towns: Ephraim, Egg Harbor, Fish Creek, Sister Bay. Pictures from a New England guidebook. No wonder they compare the Door to Cape Cod. But not an "inland Cape Cod," please; there is nothing at all "inland" about this place. Just accept the fact that the United States has a coastline to the north as well as to the east and west. Wisconsin and Michigan and Ohio and Minnesota and the rest are seaboard states. It is of very little import that the sea they lie upon happens to be saltless.

Toward evening we drew up at a small coastside park called Cave Point, found an empty picnic table, opened our ice chest, and spread out a Travelers' High Tea—crackers and cheese and apples and German sausage and cold, condensation-beaded cans of Budweiser beer. The park sloped gently eastward, like the entire peninsula; it was green, a grassy sward amid maples. The grass swarmed with picnickers. A park like any other, and yet not so: for it was chopped off. A hundred feet or so to the east of our table the land and everything on it ended abruptly in a ten-foot-high ledge, and there, suddenly and without any preamble, was the Lake. North, south, east, there was nothing but Lake. The Lake extended to the horizon; the horizon blurred and disappeared; the Lake went on. The ledge dropped straight down, and the Lake had undercut it, forming coves and caves. In the coves and caves the surf slapped and pounded, the white spray flying. Long swells swept in from beyond the horizon, pounding onto the undercut shore with a hollow booming sound, falling back with a monstrous sucking, like a huge tongue pulling away from the roof of a gigantic mouth. I had never heard that sound on a lake—only on the ocean.

Neither, apparently, had Chitwood.

"You know," he mused, "calling these things lakes is not only inaccurate, it's downright dangerous. For the Lakes, I mean. If we called them seas, it might be easier to protect them. What's the significance of losing a lake? If you lose a sea, you're losing something important. Losing a sea sounds big and serious. Losing a lake—well, it just seems too local to worry about."

That is precisely the problem. Yes, we have made some progress since the 1960's. Yes, the eutrophication problem in Lake Erie seems under control; yes, we have established National Lakeshores at Sleeping Bear, and the Pictured Rocks, and the Indiana Dunes, and the

Apostle Islands. Yes, there has been proper indignation over—and even some proper treatment for—the Waukegan Harbor PCBs and the Silver Bay asbestos tailings and the hazardous-waste dumps along the Niagara and the abomination that was once the Grand Calumet River. Yes. But we are still calling them "lakes." And we are still killing them.

When are we going to learn?

I have just returned from a summer spent wandering by car around the ten-thousand-mile perimeter of these massive seas that we have so maliciously maligned by mislabeling them "lakes." Beginning at the Door in early July, I traveled south for 200 miles down the east coasts of Wisconsin and Illinois, made an end-run around the bottom of Lake Michigan through Indiana, and headed north up the west coast of Michigan. Crossing the Strait of Mackinac on the five-mile-long suspension bridge the locals call—inevitably, I suppose—Big Mac, I entered Canada at Sault Ste. Marie, swung east and then south along the northern Lake Huron shore, angled across the neck of the Arrowhead of Upper Canada, and came down to Lake Ontario at Toronto. Gulls flew over the harbor at Toronto, and the island-borne parks that fringe the harbor on the Lakeward side were full of people. Eastward, then, to Kingston; south through the Thousand Islands and back into the United States; and finally, west—west the whole length of the U.S. north coast, west through five states and a hundred cities, through Rochester and Buffalo and Erie and Cleveland and Toledo and Detroit and Saginaw and Marquette and Houghton and Ashland, west to Duluth, where the water finally stops and the continent truly begins. There were side trips to islands and peninsulas—the Bass Islands, the Apostles, Mackinac, the Keweenaw, Isle Royale. There were miles upon miles of broad sand beach. There were nautical towns with nautical names, towns built around bays or tucked in behind headlands—Port Sanilac, Port Hope, Harbor Beach, Copper Harbor, Eagle Harbor, Baileys Harbor, Owen Sound, Sturgeon Bay, Thunder Bay. There were dunes and docks and rivers' mouths: There were broad, distant horizons of blue that glimmered and disappeared into a sky that went on forever. But the striking thing—the frightening thing—was the apathy.

Not everywhere. Not from everyone. But too much, from too

many. We have become a people that has turned its back to the sea, and the consequences—for sea and people alike—are grave.

In Cleveland, I drove for miles along a squalid gray waterfront that looked like the backside of doom. There were factories with smoking chimneys; there were rundown warehouses; there were railroad yards and wrecking yards and piles of garbage. There were sewer outfalls. Much of the land was fill, and torn chunks of concrete stuck up through it like broken bones. An oily, abused river oozed forth between pilings to spread like a stain across the broad blue-gray expanse of Lake Erie. Cleveland, Ohio, America's tenth-largest city and national running joke, the place known to wags all over the country as "Mistake on the Lake." Clevelanders, of course, detest that nickname; they are proud of their city, and they get very defensive when it is attacked. They point to their world-famous symphony orchestra, their fine museums and universities, their parks and boule-vards, their lovely tree-lined residential streets. They do not often point to their waterfront. Cleveland has unaccountably turned its back to the water, and its waterfront is a disaster area.

In Toledo and Green Bay and Duluth, the story is similar. In Buffalo it is even worse. Buffalo's waterfront looks like one of Hieronymus Bosch's visions of hell. There is an elevated freeway along the Lake there, a part of New York State Route 5, called the Buffalo Skyway; it rises on tall stilts out of a jungle of broken con-crete blocks and aimlessly tossed fifty-five-gallon drums and rusty steel beams, and it is separated from the water by eyesore after running eyesore of sprawling industrial megadevelopments, many of them abandoned. I am sure that Buffalo has any number of beautiful places, but I saw none of them. I stood on the edge of the Lake at Mount Vernon after escaping from hell, and I looked back at that broken and meaningless hulk of a skyline, and I wondered, with real anguish, what it was that caused the hell in the first place. Why do people do such things? What does it gain them? Whom does it gain it for? There are no answers; there is only Buffalo.

In Chicago and Toronto, things are a little better; the waterfronts there are a series of beaches and pleasure-boat anchorages, and they are well maintained and heavily used. But Chicago and Toronto residents, too, fail to understand what their Lakes mean to them. They flock to them on warm days, but they also fill them for urban development. Endlessly, they fill them. Toronto's waterfront extends at least two blocks into Lake Ontario beyond the original shoreline: more than 2,000 acres of the city is filled land, including such well-known local attractions as Harbourfront, Ontario Place, the Hilton Harbour Castle hotel, and the Redpath Sugar Museum. In Chicago, Soldier's Field; McCormick Place; Grant Park; the railroad yards; many of the skyscrapers along Wacker Drive—all of these, and others, are built on fill. Not many years ago, Chicago announced plans to create a new international jetport on fill five miles or so out in the Lake. That was shot down. Now the hope is for a World's Fair out there—not so far out as the unbuilt airport, but out there anyway. More daintily than Cleveland and Buffalo, but just as surely, Chicago and Toronto eat away at their Lakes, biting the hands that feed them. They protect the appearance of their waterfronts, but they have forgotten that their waterfronts are connected to water. I visited Chicago's Field Museum of Natural History, one of the world's great showcases for the earth sciences. It is built on Lake Michigan fill. It has exhibits on everything under the sun—dinosaurs, Africa, the islands of the Pacific, asteroids, the moon. It has no exhibit on the Great Lakes. I asked about that at the information booth in the main lobby. The attendant looked uninterested. "I think there used to be one," he said, "but it was taken down about six months ago, and it hasn't been put back up."

It is this apathy—this, more than any other single cause—which is at the root of the Lakes' current crisis. It is apathy that causes people to look the other way as the waters are filled with garbage; it is apathy that allows shorelines to be eaten away for industrial development, and harbor floors to become poisoned deserts, and wetlands to be turned into toxic-waste dumps. If Great Lakes water refills the Ogallala—and empties the Lakes—it will be apathy as much as pipes that gets it there. If High Plains residents care about the water, and Great Lakes residents do not, there is no doubt whatsoever in my mind as to where that water will go.

The worst thing about all this apathy, though—the worst thing, and the most frightening—is not the problems it inevitably leads to for the Lakes. It is the way the people of the Great Lakes region accept those problems so docilely.

Those who *do* care about the Lakes find this attitude both frustrating and disturbing. "I think one of the great tragedies is that people accept the fact that they can't eat Great Lakes fish," Jane Elder told me in Madison. "There ought to be protests in the *streets*. The Michigan fishing license has a warning right on it that tells you not to eat certain amounts of certain kinds of fish, and certainly not if you're a pregnant mother, or a nursing mother. And yet people are not yelling about it when they get their fishing licenses. They should be just furious to pay—whatever it is you pay these days to get one —and then get told, you can catch it, but God, don't eat it." She gestured impatiently. "There's a tremendous potential here for a major source of this nation's protein. And yet we just ignore it. It blows me away."

Lately there have been signs that this crisis of apathy, like the crisis of eutrophication in the 1960's, may yet be recognized and dealt with. Conferences have been held; articles have been written. Organizations dedicated to Lakes issues have sprouted like seedlings after a spring rain. A movement called Great Lakes United has formed under the prodding of the Michigan Federation of Outdoor Clubs; another, the Center for the Great Lakes, has grown out of Chicago's Joyce Foundation. There is an organization called Great Lakes Tomorrow and another called the Lake Michigan Federation and another called Earthweal Great Lakes. An enthusiastic group of people in Muskegon, Michigan, who call themselves Project Lakewell are building a replica of the old clipper schooner *Challenge* to sail the Lakes (much as folk singer Pete Seeger's sloop *Clearwater* sails the Hudson), carrying the gospel of environmental consciousness and pleading for united action among Lakes residents. The various state and provincial governments, not satisfied with merely meeting occasionally, have formed a political alliance called the Council of Great Lakes Governors to lobby for North Coast interests in Washington and Ottawa. National organizations such as the Sierra Club and the National Wildlife Federation have formed internal committees to deal with Lakes issues. On the surface there is ferment, movement, commitment.

On the surface. That is the sad part. Underneath, the same old apathy exists—an apathy that is particularly bad because of its tendency to be bolstered, in many cases, by political infighting of a particularly vicious nature. The various organizations rarely talk to each other; each works as if it, alone, must be the savior of the Lakes. The Center for the Great Lakes is largely duplicating the work of Great Lakes United; the Lake Michigan Federation seems to have no idea what either the Center or GLU is doing. The Sierra Club is at least attempting to coordinate with the others, but it is hampered—as many other groups are—by an organizational structure that places responsibility for the Lakes in at least three separate internal administrative regions. The Council of Great Lakes Governors—politically, perhaps, the best hope of all—is badly weakened by its pointed failure to include all Great Lakes jurisdictions. New York and Pennsylvania have not been allowed to join, for the saddest of all sad reasons: New York and Pennsylvania are also classed as Atlantic seaboard states. Consequently, there is fear on the part of the other states and provinces that they will not be able to speak properly for the Lakes on issues relating to the relatively minor item of port improvement.

All this is complicated by a sort of desperately earnest need, on the part of Great Lakes activists—developers and environmentalists alike—to believe that whatever it is they are doing in their attempts to solve problems is *right*, and is therefore not to be looked at very hard. This is a natural human tendency, and it is always aggravated in areas of economic and/or environmental suffering, but it seems to have reached some sort of new high in the Great Lakes Basin. "We just don't seem to move fast enough," complains executive secretary Vivian Maine of the Center for the Great Lakes. "I lived in California fifteen years ago, when everyone was driving a foreign car. And my parents lived in Detroit, and they would cut out weekly, from the Detroit paper, these little articles that said, 'People in the States don't want small cars, they want big cars.' Well, it was local media hype, it was local propaganda, and it wasn't true. If you got out of Detroit, people were *not* driving those huge cars. And yet, in Detroit, there was a feeling that the rest of it was just something that was put on." It is self-serving excuses for inaction such as these that have led, as much as anything, to the depression the Great Lakes region finds itself in these days.

And even when action comes, it is too often the wrong action: The story of TFM proves that. It is a story worth telling in some detail, for there is much that may be learned from it.

The tale begins in the mid-1950's, when nearly every fisheries organization in the Great Lakes Basin was working desperately to try to stave off what appeared to be certain extinction for the three most important commercial fish species in Fifth Coast waters—whitefish, Lake trout, and Lake herring—by the invading hordes of sea lampreys. Many of these agencies had been working on the problem for at least ten years; most of them were working literally around the clock. By this point, though, no one had much real hope of success. A strenuous effort would be made to salvage what could be salvaged from a dying resource, but it was unrealistic to hope that the course of the disease could be reversed. The general sentiment was expressed by the editors of the Great Lakes commercial fisheries magazine *The Fisherman:* "The trout are gone." And so it was a surprise to nearly everyone when, in the fall of 1957, a group of government biologists from the fledgling U.S. Fish and Wildlife Service, operating out of a makeshift research laboratory at a disused Coast Guard station at Hammond Bay, Michigan, announced that they had come up with something that looked as though it might actually do the trick.

The Hammond Bay research had been, at its outset in 1950, a rather lengthy shot in the dark; of the various approaches being taken to the problem around the basin, it originally had been given the lowest chance of success. Elsewhere they were trying weirs and lamprey traps, or the destruction of spawning beds, or the application of electricity to streams during the lamprey's spawning runs, turning them into gigantic watery versions of the execution chamber at Sing Sing. Poisoning the spawning beds had been considered early on, and had been rejected because of the wholesale slaughter of aquatic life any known chemical poison would cause. The lampreys' victims would perish along with the lampreys; the resource would have been, in the language of the Vietnam war, destroyed in order to save it. Despite this, however, it was a poisoning program that research chief Vernon Applegate and his crew were investigating at Hammond Bay. Not any old poisoning program, mind you, but one with a twist; by investigating as many poisons as possible, the Hammond Bay researchers hoped to come up with one that would kill lampreys without harming anything else.

The process was a little like looking through a Brobdingnagian haystack for the proverbial needle. There is no sure way to predict what twists and turns a chemical's toxicity will take from its formula alone; you have to try it out. The only way that could be done was to set up literally thousands of experiments with isolated water tanks containing lamprey larvae and at least one other animal, introducing potential poisons one at a time and seeing what—if anything—died.

Applegate and his crew obtained several hundred glass ten-liter jars, filled them with water, put lamprey larvae and rainbow trout in the water, and went to work. More than 100 different compounds were tested in every run, on a twenty-four-hour cycle of downright monotonous regularity: Set up the jars, wait around the clock to see if anything happens, write down the results, empty everything out, and start all over again. Always the results were the same—nothing died, or everything did. Months went by, and then years. Cries were raised against the Hammond Bay boondoggle; workers became bored and resigned. Vern Applegate ignored the cries and replaced the workers. The project went on, and on, and on . . . and then, finally, more than 60,000 experiments into the search, the impossible happened. Applegate was roused from paperwork in his office one day to go down to the test facility and look at one of the jars. The trout were swimming happily about; the lampreys were lying on the bottom. Stone dead.

Applegate's first words, according to his own later account, were "What the hell chemical is that?"

They checked. It turned out to a compound called 3-bromo-4-nitrophenol, one of a large group of petroleum-derived chemicals based on the benzine ring, distantly related to DDT and the PCBs. It cost $1,600 per ounce. There was perhaps two ounces of it in all of North America.

Now the problem became the relatively simple one of finding a related chemical that would do the same job as this rarity but could be produced cheaply, and in quantities. Focusing their tests on the nitrophenol family, the researchers soon came up with one. It was called 3-trifluormethyl-4-nitrophenol, or TFM, and its cost per ounce was only fifty cents. In the spring of 1958, after exhaustive tests in artificial streambeds at the Hammond Bay facility—and in the real-life streambed of nearby Billie's Creek—controlled doses of TFM were released into twelve lamprey-infested tributaries of Lake Superior. The results were exactly the same as those in the laboratory jars. Ninety-eight percent of the lamprey larvae in the tested streams died.

Nothing else appeared to be harmed. The long shot had been the one that had paid off.

Or had it?

Lately, there are those who have been wondering.

One day not long ago, on a drive from Marquette to Houghton on Michigan's Upper Peninsula, I discussed the lamprey-control program in Superior with Northern Michigan University biologist Bill Robinson. Robinson is one of the wonderers. He is not at all convinced that the lampricide method is—or ever was—the best way to control lampreys. TFM, he says, is not nearly as lamprey-specific as it was made out to be. "It's toxic to other species, too, you know —it's just more toxic to the lamprey. I don't think anyone really knows how much more. I wish they'd do more research on it, if only to find out what damage it's really doing. I'm afraid it may be a vested-interest kind of thing. The lampricide kills lampreys, and the fisheries people know how to apply it. They may not be too inter- ested in finding out if there might be a better way."

They may, however, have to do so soon. The lampreys seem to be adapting, altering their spawning patterns to conform to the new conditions we have forced upon them. "TFM still seems to be the only effective way to control the lamprey problem in the streams," remarks Wayland Swain. "The difficulty is that some other form of material is going to have to be used in the near future, because the breeding sites have apparently been driven out of the streams and into the sand beds of the Lake itself, where trying to slug with TFM or some similar material simply won't be possible. Because you can't retain the material there long enough, or predict where it's going adequately enough, to use it." There also seems to be some forced selective breeding going on, as only those individuals able to survive treatment by TFM remain alive to pass their genes on to the next generation. "Whether a resistance develops to it or not, I don't know," says Swain, "but I do know that in areas such as Batchawana Bay in Superior, for example, the amocete densities of immature larvae are much greater now than ever before."

So there you have it. Poisoning of lamprey spawning grounds, it is now clear—as it should have been clear from the beginning—was only a time-buyer until we could find a more permanent, less envi- ronmentally disruptive solution to the lamprey problem. That block of purchased time appears about ready to run out. How have we been spending it? What has it got for us? Do we care enough to find out?

Near Toronto, I toured the Pickering Nuclear Power Generating Facility with Ontario Hydro's Jack Muir. There was, I noticed, no traditional nuclear-plant cooling tower to be seen. How did they get rid of the waste heat from what he had just told me was one of the largest nuclear reactors in the Western Hemisphere? Simple, he said: They just pick up water from the Lake, run it through the cooling coils, and dump it back in. The Lake is so big that thermal pollution —the warming of a body of water by artificial means to the point that its ecology changes—is not a serious problem here. Of course, there was a plume of hot water extending out into the Lake from the outlet pipe, but its volume, in comparison with the total Lake volume, was infinitesimal. They had noticed that it attracted fish in the winter, so they thought it was probably beneficial to wildlife. "Actually," he said, "our greatest fear was that they would make us put in a cooling tower. Then there'd be all that evaporation, and the freeway would fog up in the winter. There'd be accidents. We could be held liable."

"Interesting," I said. "And how much extra evaporation is there now, from the surface of the thermal plume out there in the Lake?"

He stared at me. "I have no idea," he said.

In Cleveland, I stood at the mouth of the Cuyahoga River and talked over its problems with chemical engineer Ed Fritz, a good practicing environmentalist who once worked for the Cleveland sewage authority. He had few kind words for Cleveland's sewage system, which he termed a "Byzantine monstrosity." "It's so complicated," he said, "that you won't understand it if you go to look at it. But that's all right. Nobody else understands it, either. You know, a few years ago, engineers were building roads and dams. Now it's sewage plants. You tell us what you want, and suddenly we're experts at it.

"Now. Is the objective of the sewage system to get the Cuyahoga clean, or is it to get Lake Erie clean? They talk about reestablishing a commercial fishery in the lower river. Who are they kidding? You can walk across the mouths of most of the rivers that enter Lake Erie today, and I'm sure the Cuyahoga was that way once. But now it's a shipping channel twenty-seven feet deep and the big ships come up it all the time and keep it stirred up. The design specs for the sewage system call for a clarity of eight Jackson Turbidity Units in the effluent. But there's sixty to seventy JTU in the river from the shipping all the time. The water's brown. I'm not sure I understand the point."

In Madison, I spent several pleasant hours discussing the Lakes States' salmon-stocking programs with Jane Elder. "One of the things I've found fascinating," she told me in the course of that conversation, "is that the Pacific salmon here in the Great Lakes tend to eat a lot of alewives, which were once considered the bane of the Lakes. And they've been eating them to the point where there sometimes aren't enough to go around. So now the fisheries people are thinking of stocking alewives." She laughed. "*Ale* wives! In the Great Lakes! Now, maybe it's just a bad rumor I've heard, but I've heard it from a couple of sources. And the idea of stocking alewives in the Great Lakes, after all the trouble they've caused—I don't know. It's hard to think of anything much wilder."

Apathy can lead to worse than inaction. Apathy can lead to action —action that, because it is designed by experts, carried out by technicians, and overseen by nobody, often hopelessly complicates the situation it was meant, by its well-meaning promoters, to resolve. A research administrator, Wayland Swain once remarked, is "a nonessential individual who is capable of drawing a mathematically precise line from an unwarranted assumption to a foregone conclusion." It is the fate of the Great Lakes, as long as we remain apathetic about them, to suffer remedial programs run by research administrators.

Surely, the greatest reservoir of fresh water on earth deserves better than that.

One fine July evening in the midst of our travels around the Lakes, Rod Badger and I came to Tawas Point State Park, on the eastern Michigan coast just above Saginaw Bay. The park has as its central feature one of the most splendid sandspits in the world—a bright, open, marshy peninsula two miles long, edged by acre upon acre of magnificent Lake Huron beach. The park's campground is large, and it was full: Rod and I, arriving in the late afternoon, were just able to squeeze into the last available site. Around us were motor homes and trailers and campers and a smattering—a very small smattering, indeed—of wall tents. All of them were full of people. All of the people had television sets and radios; all of the television sets and radios were on. Rod stared around him. "This," he said wonderingly, "bears about as much resemblance to camping as an Annette Funicello Beach Blanket Bingo movie bears to a grunion hunt."

I swear to God he said that.

The beach was five minutes away by foot. We walked over there. The late afternoon sun had turned everything golden; the air was cool and pure. The surf of the great Lake, clear as a bell, tolled on the sand. For two hours we walked up and down that beach, treading the sand and surf, our shoes around our necks. The gulls screamed as we approached, and the wind and the water sang; otherwise, the beach was silent. We were the only humans in sight. We might well have been the only ones in all of Creation.

When we got back to the campground, the radios and television sets were still on. The motor homes hulked around us; the spaces between them were full of city noises—fractious children and loud music and bicycle brakes. There were beggars in gulls' clothing, but none of the beautiful wild birds we had seen on the beach. I touched Rod's elbow. "Do you ever," I said, "feel a sense of alienation from the rest of society?"

He gave me an odd look. "E.T. Phone Home," he said.

Late that night the surf rose. To our tent in the darkened, bedded-down streets of Winnebago City came the sound of breakers, quiet but powerful, like the muttering of a muted diapason. Its call was irresistible. Leaving my sleeping bag, I went alone across the dark sand toward the dark sea. Starlight shone on the white crests of the waves; a small breeze moved in the great void of the night sky. The largest skies of all are those over open water; and there is no body of water like this—hence no skies like this—anywhere else on earth.

Do we use this water and these skies? Do we preserve them? Must we make a choice?

Back there behind me in the campground, in that vast ephemeral ghetto of metal boxes on wheels, my fellow campers slept. *Wake up,* I wanted to shout to them, *Wake up and see.* The steel you surround yourselves with is Great Lakes steel; the energy that welded it together was Great Lakes energy. The fish you cooked over the campfire tonight, the salt you sprinkled on it, the sugar you put in your coffee, the plastic chair you sat in to eat and to drink—Great Lakes products, all of them. No matter where on the continent you bought them, they are almost certainly Great Lakes products. Without the Great Lakes your lives would be far different and much less comfortable. Do you understand any of this? Do you understand the appropriateness with which so many of your vehicles are labeled by their manufacturer with the word "Winnebago," which means "stinking water"?

At my feet the great animal of the surf worried the shore; overhead the stars blazed like fireflies, and with the same cold blue light. An hour I stood with my face in the distant wind, and then I went back.

Bibliography

BOOKS

Battin, J. G., and J. G. Nelson. *Man's Impact on Point Pelee National Park*. Toronto: National Provincial Parks Association, 1978.

Bogue, Margaret Beattie, and Virginia Palmer. *Around the Shores of Lake Superior: A Guide to Historic Sites*. Madison: University of Wisconsin Sea Grant Program, 1979.

Cantor, George. *The Great Lakes Guidebook* (3 vols.). Ann Arbor: University of Michigan Press, 1978, 1979, and 1980.

Daniel, Glenda, and Jerry Sullivan. *The Sierra Club Naturalist's Guide to the North Woods*. San Francisco: Sierra Club Books, 1981.

Davis, Charles M. *A Study of the Land Type*. Ann Arbor: University of Michigan Press (undated).

Dorr, John A., Jr., and Donald Eschman. *Geology of Michigan*. Ann Arbor: University of Michigan Press, 1970.

Eutrophication: Causes, Consequences, Correctives. Proceedings of a Symposium. Washington, D.C.: National Academy of Sciences, 1969.

Frey, David G., ed. *Limnology in North America*. Madison: University of Wisconsin Press, 1963.

Hatcher, Harlan, and Erich A. Walter. *A Pictorial History of the Great Lakes*. New York: Crown Publishers, 1963.

Havighurst, Walter. *The Great Lakes Reader*. New York: Collier Books, 1966.

———. *The Long Ships Passing*. New York: Macmillan, 1953.

Historic Johnston Family of Sault Ste. Marie, Michigan: Reprinted as a Service to Libraries from Michigan Pioneer and Historic Collections, Vols. 1–40. Iron Mountain, Michigan: Mid-Peninsula Library Cooperative, 1982 (uncopyrighted).

Holzhueter, John O. *Madeline Island and the Chequamegon Region*. Madison: State Historical Society of Wisconsin, 1974.

Huber, N. King. *Geologic Story of Isle Royale National Park.* Houghton, Michigan: Isle Royale Natural History Association, 1983.

Jackson, John N., and Fred A. Addis. *The Welland Canals: A Comprehensive Guide.* St. Catharines, Ontario: Welland Canal Foundation, 1982.

Kuchenberg, Tom. *Reflections in a Tarnished Mirror: The Use and Abuse of the Great Lakes.* Sturgeon Bay, Wisconsin: Golden Glow Publishing Co., 1978.

Noble, Dennis, and T. Michael O'Brien. *Sentinels of the Rocks: From "Graveyard Coast" to National Lakeshore.* Marquette, Michigan: Northern Michigan University Press, 1979.

Pincus, Howard J., ed. *Great Lakes Basin: A Symposium.* Washington, D.C.: American Association for the Advancement of Science, 1962.

Proceedings of the Conference on Changes in the Biota of Lakes Erie and Ontario. Buffalo: Buffalo Society of Natural Sciences, 1969.

Quimby, George Irving. *Indian Life in the Upper Great Lakes, 11,000 B.C. to A.D. 1800.* Chicago: University of Chicago Press, 1960.

Ratigan, William. *Great Lakes Shipwrecks and Survivals (Edmund Fitzgerald Edition).* Grand Rapids: Eerdmans Publishing Company, 1977.

Rousmaniere, John, ed. *The Enduring Great Lakes: A Natural History Book.* New York: W. W. Norton, 1979.

Saga of the Great Lakes (Facsimile of 1899 edition). Toronto: Coles Publishing Co., 1980.

Schoolcraft, Henry Rowe. *Travels through the Northwestern Regions of the United States.* Albany, N.Y.: E. & E. Hosford, 1821 (facsimile by Readex Microprint, 1966).

Stonehouse, Frederick. *The Wreck of the Edmund Fitzgerald.* Au Train, Michigan: Avery Color Studios, 1977.

Van Dusen, Larry. *Duluth-Superior: World's Largest Inland Port.* Au Train, Michigan: Avery Color Studios, 1977.

MAGAZINES AND NEWSPAPERS

Adovasio, J. M., and R. C. Carlisle. "An Indian Hunters' Camp for 20,000 Years." *Scientific American,* May 1984.

Arden, Harvey. "Chicago!" *National Geographic,* April 1978.

Argenio, Modesto. "Lake Erie." *Sierra Club Bulletin,* March 1970.

Beck, Melinda. "The Toxic-Waste Crisis." *Newsweek,* March 7, 1983.

Beeton, Alfred M. "Eutrophication of the St. Lawrence Great Lakes." *Limnology & Oceanography,* April 1965.

Bierman, Victor J., and Wayland R. Swain. "Mass Balance Modeling of DDT Dynamics in Lakes Michigan and Superior." *Environmental Science & Technology,* September 1982.

"Big and Little Two Hearted Get Lamprey Treatment." *Newberry (Minn.) News,* July 27, 1983.

Boardman, Robert C. "Taconite Dumping Ends." *Audubon,* May 1980.

Boraiko, Allen A. "The Pesticide Dilemma." *National Geographic,* February 1980.
Boyer, David S. "Minnesota, Where Water Is the Magic Word." *National Geographic,* February 1976.
Brown, Melissa. "Facing a New Challenge." *Michigan Natural Resources Magazine,* July/August 1983.
Brown, Michael H. "The Forgotten Great Lake." *Audubon,* November 1982.
Canby, Thomas Y. "Water: Our Most Precious Resource." *National Geographic,* August 1980.
"Danger on the Waterfront." *Maclean's,* August 15, 1983.
Douglas, Matthew. "A Dubious Tradeoff: Mining Bridgman Dunes." *Sierra,* January/February 1984.
Eiler, Terry and Lyntha. "Yesterday Lingers on Lake Erie's Bass Islands." *National Geographic,* July 1978.
Ela, Jonathan. "Good News for the Indiana Dunes." *Sierra Club Bulletin,* September 1977.
———. "Michigan's Upper Peninsula." *Sierra Club Bulletin,* June 1973.
———. "Shifting Sands in the Great Lakes." *Sierra Club Bulletin,* March 1973.
Ellis, William S. "The St. Lawrence: Canada's Highway to the Sea." *National Geographic,* May 1980.
"EPA Limits Toxaphene Pesticide." Ashland (Ore.) *Daily Tidings,* October 19, 1982.
"EPA Urged Great Lakes Fishing Ban." Ashland (Ore.) *Daily Tidings,* March 28, 1983.
"Family Pushes Interior to Sell Back Parkland." *National Parks and Conservation Magazine,* March/April 1983.
"Fish Stories and Empty Offices." *Time,* April 11, 1983.
Ginsburg, Robert. "The Dirt Comes Out from Under the Carpet." *CBE Environmental Review,* March/April 1983.
Golden, Frederick. "The OPEC of the Midwest: A National Water War Looms over the Great Lakes." *Time,* August 2, 1982.
"Great Lakes." A special 32-page supplement to the *Christian Science Monitor,* June 5, 1984.
Grove, Noel. "The Two Worlds of Michigan." *National Geographic,* June 1979.
Haverfield, Linda. "Winter Navigation on the Great Lakes." *Sierra,* September/October 1979.
Heydorn, Allan. "On the Urban Waterfront: Renovating the Chicago River." *Sierra,* November/December 1981.
Hill, Gladwin. "Chamber Opposes U.S. on Pollution." *The New York Times,* December 10, 1965.
———. "The Great and Dirty Lakes." *Saturday Review,* October 23, 1965.
———. "Industry Weighs Pollution Goals: Meets on Public Demand for Cleanup." *The New York Times,* December 9, 1965.
Hillen, Ernest. "A River's Deadly Current." *Maclean's,* July 25, 1983.
"How Many More Lakes Have to Die?" *Canada Today,* February 1981.
"Interior Eyes Parklands in Wisconsin." *Sierra Club National News Report,* January 26, 1983.

Johnson, William Oscar. "By the Shining Big Sea Water." *Audubon*, September 1979.
"Lake Level Forecast Revised Upward: Corps Gears up for More Home, Shoreline Damage." Frankfort (Minn.) *Ad-visor*, July 11, 1983.
"Lake Superior Eyed for Coal Slurry Water." *Duluth News-Tribune*, September 10, 1981.
Levathes, Louise. "Milwaukee: More Than Beer." *National Geographic*, August 1980.
Luoma, Jon R. "Troubled Skies, Troubled Waters." *Audubon*, November 1980.
Malcolm, Andrew H. "Great Lakes States Seek to Keep Their Water." *The New York Times*, June 13, 1982.
McCarthy, Walter J. "A Great Lakes Strategy." *Vital Speeches of the Day*, August 1, 1983.
Mitchell, John G. "U.P." *Audubon*, November 1981.
Morehead, John. "Sunken Ships of Isle Royale." *Sierra*, September/October 1980.
Norris, Ruth. "Whose Fault?" *Audubon*, March 1981.
Parker, Jack. "Tales from the Sweetwater Sea." *Michigan Natural Resources Magazine*, July/August 1983.
Plowden, David. "A Hard Place." *Audubon*, November 1981.
Powers, Charles F., and Andrew Robertson. "Aging Great Lakes." *Scientific American*, November 1966.
Prentice, Virginia. "Sleeping Bear Dunes." *Sierra Club Bulletin*, June 1969.
Rozin, Skip. "Towns Dead and Dying." *Audubon*, September 1979.
Sax, Joseph L. "Saving Indiana's Sand Dunes." *Sierra*, November/December 1983.
"Sea Lamprey in New York State." *Conservationist*, January/February 1984.
Seamonds, Jack A. "St. Lawrence Seaway—It's Still Struggling at 25." *US News & World Report*, July 2, 1984.
Sommers, Lawrence M. "Lake Michigan, Underwater." *Michigan Natural Resources Magazine*, July/August 1983.
Sonzogni, William C., and Wayland R. Swain. "Perspectives on U.S. Great Lakes Chemical Toxic Substances Research." *Journal of Great Lakes Research*, Vol. 6, No. 4 (1980).
Swain, Wayland R. "Chlorinated Organic Residues in Fish, Water and Precipitation from the Vicinity of Isle Royale, Lake Superior." *Journal of Great Lakes Research*, December 1978.
———. "The Great Lakes: An Example of International Cooperation to Control Lake Pollution." *Geojournal* 5.5, 1981.
———. "Ecosystem Monitoring in the Great Lakes: Research Needs, Public Health Implications." *Great Lakes Focus*, May 1981.
———. "Water: 'Thirst Belt' Eyes Turn Toward the Great Lakes." *Detroit Free Press*, March 15, 1983.

GOVERNMENT DOCUMENTS

1982 Annual Report—Great Lakes Research Review. Windsor, Ontario: International Joint Commission, 1982.

1982 Report—Committee on the Assessment of Human Health Effects of Great Lakes Water Quality. Windsor, Ontario: International Joint Commission, November 1982.

1982 Report on Great Lakes Water Quality. Windsor, Ontario: International Joint Commission, November 1982.

1983 Report on Great Lakes Water Quality. Windsor, Ontario: International Joint Commission, November 1983.

Assessment of Airborne Contaminants in the Great Lakes Basin Ecosystem. Toronto: International Joint Commission, November 1980.

Atmospheric Loadings to the Great Lakes: A Technical Note Prepared for the International Reference Group on Pollution of the Great Lakes from Land Use Activities. Windsor, Ontario: International Joint Commission, September 1977.

Conserving the Garden of the Great Spirit: The St. Lawrence River–Thousand Islands Area Report. Philadelphia: National Park Service, May 1983.

Control of Water Pollution from Land Use Activities in the Great Lakes Basin. Windsor, Ontario: International Joint Commission, March 1978.

Coping with Oil Spills along the Eastern Lake Ontario Shore Line: An Early Action Guide for Property Owners. Watertown, N.Y.: St. Lawrence–Eastern Ontario Commission (undated).

Damages and Threats Caused by Hazardous Material Sites. Washington, D.C.: Environmental Protection Agency Oil and Special Materials Division, May 1980.

Environmental Management Strategy for the Great Lakes System. Windsor, Ontario: International Joint Commission, July 1978.

Evaluation of Remedial Measures to Control Nonpoint Sources of Water Pollution in the Great Lakes. Windsor, Ontario: International Joint Commission, October 1977.

Final Survey Report on Navigation Season Extensions for the Great Lakes and St. Lawrence Seaway. Fort Belvoir, Va.: U.S. Army Corps of Engineers, March 18, 1981.

Final Survey Study for Great Lakes and St. Lawrence Seaway Navigation Extension. Detroit: U.S. Army Corps of Engineers, August 1979.

First Biennial Report under the Great Lakes Water Quality Agreement of 1978. Windsor, Ontario: International Joint Commission, June 1982.

Great Lakes Diversions and Consumptive Uses: Report to the International Joint Commission. Chicago: International Joint Commission, September 1981.

Great Lakes Water Quality Agreement of 1978. Ottawa: International Joint Commission, November 1978.

Hazardous Waste Contamination of Water Resources. Hearings Before the Subcommittee on Investigations and Oversight, Committee on Public Works, U.S. House of Representatives. Washington, D.C., July 1982.

Inventory of Land Use and Land Use Practices, Volume I—Great Lakes Basin. Ann Arbor: International Joint Commission, March 1976.

Inventory of Land Use and Land Use Practices, Volume I—Canadian Great Lakes Basin Summary. Windsor, Ontario: International Joint Commission, December 1977.

Land Use Activities in the Great Lakes Basin: A Citizen's Guide. Windsor, Ontario: International Joint Commission (undated).

Planning and Managing Coastal Resources—The St. Lawrence–Eastern Ontario Commission Report. Watertown, N.Y.: St. Lawrence–Eastern Ontario Commission, 1980.

Public Consultation Panel Reports—Canada. Windsor, Ontario: International Joint Commission, March 1978.

Public Consultation Panel Reports—United States. Windsor, Ontario: International Joint Commission, March 1978.

Report on Coastal Resources. Watertown, N.Y.: St. Lawrence–Eastern Ontario Commission, 1977.

Toxic Substances Control Programs in the Great Lakes Basin. Windsor, Ontario: International Joint Commission (undated).

Toxic Substances in the Great Lakes. Chicago: Environmental Protection Agency, June 1980.

BOOKLETS, PAMPHLETS, ETC.

Benton, Marjorie F. *Chequamegon Bay and Apostle Islands.* Ashland, Wisconsin: American Association of University Women (Ashland branch), 1972.

Blegen, Theodore C. *The Voyageurs and Their Songs.* St. Paul: Minnesota Historical Society, 1966.

Chrysler, Barbara L., ed. *Put an Island in Your Life.* Put-in-Bay, Ohio: Put-in-Bay Chamber of Commerce, 1983.

Copper Country Vacation Guide. Calumet, Michigan: Copper Island Graphics, August 1983.

Dent, Joan Bishop. *Surfbeat: Commentaries About the Great Lakes.* Ann Arbor: Michigan Sea Grant Program, 1979.

Downs, Margaret. *Great Lakes Policy Issues and the 98th Congress.* Chicago: Center for the Great Lakes, April 1983.

Downs, Warren. *Fish of Lake Superior.* Madison: University of Wisconsin Sea Grant Program (undated).

———. *The Sea Lamprey: Invader of the Great Lakes.* Madison: University of Wisconsin Sea Grant Program, 1982.

Downwind: The Acid Rain Story. Ottawa: Environment Canada, 1981.

Egan, Michael. *Sweetwater Seas: The Legacy of the Great Lakes.* Toronto: Ontario Ministry of the Environment (undated).

Entine, Lynn, ed. *Groundwater—Wisconsin's Buried Treasure.* Madison: Wisconsin Department of Natural Resources (undated).

Fact Sheet on Acid Rain. Washington, D.C.: Canadian Embassy (undated).

Fritzen, John. *Historic Sites and Place Names of Minnesota's North Shore.* Duluth: St. Louis County Historical Society, 1974.

————. *History of Fond du Lac and Jay Cooke Park.* Duluth: St. Louis County Historical Society, July 1978.

Fulcher, Dan, ed. *Lake Superior Circle Tour Travel Guide 1983.* Thunder Bay, Ontario: North of Superior Travel Organization, 1983.

The Fur Trade in the Minnesota Country. St. Paul: Minnesota Historical Society (undated).

Great Lakes, America. Chicago: Environmental Protection Agency, 1980.

The Great Lakes: Do We Take Them for Granted? Windsor, Ontario: International Joint Commission (undated).

Great Lakes: Yesterday, Today and Tomorrow. Toronto: Ontario Ministry of the Environment, 1982.

Green, Janet, and Gerald Niemi. *Birds of the Superior National Forest.* Duluth: Superior National Forest, 1980.

Herbert, Paul A. *Great Lakes Nature Guide.* Lansing: Michigan United Conservation Clubs (undated).

Hill, John R. *The Indiana Dunes—Legacy of Sand.* Bloomington: Indiana Department of Natural Resources, 1974.

Keweenaw's Beautiful South Shoreline Drive. Lake Linden, Michigan: Torch Lake Chamber of Commerce (undated).

Lukes, Roy. *Trail Guide: Ridges Sanctuary.* Baileys Harbor, Wis.: Ridges Sanctuary, Inc., 1981.

Lydecker, Ryck. *Pigboat . . . The Story of the Whalebacks.* Superior, Wis.: Head of the Lakes Maritime Society, 1981.

MacMullin, R. B. *A Walker's Guide to the Niagara Gorge.* Niagara Falls, N.Y.: Schoellkopf Museum, 1975.

Mammals of the Superior National Forest. Duluth: Superior National Forest, 1981.

Man's Impact on Lake Michigan. Chicago: Lake Michigan Federation, 1975.

Michigan Outdoor Guide. Dearborn: Automobile Club of Michigan, 1982.

Nekvasil, Glen G. "Great Lakes Fleets Do Not Advocate Year-Round Navigation" (news release). Cleveland: Lake Carriers' Association, September 7, 1983.

Ontario/Canada Traveller's Encyclopaedia. Toronto: Ontario Ministry of Tourism, 1983.

Petersen, Eugene T. *Guide Book for Mackinac Island Visitors.* Mackinac Island, Michigan: Mackinac Island State Park Commission, 1979.

Pickering Generating Station. Toronto: Ontario Hydro (undated).

Rakestraw, Lawrence. *Historic Mining on Isle Royale.* Houghton, Michigan: Isle Royale Natural History Association, 1965.

Rawson, A. L. *Historic Legend of the Pictured Rocks of Lake Superior.* Au Train, Michigan: Avery Color Studios, 1971.

Read, Robert H. *Vascular Plants of Pictured Rocks National Lakeshore.* Ann Arbor: Michigan Botanical Club, 1975.

Ryan, George J. "Remarks Before the International Joint Commission Meetings on Great Lakes Water Uses" (speech transcript). Cleveland, June 13, 1983.

The Sea Lamprey and Its Control in the Great Lakes. Marquette: U.S. Fish and Wildlife Service, 1980.

A Short History of the Ice Age in Wisconsin. Madison: University of Wisconsin Geological and Natural History Service, 1964.

Soo Locks, Sault Ste. Marie, Michigan. Detroit: U.S. Army Corps of Engineers (undated).

Stacey, C. P. *The Undefended Border: The Myth and the Reality.* Ottawa: Canadian Historical Association, 1953.

Strzok, Dave. *Apostle Islands National Lakeshore: A Visitor's Guide.* Bayfield, Wisconsin: Strzok Publishers, 1981.

Swain, Wayland R. "Superior, Serendipity, and the Toxic Substances Snipe Hunt" (unpublished paper) (undated).

Toxic Substances: The Subject Is Poison. Windsor, Ontario: International Joint Commission, 1981.

Trautman, Milton B. *The Ohio Country from 1750 to 1977—A Naturalist's View.* Columbus: Ohio Biological Survey, 1977.

Waves Against the Shore: An Erosion Manual for the Great Lakes Region. Chicago: Lake Michigan Federation, 1978.

Weimer, Linda, et al. *ABC's of PCB's.* Madison: University of Wisconsin Sea Grant Program, 1976.

————. *Our Great Lakes.* Madison: University of Wisconsin Sea Grant Program, September 1973.

Wilderness Trails: A Guide to the Trails in Isle Royale National Park. Houghton, Michigan: Isle Royale Natural History Association, 1977.

Willman, Charles. *Ontonagon Boulder.* Ontonagon, Michigan: Ontonagon Chamber of Commerce, 1962.

Acknowledgments

Peggy Tsukahira, for getting me started on this project in the first place;

Max Gartenberg, for believing in it enough to make me push it to completion;

Larry Chitwood and Rod Badger, for their companionship, insights, and constant good humor along ten thousand miles of freshwater coast;

Kary Hyre in Madison, Wisconsin; Conrad and Dorothy White in Chicago; Curtis and Kathy Curtis-Smith in Kalamazoo, Michigan; Steve and Mina Otto in Toronto; Ed and Anna Fritz in Cleveland; the Quentin Holmes and Steve Olson families in Ann Arbor, Michigan; and Bill and Glenda Robinson in Marquette, Michigan, for hospitality above and beyond the call of duty;

Bob Wilson at the Ashland (Oregon) Public Library and to Ann Richards and Harold Ottness at the Southern Oregon State College Library for assistance in research;

AND all those who provided me with the information and anecdotes that eventually became this book, including especially the following (listed alphabetically).

Leonard Asselin, Prairie Village, Kansas (for sharing his memories of a Keweenaw Peninsula childhood); Brenda Behm, Chicago (Lake Michigan Federation); Bob Beltran, Chicago (Environmental Protection Agency); Frank Bevacqua, Washington, D.C. (International Joint Commission); Pat Bonner, Windsor, Ontario (International Joint Commission); Don Brown, Bayfield, Wisconsin (Apostle Islands National Lakeshore); Don Carney, Grand Marais, Minnesota (Grand Portage National Monument); Stuart Croll, Isle Royale, Michigan (Isle Royale National Park); Tom Cutter, Watertown, New York (St. Lawrence–Eastern Ontario Commission); Roland Eisenbeis, Chicago (Forest Preserve District of Cook County); Jane Elder, Madison (Sierra Club); Larry Fink, Chicago (Environmental Protection Agency); Robert Fudge, Porter, Indiana (Indiana Dunes National Lakeshore); Kent Fuller, Chicago (Environmental Protection Agency); DuWayne Gebken, Madison (Wisconsin Department of Natural Resources); Robert Ginsburg, Chicago (Citizens for a Better Environment);

Charles Herdendorf, Put-in-Bay, Ohio (Franz Theodore Stone Memorial Laboratory, Ohio State University); Ron Hiebert, Porter, Indiana (Indiana Dunes National Lakeshore); Max Holden, Frankfort, Michigan (Sleeping Bear Dunes National Lakeshore); David Jasperse, Holland, Michigan (Project Lakewell); Vivian Maine, Chicago (Center for the Great Lakes); Bob "Fisherman Bob" Martignon, Marquette, Michigan; Alec McKay, Edmonton, Alberta (for providing Great Lakes materials collected during his years in London, Ontario); Jack Muir, Pickering, Ontario (Ontario Hydro–Pickering Generating Station); Glen Nekvasil, Cleveland (Lake Carriers' Association); Jerry Paulson, Chicago (Lake Michigan Federation); Ken Peebles, Muskegon, Michigan (Project Lakewell); Bill Schlemir, Oswego, New York (WSGO Radio); Greg Skillman, Washington, D.C. (office of Congressman Jim Weaver, D-Ore.); Sally Spiers, Washington, D.C. (International Joint Commission); Wayland Swain, Amsterdam, The Netherlands (for providing materials and insights from his tenure as head of the Large Lakes Laboratory at Grosse Ile, Michigan); Bob Sweeney, Buffalo, New York (Ecology and Environment, Inc.); and Tim Weston, Harrisburg, Pennsylvania (Pennsylvania Department of Environmental Protection).

For more information on the current status of the Great Lakes and how you can help, contact:

The Lake Michigan Federation
8 South Michigan Avenue
Suite 2010
Chicago, Illinois 60603

Great Lakes United
24 Agassiz Circle
Parkside Avenue & Route 198
Medaille College
Buffalo, New York 14214

United States Environmental
  Protection Agency
Great Lakes National Program
  Office
536 South Clark Street
Chicago, Illinois 60605

The Center for the Great Lakes
435 North Michigan Avenue
Suite 1733
Chicago, Illinois 60611

The Center for the Great Lakes
  Foundation
3 Church Street
Suite 500
Toronto, Ontario M5E 1M2
Canada

Sierra Club
Midwest Regional Office
214 North Henry Street
Suite 203
Madison, Wisconsin 53703

International Joint Commission
Great Lakes Regional Office
100 Oulette Avenue
8th floor
Windsor, Ontario N9A 6T3
Canada

Great Lakes Commission
2200 Bonisteel Boulevard
Ann Arbor, Michigan 48109

Index

Index

A NOTE ABOUT THE AUTHOR

One of our leading writers on environmental subjects, William Ashworth is the author of several books on water-resource politics and the American water crisis, including the acclaimed *Nor Any Drop to Drink* (1982). He has served as vice-chairman, secretary, and conservation coordinator for the Oregon chapter of the Sierra Club, and in 1982 received the chapter's annual Award for Outstanding Achievement. Mr. Ashworth lives in Ashland, Oregon.

A NOTE ON THE TYPE

This book was set in a digitized version of Janson, a redrawing of type cast from matrices long thought to have been made by the Dutchman Anton Janson, who was a practicing type founder in Leipzig during the years 1668–87. However, it has been conclusively demonstrated that these types are actually the work of Nicholas Kis (1650–1702), a Hungarian, who most probably learned his trade from the master Dutch type founder Dirk Voskens. The type is an excellent example of the influential and sturdy Dutch types that prevailed in England up to the time William Caslon developed his own incomparable designs from them.

Composed, printed and bound by The Haddon Craftsmen,
Scranton, Pennsylvania

Typography and binding design
by Dorothy Schmiderer

Thunder Bay

*Isle
Royale*

Grand Portage

MINNESOTA

LAKE SUPERIOR

*Apostle
Islands*

*Keweenaw
Peninsula*

Copper
Harbor

Duluth

Ashland

Marquette

*Pictured
Rocks*

Sault Ste.
Marie

MICHIGAN
(U.P.)

Mackinac

WISCONSIN

Door Peninsula

*Sleeping
Bear Dunes*

Green Bay

Traverse
City

MICHIGAN
(L.P.)

LAKE MICHIGAN

Muskegon

Milwaukee

Waukegan